THE BEST OF
MONTREAL QUEBEC & CITY

THE BEST OF

MONTREAL QUEBEC & CITY

A Guide to the Places, Peoples and Pleasures of French Canada

— ⚜ —

MARTIN KEVAN

CROWN PUBLISHERS, INC.
New York

Published by Crown Publishers, Inc., 201 East 50th Street, New York, New York 10022. Member of the Crown Publishing Group.

CROWN is a trademark of Crown Publishers, Inc.

Manufactured in the United States of America

Designed by Rhea Braunstein

Cartography by Jacques Chazaud

Library of Congress Cataloging-in-Publication Data

Kevan, Martin.
The best of Montreal and Quebec City: a guide to the places, peoples and pleasures of French Canada/Martin Kevan.—1st ed.
Includes index.
1. Montréal (Québec)—Description—Guidebooks. 2. Québec (Québec)—Description—Guidebooks. 3. Québec Region (Québec)—Description and travel—Guidebooks.
I. Title.
F1054.5.M83K48   1992
917.14′27044—dc20   91-43297   CIP

ISBN 0-517-58230-9

10 9 8 7 6 5 4 3 2 1
First Edition

Contents

Maps

Introduction

WHY THIS GUIDE BOOK?

I am a person who loves stories. I am a person who loves the people of Quebec, and the people of Quebec have many stories that I love. If you love stories, architecture and food, and want the romance of French culture in North America, Montreal and Quebec City are places you should visit.

To love a person or a place, it is necessary to know the changing pattern of dreams that have molded and continue to mold that person or place. Many a guide book will tell you what sights are important to see in a city, but they will very often fail to put these sights into a context that makes them memorable. The dreams that glue a culture together are forgotten. Many a guide book reads like a checklist of names and monuments. There are a number of good, efficient, pocket-size guides to Montreal and Quebec. I have looked at them all, and if you want one that gives you facts, lists monuments and makes limited suggestions about restaurants and the nightlife of the two great French-speaking cities of North America, I suggest that you go for the ones published by American Express or Fodor's; better still, if you are in the continental United States or Canada, telephone 1-800-363-7777 and ask Tourisme Québec to send you their very adequate and free guides. If you wish to write, their address is P.O. Box 2000, Quebec City, Quebec, Canada G1K 7X2.

However, these free booklets include no guides to restaurants or night spots, and the attractions are organized according to function, that is, museums are grouped together. As a result, they present little of the cultural and architectural development of neighborhoods and, because they are not deeply researched, they avoid controversial issues, ignore scandals, omit legends and give no sweep of history.

The Best of Montreal and Quebec City is divided into two parts, the main bodies of which are made up of leisurely, half-day walking tours of the two cities. Each part includes a chapter of historical essays that give brief accounts of events that are either too sweeping or too important to be comfortably woven into the text of the walking tours, each of which has, as far as possible, a thematic core. The tours point out the architectural and historical significance of neighborhoods, buildings and squares, and include, where appropriate, short accounts and brief biographies of those events and people who have built (and occasionally destroyed and defamed) the institutions of the two cities. It is my hope that this organization stimulates readers' imaginations as they actively explore the two cities.

The Best of Montreal and Quebec City is, in part, written for the armchair tourist who is planning a visit; it is also written for the residents of Montreal and Quebec who wish to know their cities and province better. For the most part, however, it is written for the visitor who wishes to discover and enjoy an unfolding pattern of cultural significance. It is for active people who are willing to walk, reflect, eat, talk, shop, drink and be amused.

BASIC INFORMATION

Accommodations

Tourisme Québec determines the maximum amount that any hotel may charge for a room. These prices should be posted in the room.

Bank Machines

Many Canadian banking machines (and there are many) are connected to PLUS System and Interac.

Clothes and Climate

Mid-June through mid-September: Summer clothes are all that are needed, although one jacket or light coat is advisable for some nights. Average maximum temperature: 77°F (25°C). Average minimum temperature: 60°F (15°C).

Mid-September through October, and April and May: Fall and spring clothes are needed. Average maximum temperature: 60°F (15°C). Average minimum temperature: 46°F (8°C).

Mid-November through March: Good winter clothes, boots and hats are required. In March and April, practical waterproof boots are a necessity. Don't wear your best leather ones—the salt used to melt snow will badly stain them. Average maximum temperature: 27°F (−4°C). Average minimum temperature: 14°F (−10°C).

If you plan a trip to the Gaspé, take a sweater, for the evenings can be chilly even in the height of summer.

Credit Cards

Visa and MasterCard are almost always accepted. American Express runs a close third. Diners Club/Carte Blanche and en Route are sometimes accepted.

Currency Exchange and Money

Ordinary Canadian bills come in $2, $5, $10, $20, $50 and $100 denominations. The $1 coin is nicknamed "the loonie" after the bird engraved on the back.

American dollars: U.S. currency is almost universally accepted in shops, restaurants and hotels, and will often be valued at a rate close to the current exchange levels. Generally, it is more expensive to buy Canadian currency in the United States than in Canada, where almost every bank branch will do the transaction.

Other foreign currencies: Deak Perrara, 1218 rue McGill, is in Old Montreal. National Coin Exchange, 1240 rue Peel, and Guardian, 950 Ste-Catherine O., are downtown. Quebec City has an exchange office at Banque d'Amérique du Canada, 24 côte de la Fabrique.

Customs

Each visitor over eighteen years old is allowed to bring 1.1 liters (40 ounces) of liquor or wine, or 8.2 liters (24 small cans or bottles) of beer. Those over sixteen can bring 200 cigarettes, 50 cigars or cigarillos and 0.9 kilograms (2 pounds) of tobacco. Smokers are advised to bring their maximum allotment—in Quebec, a pack of 20 cigarettes costs between $5 and $6.

Dental Emergencies

Telephone 288-8888 in Montreal, 653-5412 in Quebec.

Driving

Gasoline is sold in liters and is much more expensive in Canada than in the United States. One gallon is 3.785 liters. Tank up before you cross the border!

Parking on streets requires a knowledge of the French abbreviations of the days of the week and familiarity with the twenty-four-hour clock. If a parking meter gives you a ticket, place it on the windshield in front of the driver's seat.

Dim. (*Dimanche*) = Sunday
Lun. (*Lundi*) = Monday
Mar. (*Mardi*) = Tuesday
Mec. (*Mercredi*) = Wednesday
Jeu. (*Jeudi*) = Thursday
Ven. (*Vendredi*) = Friday
Sam. (*Samedi*) = Saturday

Radar detection devices are illegal in Quebec and will be confiscated at the border.

Road signs, although written in French, use the standard North American designs.

Speed limits and distances are marked in kilometers (km):

1 kilometer = .621 miles
60 kilometers per hour = 37.26 miles per hour
100 kilometers per hour = 62 miles per hour

Turning right on a red light is illegal in Quebec.

Language

Quebec is officially a unilingual, French-speaking province with a large English-speaking minority that has its own schools, hospitals and social services. Although road signs, parking instructions and outdoor advertisements are written only in French, the greater part of the population of Montreal and almost all people in the tourist industry of the province also speak English. A visitor who has studied Parisian French will find Québecois-accented French hard to comprehend and will often have to be persistent in order to stop replies in English.

Medical Services

Quebec has excellent free health-care services for its own residents only. Visitors should have insurance from either other provincial governments of Canada or private companies.

Museums

The exhibits in many museums are labeled only in French, but there is almost always a printed English translation that visitors are invited to use as they examine the displays.

Newspapers—English Language

The *Montreal Gazette* is a comprehensive daily English-language newspaper; the *Montreal Mirror* is an excellent weekly English guide to the cultural events in the city.

Passports and Visas

American tourists are not required to have a passport or visa to enter Canada—valid identification that indicates American residence is usually all that is necessary. If you are traveling on public transport and have no credit cards, a return ticket is advisable. Visitors from other countries should check with the Canadian Embassy to find out if visas are needed. Dogs and cats need to have proof of vaccination against rabies.

Restaurants

Menus and prices are posted outside the entrances. For help in translating a French menu see the appendix at the end of this book.

Taxes

It was Mark Twain who said that there are two things you can't escape: death and taxes. You certainly won't escape taxes in Quebec. The federal government levies a 7 percent tax and the provincial government adds an 8 percent tax (GST or TPS) on all goods and services except grocery foods. Do not despair, however—all tourists from foreign countries are entitled to a rebate of the 7 percent federal tax on all goods and services (except gasoline, alcohol, tobacco and more than thirty nights of hotel accommodation) that cost more than $7. On entering the country, ask Canada Customs for an application form (GST 176E). Hotels and shopping centers will also provide the application form. Refunds to the United States will be made in American currency and those to other countries in Canadian money. Save your receipts!

Telephones

Public telephones are numerous, cost twenty-five cents and are supplied with both yellow and white pages.

The area code for Montreal is 514 and the area code for Quebec City is 418. In this book, area codes are only given for numbers that do not fall within the Montreal or Quebec City areas.

Tipping

Because it is assumed that the bulk of their income comes from tips, waiters are paid less than the normal minimum wage. A tip of 5 percent indicates very dissatisfactory service; 10 percent indicates passable service; 15 percent indicates good service; 20 percent means that you felt pampered. The acronym TPS at the bottom of a bill indicates the 15 percent goods-and-services tax, not the tip. Taxi drivers used to expect a tip of 10 to 15 percent, but since the drop rate and per-kilometer charge have risen to among the highest in North America, tips have fallen. If I am in a big, quiet, comfortable car, I tend to tip at 15 percent, but if I'm squeezed into the back seat of a noisy, diesel-engined compact, I tip less.

Emergencies

Telephone 911 in Montreal; and the police, 694-6123, in Quebec City.

THE BEST SEASONS TO VISIT MONTREAL AND QUEBEC

Mention Canada to Americans and the first thing they think of is a TV weather map. "It's the place that all that cold comes from," they say. And it's true; in July, many come north seeking relief from the heat—relief they sometimes don't find. There's an old joke in Canada: How do you recognize an American tourist in July? Answer: He's the one on skis. Joking aside, in all seasons, Montreal is generally ten Fahrenheit degrees colder than New York City; Quebec City is twelve degrees colder.

So when is the best time to visit Montreal and Quebec? What has to be remembered is that Quebec has only three seasons: summer, fall and winter. All three are great. Spring is so rapid that it hardly seems to exist. In mid-May, often within a week, the trees burst into full foliage and people divest themselves of waterproof boots and heavy coats. The first shorts of summer make the heart beat faster, and even Canadians can sing Gershwin and think that living is easy. Both in Montreal and Quebec City, which moves at a slower pace, the bars, restaurants and cafés spill out onto patios, terraces and balconies, and visitors discover two cultural oases—safe North American urban centers with distinctly European traditions, places where the citizens glory in the sun, cultural festivals, sports, drinking and dining.

In late May and early June, Montreal and Quebec City alternately host the annual **International Theatre Fortnight** and Montreal explodes with the **Benson & Hedges International Fireworks Festival.** By June, the Montreal International Music Competitions are under way and the season bounds on with Grand Prix racing on the island park in the middle of the St. Lawrence River and the Festival of New World Music. There's baseball at the Olympic Stadium and then, on June 24, the citizens of both cities take to the streets to celebrate the traditional national holiday, St. Jean Baptiste Day. A week later, Montreal's black community celebrates Carib-fest and Canadians honor Canada Day.

By the end of June the **Montreal International Jazz Festival,** which attracts 650,000 people, is in full swing. And, if you can't afford the indoor shows by stars like Wynton Marsalis, Charlie Haden or Oscar Peterson, just hang out on the streets—among the many outdoor stages, buskers and kiosks, the entertainment is overwhelm-

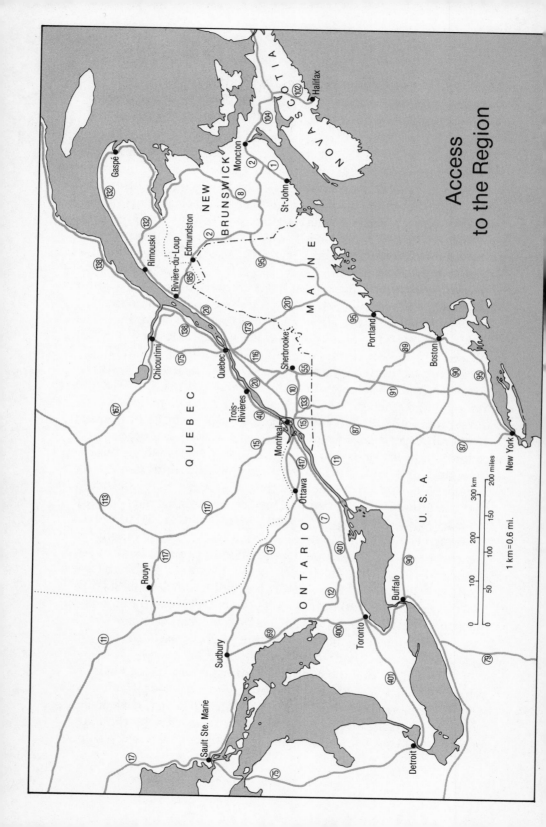

Access
to the Region

ing. No sooner has Montreal played host to the jazz musicians than the comics arrive for the **Just for Laughs Comedy Festival,** which also happens as much in the streets as it does in the theaters. Again, if you can't afford the tickets to see the stars, 350 outdoor performances are given on five stages and impromptu comedy erupts in the parks. Over 450,000 people attend this festival, which is, in part, broadcast to Europe by Britain's Channel 4 and to the United States by HBO.

Meanwhile, Quebec begins its **Les nuits Bleues internationales de jazz** and follows it up with **The Quebec International Summer Festival**, a ten-day cultural feast.

At the end of July, the summer is in high gear for the International Regatta at Valleyfield, the Player's International Tennis Tournament, the Tour du Monde bicycle race and the outdoor rock concerts, until it is brought to a close, in the last two weeks of August, by the **Montreal World Film Festival,** during which a quarter of a million people attend screenings of 250 films from around the world.

These summer festivals are not just for visitors; many residents plan their vacations around the blowouts. It's one way to deal with six months of winter.

The fall is quieter, but Quebec City does host its own film festival in early September, a lovely month that seems to caress the end of summer as the trees prepare themselves for their most spectacular display of reds, golds, oranges and browns. The hockey season begins in both cities, and at the end of the month, dancers from Europe and America gather to attend Montreal's biannual festival of modern dance. The population begins to debate: "Is this heat wave Indian summer, or will there be another in October?"

The nights become longer and colder as we approach Halloween and Canadian Thanksgiving. In November, Montreal hosts a festival of new theater and we pull out our scarves, gloves, coats and boots. The drizzles arrive and our climate resembles an English winter. There is a certain romance to it, and I have often thought that I prefer the French word *brume* to the English "fog."

Early December is not memorable: The snow rarely settles, the trees are bare and the nights long. It is during the Christmas season that the first of the huge snowstorms usually occurs. The sounds of the city become muffled, and some folk grab the opportunity to ski down main thoroughfares devoid of cars. We know that for the next four months cold and snow will dominate our lives, forcing us to take to the slopes and rinks, swim in the indoor pools, take courses at universities and do aerobics. Some days can be so bitterly cold that it's best to stay in bed.

In February, the greatest winter festival in the world bursts open in the old walled city of Quebec. An ice palace is built and a beauty queen is chosen. **Carnivale** is a joyous celebration of the tenacity of the French-speaking people of Quebec, who have lived through every arduous winter since 1608.

Unless you are a lover of spring skiing, forget the end of March and all of April. I admit that it is astounding to experience what we call an ice storm, when rain freezes on contact with the ground. Trees and wires become heavy with glistening ice, creating a winter fairyland, but branches, under the weight, can come crashing to the ground, and city sidewalks become more suitable for skates than for boots. On the warmer days, large puddles form between melting piles of ice. I had an uncle who visited in an April that mixed ice, slush, snow, rain and winds. He was relieved to go back to Liverpool, England, a place not famous for its weather. Unless you are a complete romantic, avoid this corner of the continent from the end of March through April. Wait for the fabulous summer, the gorgeous autumn and the invigorating and exciting winter.

Addresses to write to for the programs of the major festivals:

Festival de Nouvelle Danse: *Suite 204, 4060 St-Laurent, Montreal, Quebec H2W 1Y9. Tel.: 287-1423.*

Festival de Théâtre des Amériques: *4672 St-Denis, Montreal, Quebec. Tel.: 842-0704.*

Just for Laughs Comedy Festival: *301 de Maisonneuve O., Montreal, Quebec H2X 4L4. Tel.: 845-3155.*

Montreal International Jazz Festival: *355 Ste-Catherine O., Montreal, Quebec H3B 1A5. Tel.: 871-1881.*

Montreal World Film Festival: *Suite H109, 4055 de Maisonneuve O., Montreal, Quebec H3G 1M8. Tel.: 933-9699.*

Quebec Winter Carnival: *29 Joly, Quebec, Quebec G1L 1N8. Tel.: 626-3716.*

WHO ARE THE QUÉBECOIS?

I went into several Montreal bars and asked, supplying pen and paper, "What is it to be a Canadian?" The two most repeated replies were "Not to be an American" and "I'm not a Canadian; I'm a Québecois."

It's not easy to define any national identity, but it's generally accepted, whether it be true or not, that Americans are friendly, but sometimes pushy; the British humorous, but sometimes snobbish; and the French cultured, but sometimes arrogant. To the consternation of many English-Canadians, they have been described as "well-meaning, but sometimes dull." The Québecois (pronounced "kay-bek-wah"), on the other hand, are "vivacious, but sometimes stubborn." It is this stubbornness that has allowed Quebec to survive, to prosper and, lately, to believe herself enough of "a distinct society" to contemplate national independence.

What is meant by the phrase "a distinct society"? It is not just that there are almost 6 million French-speaking people with a clearly defined territory in the northeast corner of the Americas. The phrase reaches deep into Quebec's well-remembered history (the motto of the province, which appears on all car license plates, is *Je me souviens*—"I remember"), and the popular history of Quebec is fundamentally different from that of the United States and English Canada. Americans trace their country's roots to immigrants fleeing England for religious freedom, a revolution for political freedom, and people, of many nations, fleeing their homelands in the hope of finding economic freedom. English Canada also traces many of its roots to flight—at first it was largely populated by Americans who fled the Revolution, and then by Scots, Irish, Jewish, Ukrainian and other people who fled economic and political oppression. The popular history of Quebec, on the other hand, is very different. The early settlers did not flee France but came to convert the Amerindians to Catholicism.

Quebec's culture and nationalism have been slowly evolving for almost four hundred years. The question of survival has always been primary. For the first hundred years, the Iroquois threatened the small French colonies. For the next fifty years, the British, including the American colonies, were the primary enemy. The French regime gave Quebec its language, religion and a preferred style of architecture, but encouraged almost no artistic, literary or political expression—not even a newspaper. The people survived against great natural odds, but Quebec did not have a revolution against a motherland. Instead, it was conquered.

Quebec's history never talks of flight. The seventy thousand colonists responded to the British takeover by having one of the highest birthrates ever recorded. By sheer stubbornness, their descendants have refused, ever since, to be assimilated into the English majority of North America. For the first sixty years of the British period, the people, led by their priests, successfully fought off halfhearted attempts to assimilate them. They were aided by British preoccupations with the American War of Independence, the French Revolution, the Napoleonic Wars and the War of 1812. In the early 1800s Quebec began to express itself in print, and even though there was some racist rhetoric preceding the Rebellion of 1837, this insurrection was as much inspired by Louis-Joseph Papineau's understanding of the constitutional rights of an elected assembly as it was by a sense of local nationalism.

It is said that a people without a history has no future. The 1845 publication of the first volume of François-Xavier Garneau's *Histoire du Canada* marks the beginning of Quebec's artistic expression and prepared the ground on which its nationalism would grow. It did not, however, immediately lead to the flowering of a vibrant culture. The largely rural population remained illiterate and dominated by a conservative clergy that believed in the supremacy of Rome. English-speaking businessmen controlled the economic levers of the province and the church actively discouraged liberal thought and original artistic expression.

The formation of modern Canada in 1867 was generally celebrated by a Quebec that had been led into confederation by George-Etienne Cartier. Cartier had fought for French and Catholic rights (especially in education) across Canada, but after his death these rights in Manitoba, Ontario and New Brunswick began to be eroded. After Louis Riel, the French-speaking leader of Manitoba, was hanged in 1885, Montrealers protested and Honoré Mercier, who flirted with both Rome and France, was elected into office. His career was shortened by scandal.

In the 1890s, Henri Bourassa, a liberal journalist and politician, was the first to express a form of nationalism that can be considered modern. He was a hero to students but was feared by the clergy. Although a severe critic of both Canada and Britain, he did not advocate independence—he felt that American materialism was more dangerous to Quebec than an evolving position inside the British Empire. He believed in a bilingual Canada.

Before World War I, it could be said that *un vrai Canadien* ("a real Canadian") was a French-speaking citizen of British North America

—hence the name of Montreal's hockey team, Les Canadiens. Canada's national anthem, both words and music, was written by *un Canadien*. The country's national symbol, the maple leaf, was first adopted in Quebec. After the war (during which the majority of French-Canadians refused to fight overseas), many of the English-Canadian soldiers found that they had more affinity with the Americans than with the British. With the arrival of hundreds of thousands of immigrants from continental Europe, British North America slowly began to forget the Union Jack and the monarchy (although Queen Elizabeth is still head of state and appears on all the coinage), and as a result, the hyphenated term "French-Canadian" came into more common usage.

In 1921, Abbé Lionel Groulx was the first public figure to imagine an independent French state in North America. However, his vision was not in the liberal tradition of Bourassa. Groulx believed that it was Quebec's destiny to become a perfect Catholic nation, free of the liberalism of Europe and the United States. Meanwhile, American investors were beginning to dominate the province.

During the Great Depression, economic hardship altered the development of Quebec's culture. The church began to lose some of its control as the union movement gathered strength, yet Maurice Duplessis, a conservative who fought the unions, came to power in 1936. The legacy of Duplessis, who controlled the province (except during World War II) until his death in 1959, is mixed. He jealously guarded provincial rights from incursions by Ottawa, yet allowed American, British and English-Canadian investors to gain greater control of the economy.

It was *La Révolution Tranquille* ("The Quiet Revolution"), which began with the election of the Liberal government of Jean Lesage in 1960, that led to the unraveling of the conservative forces of big business and the church. Hydro-Québec, the power company, was nationalized; married women were allowed to own property; the education system was reorganized and freed from censorship; free health care became a right; and artistic expression (including nationalist fervor) flowered. It was during the 1960s that the hyphenated term "French-Canadian" began to be seen as demeaning. The name Québecois became widely used. By 1970, some Québecois were referring to themselves as *Les Nègres blancs de l'Amérique du Nord*—"White Niggers of North America."

Until the late 1960s, the English-speaking minority were completely secure in their privileged position and felt no need to learn French. Their community continued to grow as most immigrant families elected to send their children to English schools. Their position began to change when a terrorist group, le Front de libération du Québec (FLQ), began placing bombs in mailboxes. Quebec nationalism continued to grow. In 1968, René Lévesque founded the Parti Québecois, a political party that advocated Quebec's separation from the rest of Canada through democratic means. In 1970, the FLQ kidnapped and murdered Pierre Laporte, a Quebec cabinet minister. The terrorists were quickly suppressed when the province was put under martial law by the prime minister of Canada, Pierre Eliot Trudeau, who (like Henri Bourassa) advocated a bilingual Canada. The Liberal government of Quebec began enacting legislation that was designed to strengthen the use of the French language. The laws were not considered strong enough and in 1976 the Parti Québecois was elected into office. Thousands of anglophones sold their homes and fled west to Toronto.

In 1980, the provincial government conducted a referendum asking the people if they wished to have "sovereignty-association" with the rest of Canada. Forty percent of the population did. Quebec did not separate then, but when Prime Minister Trudeau patriated the Canadian constitution from Britain, in 1984, Quebec refused to sign it unless its fears of assimilation were addressed and it was given some guarantees that its "distinct society" would be preserved. Today, most Québecois feel that the French language will disappear from North America unless Quebec forms a new relationship with Canada. Businesses are required to communicate in French, English outdoor signs are illegal and immigrants, including Americans and the British, are required to go to French schools. As a result, the English community has been steadily shrinking. Nonetheless, a visitor to Montreal and Quebec will encounter a generous people who may, through stubborn persistence, be on the verge of forging a new and independent identity. It's an exciting time to visit Quebec.

Part One

MONTREAL

❧ I ❧

An Introduction to Montreal

GEOGRAPHY AND CHARACTER

Montreal is on an island just to the west of where the Ottawa River meets the St. Lawrence River. In the center of the island and the city is a 739-foot (225-meter) "mountain," Mont-Royal, after which the city is named.

According to the Population Crisis Committee of Washington, D.C., Montreal's metropolitan area, with a population of roughly 2½ million, is considered, with Melbourne, Australia, and Seattle-Tacoma, Washington, to be the most livable in the world. Montreal has been called the Paris of North America. That's rubbish! It may be like San Francisco; it may be like New Orleans; it may be like Boston; it may be like Edinburgh, Scotland; it may even be a little like Paris; but the truth of the matter is that Montreal is Montreal. Montrealers are confident in who they are. They know how to dress, eat and have fun, without letting productivity get too much in the way.

Geographically, it is a disorienting city: north is not north, south is not south, nor is east, east or west, west. You can look "north" on a street like avenue du Parc, boulevard St-Laurent or rue St-Denis and see the sun setting; you can look "south" and see it rise. There is a reason for this: Early town planners wrongly designated the St. Lawrence River as running from west to east when, in fact, off the old port, it runs from south to north.

Boulevard St-Laurent, just to the east of Mont-Royal, divides the addresses of the city from "east" to "west." Rue Sherbrooke, the longest street, runs through downtown from "east" to "west" and at the base of the "southern" slope of Mont-Royal. Got it? If not, try again.

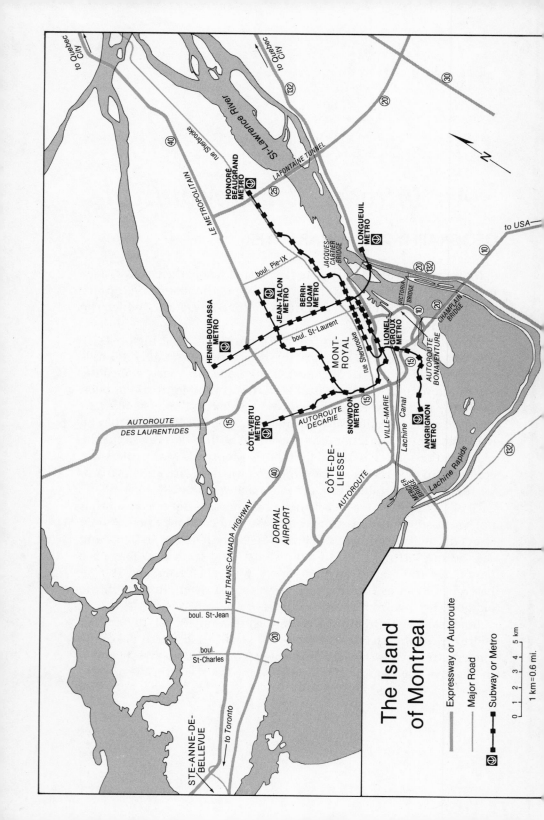

The Island
of Montreal

Expressway or Autoroute
Major Road
Subway or Metro

0 1 2 3 4 5 km

1 km = 0.6 mi.

ARRIVAL IN MONTREAL

By air: Europeans and South Americans will arrive at Mirabel, to the north of Montreal. It was designed to relieve the congestion of the city's more conveniently located Dorval, where flights from the United States and Canada debark. Both airports have rapid bus service to downtown hotels and the metro (subway) system. For information, telephone Aeroplus, 476-1100.

By train: Trains arrive at Central Station in downtown Montreal (Bonaventure metro station).

The Amtrak day-train from New York has long been considered one of the great scenic train rides of the world. It speeds up the Hudson River, passing the underpass at Sing-Sing prison and a couple of abandoned, fake and half-completed castles that were built by American industrialists in the later part of the nineteenth century. It stops for a while in Albany, where Nelson Rockefeller's understanding of modern architecture is expressed in the State Buildings, and then begins to wander along the beautiful shores of Lake Champlain. It is a long (ten-hour) ride, but it is beautiful in all seasons, and you arrive with enough time to check into a hotel, have a late supper and then sleep, ready to "tourist" the next day.

By bus: Buses arrive at the Voyageur Terminal, which is not only downtown but also directly above the Berri-UQAM metro station.

By car from points west: The Trans-Canada Highway, Route 40, confusingly becomes Le Metropolitain in Montreal and will leave you six kilometers (or four miles) north of downtown (Centre-Ville). I suggest that once you cross onto the island of Montreal, you turn off Route 40 and take the parallel Highway 2 and 20, which leads you directly downtown. You can turn off at Ste-Anne-de-Bellevue (just after the bridge) and wander down to an underpass, after which you will take a sharp left. If you didn't make the Ste-Anne-de-Bellevue turnoff, continue eight kilometers, and go down Boulevard St-Charles or St-Jean. If you missed all of these, continue another thirteen kilometers to Decarie (the exit is on the left), a submerged metropolitan expressway that will lead you to rue Sherbrooke, to the west of downtown. The next useful and simple exit is at boulevard St-Laurent (some seven kilometers further east) by which you can make your way, through the city, to rue Sherbrooke or boulevard René-Lévesque. If you did elect to arrive by Highway 2 and 20, you will find yourself on the Ville-Marie Expressway as you approach downtown. The Atwater and Guy exits lead to the west end. If you find yourself going into a tunnel that passes under downtown, don't panic—University, St-Laurent and Berri are streets that run north through the central core.

By car from Vermont or New York State: Don't be discouraged by the rather dull and unattractive country just north of the border. It's a bit of a shock; but remember that, at night, the glow of the distant lights of Montreal can be seen from Customs and Immigration. As you approach the city be alert and ready to get into the lanes leading to Centre-Ville and/or Pont Champlain—the Highway 15 exit—which will quickly lead you to an exit to the Bonaventure Expressway, which ends on rue University in the center of the downtown core. If you miss the Bonaventure, the Ville-Marie Expressway will lead you downtown by the route for those coming from points west.

By plane, boat and train: The most exciting way to come to Montreal is to fly to Burlington, Vermont, take a taxi to the ferry that crosses Lake Champlain, spend close to an hour on the lake and then flag down the Amtrak train that has come from New York City. This takes timing, and if you mess it up, you are stuck in the wilderness of upper New York State. If you take the risk, plan carefully and don't have much luggage—you'll be rewarded.

LE CHASSE-GALERIE

I have told you about the more mundane ways to arrive in Montreal; but there is one other way—by *chasse-galerie.* This requires that you have a large canoe, seating eight to twelve people, and that you and your friends are willing to make a contract with the Devil. I have never tried this mode of transportation myself, but Quebec's most famous folk legend assures that it is possible.

In the nineteenth century, many Quebec men were employed in the logging camps in the Ottawa Valley, west of Montreal. From time to time, they would get bored with their work and their almost exclusively male companionship, get drunk and think about seeing their girlfriends at parties in their hometowns on the shores of the St. Lawrence, east of Montreal. Enter the Devil!

The Prince of Darkness, probably waxing his mustache and wringing his hands, would offer them a free flight home in a *chasse-galerie,* a flying canoe, on the conditions that they not crash the boat into a cross and that they return by dawn. Many men were willing to risk their souls to see their loved ones, and as long as everyone was drunk enough, they would paddle, skimming the sky until they came to Montreal. Now, Montreal had a lot of churches with crosses on the top of their steeples, and the *voyageurs* were repeatedly threatened with crashing and falling into a life of sin in the city below. Yet, of all reports we have, not one *chasse-galerie* crashed. The men went on safely to their villages, danced with their *blondes* and the most beautiful girls, and then, in panic, realizing that dawn was approaching, would tumble into their canoes and paddle like crazy. Occasionally, they would mistake Mount St. Bruno, south of Montreal, for Mont-Royal and have to paddle all the harder, but there is not one report of a soul being lost.

And so, if you are in Montreal at night and see an airplane fly overhead, think of the red light as the glow in a *voyageur*'s pipe and the white as the gleam in his eye as he heads home to see his *blonde.*

TRAVEL IN THE CITY

Public Transportation: Montreal is justly proud of its public transportation. The metro (subway) system is efficient, quiet, clean and safe, with each station architecturally unique. Opened in 1966, it is credited with the renaissance of underground train systems throughout the world. Inside every station there are maps of the entire island's interconnected system of public transportation. Near the entrances are maps indicating the major buildings in the immediate area. At no extra cost, you can change from the metro to buses and vice versa by showing a transfer ticket that you take from machines at the station entrances or that are given to you by bus drivers. Transfers are valid for one and a half hours. Bus stops are posted with daytime schedules. Taxis are plentiful at most times of day and night. **Metro hours:** First and last departures from the end of the lines, Sunday to

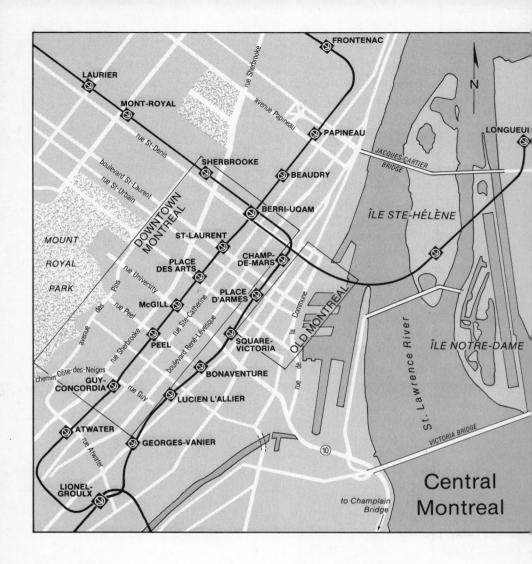

A detailed map of Old Montreal is on page 40. Downtown is on page 88. Île Ste-Hélène and île Notre-Dame are on page 138. Mount Royal Park is on page 144.

Sherbrooke, René-Lévesque, Guy, Peel, University (below Sherbrooke), St-Denis (above Sherbrooke) and Papineau have traffic in both directions.

St-Urbain and St-Denis (below Sherbrooke) run south.

St-Laurent and Berri (below Sherbrooke) run north. Berri is over the metro line.

Ste-Catherine runs east.

de Maisonneuve, over the metro, runs west.

Friday, 5:30 A.M. and 12:30 A.M.; Saturday, 5:30 A.M. and 1:00 A.M.
Bus hours: Buses on almost all major streets run all night. Service on less-traveled routes generally begins at 5:00 A.M. and ends at 1:00 A.M. For detailed information, telephone 288-6287 (AUT-OBUS).
Private Car: Montreal is not noted for its considerate drivers. Pedestrians jaywalk and bicyclists weave in and out of traffic. Also, as in most major cities, parking can be problematic. Residential areas in the city have overnight street parking, but most busy streets are lined with meters. Because of the color of their uniforms, the people who give out parking tickets are nicknamed "green onions."

✤ 2 ✤

The Story of Montreal

THE FOUNDING: MIRACLES AND WAR

In September 1535, Donnacona, the chief of the village Stadacona (present-day Quebec City), told Jacques Cartier, a native of St-Malo, France, about a walled town, Hochelaga, situated on an island and close to some violent rapids. Soon after Cartier had decided to take some small boats upriver to see the town, a canoe was sighted. In the canoe were three men wearing "horns" and dressed as "devils." These men harangued Cartier as they passed his ship and fell, as if dead, as soon as their boat reached the shore. They were carried into the forest. After some hours, Cartier was told that the god Cudouagni had spoken at Hochelaga and said that "the ice and snow were so deep that not a man would survive." Cartier laughed.

On October 2, after sailing against the river current for ten days, Captain Cartier and his men arrived at Hochelaga, where they were exuberantly welcomed by a thousand men, women and children. Clearly, reports of metal pots, gunpowder and other "miracles" had preceded them, for the natives were so pleased by the visit that they danced around campfires all night. The next day, Cartier, wearing his armor, was escorted along a trail that ran through cultivated fields to the center of a walled town of fifty longhouses. Agouhanna, the ailing chief, was carried on a litter and greeted the Frenchmen. The blind, lame, old and ill were brought for Cartier to touch and heal. Perplexed, the captain recited the Gospel of St. John, gave away knives, hatchets, rings and trinkets, and ordered musical instruments to be played. He healed no one, but the Hochelagans were pleased. The next day, they guided him up Mont-Royal, which he named for Francis I. He saw the fertile valley, the Laurentians to the north and the Green Mountains in Vermont. He left the island of Montreal on October 5, 1535.

Over the next sixty-six years, ever more fantastic stories about Hochelaga circulated in Europe. According to historians at the turn of the seventeenth century, the town was said to have fifty palaces, as well as a royal dwelling, with three stories. However, when Samuel de Champlain visited in 1611, there was no sign of any town. In France, however, the island of Montreal continued to stimulate the imagination.

In February 1630, during the Feast of the Purification of the Virgin, Jerome Le Royer de la Dauversière, a provincial tax collector and the father of five, heard a voice telling him to found a society to convert the "savages" in the wilderness of North America. Although a pious man, he was unprepared for such a calling; but, on the same holy feast of the following year, so it is said, the voice dictated the constitution of the society: ". . . what we can't do in one year, we shall do in ten; if we can do nothing in ten, we shall take a hundred. . . ." Perplexed, the tax collector consulted a priest, who told him not to heed the voice. Dauversière, however, could not forget. Religious fervor during the Counter-Reformation was highly appreciated. One of Dauversière's friends, a wealthy Parisian named Marie de la Ferre, paid for a mass for the sick and dying and prayed for clarification of the voice's message. Soon after, Dauversière had a clear and precise vision of an uninhabited and forested river-island with a mountain in its center. He was convinced that he had seen Mont-Royal and resolved to raise capital to found a mission-colony.

One day, while walking up the steps to visit the chancellor of France's palace, Dauversière met, for the first time, Father Jean-Jacques Olier, founder of a religious community, the Gentlemen of the Sulpician Order. It is said that both men found themselves bathed in celestial light, embraced each other like St. Francis and St. Dominic, and knew the deepest recesses of each other's hearts. A year later, they and five other patrons founded La Société de Nôtre-Dame de Montréal.

Not intending to leave France themselves, the wealthy friends began searching for a sober, pious gentleman to lead their mission-colony. Hearing from a Jesuit priest about a twenty-eight-year-old soldier who was tired of being surrounded by the dissolute drunks of the army, Dauversière and his richest supporter, Baron Fancamp, went to the inn where the soldier, Paul de Chomedey de Maison-neuve, was living. At first, they casually engaged him in conversation. After a subsequent and more formal interview, they asked him to found, in the name of the Virgin Mary, a colony. De Maisonneuve accepted the offer.

Meanwhile, a thirty-four-year-old woman, Jeanne Mance, of Langres, a village in the hills of northwest France, was wondering what to do with her life. Her parents had died some years before. She had never married and had raised her brothers and sisters, who were now old enough to take care of themselves. In 1640, after having learned that a cousin, a Jesuit missionary, was going to New France, she decided that her destiny was bound for the New World. Alone, telling no one of her vague plans, she went to Paris. During the winter of 1640–41, because of her piety and seemingly mad ambition, she became a celebrity in the salons of wealthy aristocrats. She was even received by the queen.

Jeanne Mance had little idea of what she would do in New France until she met Madame de Bullion, widow of the tax collector general, who had decided to emulate the niece of Cardinal Richelieu, the Duchess of Aiguillon, who had anonymously endowed a hospital at Quebec. Madame de Bullion decided to put Jeanne Mance in charge of the project that would be realized in Dauversière's yet-to-be-founded colony of Ville-Marie.

Mlle. Mance set out for La Rochelle to find a ship. While in the town, at the door of a church, she met Dauversière for the first time. On seeing each other, so the story goes, they were bathed in celestial light and knew the recesses of each other's hearts. That summer, Mlle. Mance and de Maisonneuve, along with thirty-six other men and three other women, set sail in two ships.

The colonists wintered in Quebec, which had been founded in 1608 by Samuel de Champlain. There, the governor, M. de Montmagny, tried to convince them that it was foolhardy to settle in territory threatened by enemy "savages." Neither de Maisonneuve, who declared that "if every tree were an Iroquois" he would still found Ville-Marie, nor Jeanne Mance could be dissuaded from their Christian destiny. On May 17, 1642, with more recruits from Quebec, the colonists arrived on the island of Montreal. They shot guns to frighten away the evil spirits, celebrated mass and dedicated the island to the Virgin. That evening, the host was left open to the air and Jeanne Mance decorated the altar with fireflies in jars.

When Europeans began to settle in North America, they found themselves reacting to preexisting loose alliances of native tribes. The Montreal area, in Cartier's time, had been sparsely settled by agricultural, Iroquois-speaking people, but by the turn of the seventeenth century, the hunting-gathering Algonquins had forced them south. Samuel de Champlain allied himself with the Algonquins and waged war against the Iroquois almost as soon as he arrived. To defend themselves, the Iroquois were forced to get guns from the English and Dutch.

In Europe, beaver pelts had a high trading value in a fashion industry that favored wide-brimmed fur hats for men. Until the mid-1620s, there had been enough furs for all, but, as demand grew, the Iroquois began to realize that their territory was limited in resources. They began to raid the traditional lands of their neighbors. By 1626, they had gained control of the Hudson River from the Mohicans. Ten years later, they were threatening the rich fur-bearing country of the Algonquins and the more westerly Hurons, who had developed a trading network that ran from Lake Superior to the Saguenay River. When, in 1641, the Dutch decided they would no longer trade guns for pelts, the Iroquois found their economic well-being threatened and tried to ally themselves with the French at Quebec. After they were refused, they intensified their attacks on the canoe-loads of furs that descended the Ottawa River and passed the island of Montreal.

Strangely, in the summer of 1642, as the colonists were building their communal home beside the river, the Iroquois were not seen. That winter, the danger to the missionaries came from nature, not "savages." In late December, the river began to rise. Flooding seemed inevitable. Isolated and facing a frighteningly cold winter, de Maisonneuve made a holy vow to carry a heavy cross up the mountain if the waters receded. The next day, Christmas Day, the river miraculously obliged. That spring, he and all the other colonists trekked through the woods and fulfilled his vow. The present cross on Mont-Royal commemorates this event.

In early June 1643, a large party of Iroquois, in pursuit of Hurons bearing furs, were surprised to come across the new colony. They retreated, returned upriver and captured another shipment. There must have been, however, some debate about what to do about the interloping colony, for a small party stealthily crept up to look at the new settlement. When they saw six colonists, who were preparing gardens outside the palisade, they killed three and took the others prisoner. Such was the skill of their attack, that the colonists were not immediately missed.

A few days later, one of the prisoners, who had been taken across the river, returned to the colony. His companions had been killed, but he had managed to escape and hide. He said that the Iroquois had taken only half the furs and gone to trade with the Dutch. The colonists (but not de Maisonneuve, who was above reproach) got into their boats, stole the remaining pelts and then, at a handsome profit, sold them to the traders in Quebec.

That summer, fortifications consisting of four bulwarks were erected around the colony and a pilgrimage was made to the cross on the mountain. New colonists arrived. Madame d'Aillebout and her husband had vowed to emigrate to Ville-Marie if she were miraculously cured of a terminal illness. Another new arrival was a pregnant dog, Pilote, who promptly gave birth to a litter of pups. Pilote would go down in history, because for ten years she repeatedly gave the first warning of Iroquois attacks. Also that summer, to the joy of the missionaries, Algonquins and Hurons arrived to have children baptized. The colony's first native settlers, Le Borgne de l'Île (One-Eye of the Island) and his wife, converted and were given a Christian marriage. Montreal had its first party.

Sixteen forty-four was not as happy a year. In March, what seemed to be a small group of Iroquois were seen lurking in the woods. De Maisonneuve, after being accused of cowardice, led a party of armed men out into the deep snow. They were surprised by a larger force than expected. As de Maisonneuve retreated, he shot the Iroquois leader at point-blank range. That summer, the "savages" skulked outside the stockade. They threatened, mocked, mimicked and laughed at the Europeans, but did not attack. The colonists described them as "devils" and "hobgoblins." They interpreted the harassment as a continuing test of faith that fortified their religious zeal. They bemoaned only that no conversions were made.

For the fur traders at Quebec, however, Iroquois control of the river meant that no shipments got through, and the following year they agreed that the "enemy" had won the right to be official middlemen. On their side, the Iroquois agreed to accept a Jesuit missionary, Father Jogues, into one of their villages.

The peace with the Iroquois did not last. In the spring of 1645, the Hurons brought a huge shipment of furs to Ville-Marie and the traders did not inform the "middlemen." Then the Iroquois harvest of maize was infested by worms. Father Jogues was accused of having used a magical black box to destroy the crop. He was attacked from the back, a hatchet cleaving his skull. That winter the Mohawks (one of the five Iroquois tribes) returned to harass Ville-Marie.

Over the next years, the Iroquois had more problems than poor crops and loss of trade. In 1647, they learned that the Hurons to the north and the Susquehanna to the south had forged an alliance. There was no room to move east—the English were there. There was no room to move west—the Illinois were there. The Council of Five Nations began to plan. In 1648, they allowed the Hurons to deliver another rich shipment of furs to Ville-Marie, but in January 1649 (winter was an unconventional time for an Amerindian attack) they launched a full-scale guerrilla campaign against the Huron villages. They decimated the tribe, sending scattered groups to ask for protection from the French. The Jesuit missionaries, including Father Bré- beuf, Canada's most famous martyr, were spared no quarter—they were tortured, burned alive and even eaten. For the next few years, while maintaining alternating campaigns of bloodcurdling frontal attacks, sneaking forays and ordinary harassment of New France, they went on to destroy both the Neutrals, a tribe of southern Ontario, and the Erie of northern New York, both of which had been Huron trading partners.

Sixteen fifty-one was the bleakest year of Ville-Marie's existence. Not only was the winter severe, but the attacks were frequent. Jeanne Mance's Hôtel-Dieu hospital was turned into a fortress with the chapel becoming a powder magazine. Some nuns would hide, frozen in fear, under beds or in the belfry. Other braver sisters would rush out of the palisade and drag the wounded back to safety. On May 19, Jeanne Mance saved a man who had been half scalped and left for dead. Lambert Closse, "friend of the brave and scourge of the cow- ard," who never let his dog, Pilote, from his sight, killed thirty Mohawks in one day but lost five of his men. On July 26, he fought off another attack of two hundred Mohawks. With the colony reduced to fifty people, Jeanne Mance and de Maisonneuve felt doomed. In desperation, she suggested that he return to France with 22,000 livres that she still had at her disposal and, if Madame de Bullion agreed, to use the money to find one hundred new and virtuous colonists. Madame de Bullion agreed. One of de Maisonneuve's new recruits was Marguerite Bourgeoys (see page 65).

Back in Ville-Marie, the Iroquois attacks continued. But the sense of holy mission was strong: If a "savage" was captured, baptized and burned alive, his soul was saved. Signs from God were actively sought. In the spring of 1653, the intercession of the Virgin was credited with causing every shot of a surprise attack by two hundred Iroquois to miss its mark. Then suddenly, on June 26, a chief of the Onondaga, one of the Iroquois tribes, offered peace. An Oneida chief followed suit, and on the Day of the Assumption of the Virgin, Queen of Angels, the Mohawks also agreed to stop fighting. The peace seemed miraculous. Numerological explanations, based on the number nine, were used to describe why the tribes had ceased hostilities. But there were more mundane reasons for peace: Squabbles had broken out among the Iroquois tribes.

De Maisonneuve and Marguerite Bourgeoys arrived with fifty new colonists. They made a pilgrimage to the cross on the mountain. When they found that it was toppled and broken, they replaced it.

An uneasy and uneven peace reigned until 1658. The colonists built the foundations, but not the walls, of Nôtre-Dame-de-Bonsecours, a tiny, open chapel where Amerindians were encouraged to pray to a picture of the Virgin.

In 1660, probably encouraged by the Dutch and English and certainly surrounded by enemies, the Iroquois decided to make a massive assault on Ville-Marie. News of their plans reached the colony. In a heroic and effective gesture, sixteen young colonists and about forty Algonquins and Hurons, under the leadership of Dollard des Ormeaux, ambushed eight hundred Iroquois warriors who were paddling down the Ottawa River toward the colony. Save for a few of the Algonquins, the entire French force died during the four-day battle. Montreal was never again threatened with total annihilation.

Vulnerable at home, where the women and children had been left to care for the crops, the Iroquois caused little trouble in 1661. The following year, they were decimated by smallpox, a disease that had been brought from Europe.

The early history of Montreal is filled with miraculous events, none of which can top the incredible meteor showers, repeated sun dogs, spectacular displays of the aurora borealis and the Great Earthquake—which all took place in 1663, the year that Louis XIV took the colony under his direct control. "Earth and Heaven spoke to us many times this year," wrote one witness. "Last autumn we saw serpents in the sky which entwined themselves into one another and flew through the air bearing wings of fire." The six months of earthquakes produced tremors strong enough to throw people face-first into the snow and to make the palisade around the fort "dance like the devil." While white porpoises "screamed" in the river, the Algonquins said the forest was drunk and the missionaries claimed that it was a miraculous time of visitation for the sins of America.

For twenty-four years de Maisonneuve led the mission-colony of Ville-Marie, but in 1666, because of false accusations laid against him by the Jesuit-favoring bishop of Quebec and the growing influence of royal ministers, he was forced to retire to France. Ville-Marie had become Montreal and the direction of the colony was handed over to the Sulpician Fathers.

Montreal, dedicated to the Virgin, was founded by people sworn to chastity. Jeanne Mance, who was never a nun, had made her vow at age seven. She died in 1673 and is buried under the chapel of the hospital that she founded. De Maisonneuve, after a period of great disquietude, rejected marriage and, on the advice of Marguerite Bourgeoys, who was also chaste, took a holy vow in 1654. He died forgotten and in poverty in Paris in 1678. The Sulpician Fathers, who controlled the colony for fifty years after de Maisonneuve retired, presumably were also chaste.

It is ironic that residents of Montreal went on to inseminate the greater part of North America with European settlement. During the French regime, Montrealers founded the forts and trading posts that became the cities of Chicago, Des Moines, Detroit, Duluth, Indianapolis, Louisville, Memphis, Mobile, New Orleans, Niagara, Omaha, Pittsburgh, St. Louis and Toronto. Their explorations took them north to Hudson's Bay and west to Alberta, the Dakotas, Manitoba, Montana, Saskatchewan and Wyoming. During the British period, Montreal residents were the first people to cross the continent to the Pacific Ocean and travel by land from the Great Lakes to the Arctic Ocean.

FROM TOWN TO CITY

De Maisonneuve had nurtured Montreal through its most difficult times, yet its population increased very slowly during the remaining one hundred years of the French regime. In the last half of the seventeenth century, Louis XIV and his minister, Colbert, actively encouraged the development of Quebec, where Louis Buade, Comte de Frontenac, was governor and Jean Talon was intendant. They encouraged immigration, the fur trade, the exploration of the interior of North America and the building of roads, forts and industry. Yet no matter how great their efforts, the development of New France did not compare to that in the English colonies to the south. In 1689, when the struggle for the continent began, two hundred thousand Anglo-Americans faced ten thousand French. At the same time, development of Montreal was stifled by the Sulpician Fathers who had little interest in commerce.

In the first half of the eighteenth century, the English became more and more aware of the geographical importance of the St. Lawrence River, but the court in France had lost much of its interest in its vast North American territories. Only four or five thousand immigrants arrived between 1715 and 1756 and French claims to the Ohio and Mississippi river basins became more and more tenuous. At the same time, the commerce of New France was becoming ever more poorly managed. In 1714, the royal monopoly that controlled the fur trade from Paris went bankrupt and caused much hardship in Montreal. And as the court in France became increasingly corrupt, the administrators sent to govern the colony saw their posts as a means to enrich themselves. By the 1750s, when 1,200,000 Anglo-Americans faced seventy thousand French, the British saw that it was in their power to conquer the whole of New France. The dramatic story of their siege and invasion of 1759 is included as a separate essay on Quebec City. The invasion of Montreal was a simple affair: General Amherst, with ten thousand men, camped outside the city and waited for the surrender of the town and its population of five thousand.

Over the next fifteen years, merchants arrived from Britain and New England to take over the fur trade. Mostly Scottish in origin, they brought some democratic values, but began to resent that the greater part of the government's business was conducted in French. The first British governor, who was at ease with a feudal society, called them "Licentious Fanaticks."

As the Thirteen Colonies began agitating for greater democracy, the British administration at Quebec decided that an elected assembly would not function in a recently conquered country where questions of language, religion and custom were already causing tension. The American Revolution confused most Montrealers—the First Congress had invited Quebec to join them, yet had declared that the Catholic religion "dispersed impiety, bigotry, persecution, murder and rebellion." When the Americans, with the help of some French-speaking volunteers, invaded and occupied Montreal during the winter of 1775, the citizens did not embrace "freedom." When the American soldiers started to try to pay their bills with paper money, the population began to favor British gold. When some Canadians were arrested and taken across the border to Vermont, Montrealers began to dig in their heels. The Americans retreated when British reinforcements arrived at Quebec in the spring.

American independence at first altered little in Montreal. The Ohio River Basin was lost, but the fur trade continued uninterrupted. What Canadians had not anticipated was the arrival of thousands of Empire Loyalists (royalist Americans fleeing the revolution), who, in return for their loyalty, were awarded vast tracts of land, financial help and the most lucrative jobs in the administration. By 1788, they made up almost 20 percent of the population. The Loyalists also brought a strange mixture of aristocratic and democratic values. They saw both the French *habitants* and the British soldiers as peasants, yet wanted an elected parliament. To accommodate them, Quebec was divided along linguistic lines into Upper and Lower Canada (today's Ontario and Quebec). Both were given assemblies with limited powers.

In 1791, anglophones made up only 7 percent of the population of Lower Canada, but wished the assembly at Quebec to conduct its business only in English. The French were quicker to understand democracy than the new arrivals had imagined—they not only won a bilingual parliament but also insisted on electing their choice of speaker. This was not to the liking of the merchants of Montreal. Having lost control of the assembly, they made sure that they dominated the appointed executive council and would continually thwart the elected representatives for the next fifty years.

The French Revolution was the next historical event to influence Quebec. The Reign of Terror frightened the priests and broke many of the remaining emotional ties with France. More important, when Napoleon cut off Britain's Scandinavian supplies of lumber, the colony developed an industry that was dependent on the new "motherland." More English merchants arrived. The emotional scars left by the Napoleonic Wars caused them to propose that the French should be assimilated by giving every parish an English school. The priests refused the offer.

During the War of 1812, both English and French were united in the defense of Canada, but patterns of trade were disrupted. Before the war, two-thirds of Montreal's imports were destined for the United States; but ten years later, because of the completion of the Champlain and Erie canals, the city lost its advantage of being the gateway to the continent. The Montreal merchants sought to regain their position but felt hampered by the French. In 1823, they proposed a union of Upper and Lower Canada that would have given the French-speaking majority a minority of seats in the united assembly, taxed land rather than trade, ended the French land-tenure system and phased out the use of French in fifteen years. When the British government decided against the union in 1828, the merchants began to advocate that Montreal be made part of Upper Canada.

During the same period, immigration from the British Isles increased dramatically—by 1828, English-speakers made up 20 percent of the population of Lower Canada. Vast tracts of land were set aside for "loyal" immigrants, while the *habitants* were dividing their land into smaller and smaller farms. Meanwhile, merchants were buying *seigneuries* and becoming lords of the manors. British governors came and went, as tension between the Montreal businessmen and the French-speaking professional class grew.

The next great wave of immigrants came from famine-stricken Ireland. Fifty thousand arrived in 1831. The following year, when they unwittingly brought with them a plague of cholera that killed 10 percent of the population of Montreal, some French-speakers saw the disease as part of an insidious plot to destroy their culture. When, during a by-election, three Canadians were killed by militiamen who had been called out to control a rioting mob in Place d'Armes, the radical French-language newspapers created three "martyrs." By 1834, the antagonism between the races was being inflamed by the likes of Adam Thom, a Montreal newspaper editor, who began to openly suggest that the destruction of French-Canada could be achieved by having gunboats shell the settlements along the St. Lawrence River. Repeated crop failures from 1834 to 1838 and another outburst of cholera reduced the colony to further misery.

French and English radicals united against the oligarchy of mer-

chants and bureaucrats and looked to Louis-Joseph Papineau, a constitutionalist with little belief in militarism, to lead them. In the
summer of 1837, he visited many towns and spoke openly against the
administration at well-attended, popular assemblies. Meanwhile, in
Montreal, Adam Thom organized a paramilitary force, the British
Rifles, who were willing to take the law into their own hands. The
governor, Lord Gosford, declared the organization illegal, but it went
underground and took the name The Doric Club. When a banking
crisis paralyzed the United States and sent Montreal into deeper
economic depression, talk of armed resistance became open. Thomas
Storrow Brown, an ex–New Englander, organized Les Fils de la
Liberté (The Sons of Freedom) to counteract The Doric Club. Both
organizations openly practiced military maneuvers just outside the
city. In November 1837, they came to blows, and skirmishes between
the two groups took place throughout Montreal. The governor issued
warrants for the arrest of leading radicals, including Papineau, who
had never advocated armed resistance. The large military presence
and English population in Montreal made revolution impossible in
the city, but towns to the south and north of the island prepared for
battle. Martial law was declared.

The patriots were to enjoy one brief victory. Within days the
British army had largely destroyed two towns to the southeast of
Montreal. To the northwest, the Montreal Militia defeated the radicals in the church of St. Eustache and were reported to have not only
thrown the bodies of radicals to pigs to be eaten, but also to have put
the head of one of the leaders on a pike that they carried in front of
them as they marched to two neighboring towns that they burned to
the ground.

Of the insurgents who were captured alive, a few of the most active
leaders were hanged, some were exiled to Bermuda, and a fair number were sent to the prison colonies in Australia. The majority,
however, including a future prime minister, Louis-Hippolyte Lafontaine, were given amnesty by the new governor, Lord Durham.
Eventually, this amnesty was extended to those, including Papineau
and Brown, who had fled. Adam Thom, who had done so much to
provoke the confrontation, eventually became a judge for the Hudson's Bay Company in Manitoba. There, he so offended the French-
speaking Métis that he was bitterly remembered by Louis Riel, who
was to lead Canada's only other rebellion. Thom's only other claim to

fame is a numerological study of the Bible, which predicts that the millennium (the end of the Devil's reign on Earth) will arrive in 1996.

FROM CITY TO METROPOLIS

The Rebellions of 1837 did not alter the economic development of Montreal. By 1820, the walls around the old city had been torn down and the farmland to the west, east and north was being developed. Large numbers of Irish immigrants settled to the west, while the growing English and Scottish bourgeoisie preferred the higher land to the north. The Canadians began their expansion to the east, around a public market that had been given to the city by a radical lawyer and politician, Denis-Benjamin Viger, who was to be locked in prison for eighteen months after the rebellions.

In 1823, when the Catholic diocese decided to build its first cathedral at the corner of present-day rue St-Denis and rue Ste-Catherine, development was greatly stimulated. Within twenty years dirt paths had become streets and the Irish had built their main church overlooking Old Montreal. In 1853, when fire destroyed the Catholic cathedral and the greater part of the St-Denis neighborhood, ten thousand people, including the bishop, were left homeless.

The Canadian bourgeoisie immediately started rebuilding along rue St-Denis, but Bishop Bourget, realizing that the city was becoming divided along linguistic lines, made the controversial decision to build the new cathedral on present-day Dorchester Square, in a growing British neighborhood. In 1857, the new Anglican cathedral was built on rue Ste-Catherine. In 1860, the Hôtel-Dieu, the hospital that had been founded by Jeanne Mance, moved out of Old Montreal to avenue des Pins, even further north. During the 1860s and 1870s wealthy merchants and religious organizations built homes, churches and schools in the western part of today's downtown, but it was not until the 1880s that the new area began to boom.

Rue Ste-Catherine began to assume its position as a major shopping street when Henry Morgan moved away from Victoria Square in 1890, but it was not until the turn of the century, with the opening of Windsor Station, that major economic activity can be said to have moved out of Old Montreal. Donald Smith, who later became Lord Strathcona and Mount Royal, left a heavier imprint on the city than any other Victorian. By many accounts, this great philanthropist was a cagey entrepreneur who built his fortune through duplicity and dedicated self-interest. As you tour the downtown core, you will be continually reminded of his presence.

In 1878, when Laval University (of Quebec City) opened its Montreal campus for medicine, theology and law, the area around St-Denis started to become known as the Latin (or Student) Quarter. As the campus grew, more educational facilities were opened. Bars and cafés began to thrive around the campus, and writers, actors, painters, musicians and other artists began to gather and define the modern cultural expressions of the Québecois.

In the 1890s, thousands of Jewish people, fleeing the pogroms of Russia, arrived and settled around boulevard St-Laurent, which pretty well divided the city into French and English halves. Montreal started to become a booming metropolis as Jews, rural French-Canadians and other immigrants began to flood into the city. By the 1920s, Dorchester Square was the center of a city that was growing in importance and diversity. During the 1930s and 1940s, the city's medical facilities were among the best in the world, and the nightlife was internationally appreciated.

The latest phase in Montreal's development began in 1959 with the opening of Place-Ville-Marie, an integrated block of offices and underground shops. Since the construction of the metro in 1966, this pattern of development has accelerated and resulted in the creation of the famed underground city, which has influenced urban planners all over the world.

The concept of indoor shopping goes back to Roman times and the bazaars of early Islamic cities. In nineteenth-century Europe, market arcades became common—Old Montreal's Bonsecours Market can be seen as one of the earliest of this type of building. In the early twentieth century, shops often became an integrated, street-level part of large buildings, some of which, including Montreal's Dominion Building on Dorchester Square, even included pedestrian malls. Rockefeller Center, in New York City, added to the concept of multi-purpose buildings by including the Radio City Music Hall and an outdoor skating rink. But it would be Place-Ville-Marie that would first lead to an integrated indoor city.

Today in Montreal, well-lit and safe pedestrian walkways connect (except for three short breaks) forty-two city blocks in which there are more than 1.7 million square feet of office space, 1,400 shops and restaurants, 2 department stores, 3,800 hotel rooms, 11,500 parking spaces, 2 rail stations, 3 concert halls, hundreds of apartments, 15 movie houses and 6 metro stations on two different lines. It is possible for thousands of people to live entire lives of consumer spending and never see the light of day.

---- ✤ **3** ✤ ----

Four Walking Tours In Old Montreal

INTRODUCTION TO OLD MONTREAL

Old Montreal is considered to be one of the largest architecturally and historically unified urban areas in North America. It is a nineteenth-century city that on a deep winter snowy night has the feel of Dickens's *Christmas Carol*. Only 1.2 kilometers (.8 mile) in length and less than half as wide, its story-filled streets can be toured in a day. I have organized the places of interest into a sequence that forms a comprehensive walking tour that is, as much as possible, historically consecutive. It is divided into four parts: "Religion and Charity," "The Waterfront," "Government and Guns" and "The Financial Capital of Canada."

OLD MONTREAL AT A GLANCE

Restaurants are listed on pages 167 to 175.

Art Museums: Notre-Dame Museum—religious art and artifacts (4). **Marc-Aurèle Fortin Museum**—twentieth-century landscapes (12).

Bicycle Rentals: The Old Port (17).

Churches: Notre-Dame Basilica (4). **The Sailors' Chapel** (21).

Design Center: Twentieth-century furnishings (6).

Flea Market: The Old Port (16).

Greenspaces: Champ-de-Mars (33). **Victoria Square** (45). **Bonsecours Basin Park** (19).

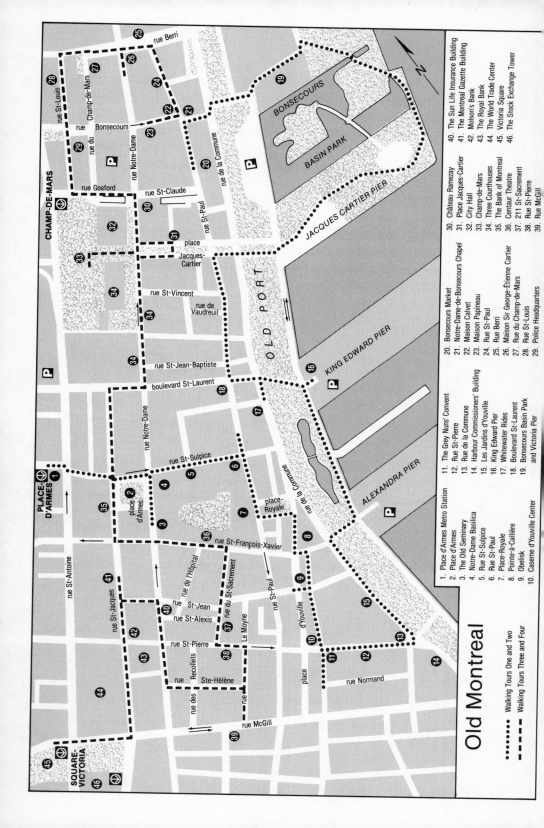

Old Montreal

Walking Tours One and Two

Walking Tours Three and Four

1. Place d'Armes Metro Station
2. Place d'Armes
3. The Old Seminary
4. Notre-Dame Basilica
5. Rue St-Sulpice
6. Rue St-Paul
7. Place-Royale
8. Pointe-à-Callière
9. Obelisk
10. Caserne d'Youville Center
11. The Grey Nuns' Convent
12. Rue St-Pierre
13. Rue de la Commune
14. Harbour Commissioners' Building
15. Les Jardins d'Youville
16. King Edward Pier
17. Whitewater Rides
18. Boulevard St-Laurent
19. Bonsecours Basin Park and Victoria Pier
20. Bonsecours Market
21. Notre-Dame-de-Bonsecours Chapel
22. Maison Calvet
23. Maison Papineau
24. Rue St-Paul
25. Rue Berri
26. Maison Sir George-Étienne Cartier
27. Rue du Champ-de-Mars
28. Rue St-Louis
29. Police Headquarters
30. Château Ramezay
31. Place Jacques-Cartier
32. City Hall
33. Champ-de-Mars
34. Three Courthouses
35. The Bank of Montreal
36. Centaur Theatre
37. 211 St-Sacrement
38. Rue St-Pierre
39. Rue McGill
40. The Sun Life Insurance Building
41. The Montreal Gazette Building
42. Molson's Bank
43. The Royal Bank
44. The World Trade Center
45. Victoria Square
46. The Stock Exchange Tower

Harbor Cruises: Victoria Pier (19).

Historical Museums: Pointe-à-Callière (8) and **Caserne d'Youville Center** (10)—exhibition centers. **Maison Sir George-Etienne Cartier**—refurbished Victorian home (26). **Château Ramezay**—refurbished eighteenth-century governor's mansion (30).

Interiors: Notre-Dame Basilica—Gothic Revival (4). **Maison Ernest Cormier**—Art Deco (34). **Bank of Montreal**—Roman Revival (35). **The Royal Bank**—Florentine Revival (43). **The World Trade Center**—Postmodern (44).

Panoramas: Rue St-Pierre (12) and **Rue de la Commune** (13). **Notre-Dame-de-Bonsecours** (21).

Shopping: Rue St-Paul (18 to 31).

Sidewalk Cafés: Place Jacques-Cartier (31).

Whitewater Rides: Saute-mouton, 105 de la Commune O. (17)

WALKING TOUR ONE: RELIGION AND CHARITY

Place d'Armes metro station (1) opens onto rue St-Urbain. Don't be shocked by the roar of traffic racing in the sunken Ville-Marie Expressway, which, a few blocks west, disappears into a tunnel. The large building that straddles the highway and dwarfs the station is Montreal's modern convention center. To the north is Chinatown; the quiet of Old Montreal is across the highway and up the small hill.

St. Martin's Brook lies under rue St-Antoine. In the seventeenth and eighteenth centuries, this stream was Montreal's first line of defense from Iroquois, British and American attacks. As you climb the small slope, the alley on the right, rue des Fortifications, marks the old city wall, built from 1716 to 1736, which, before being torn down in 1817, was upward of twenty feet tall in places, with protective bastions and six fortified gates.

Place d'Armes (2) has been the heart of Montreal for 350 years. It almost certainly gets its name from the time that de Maisonneuve shot the leader of an Iroquois band that was lurking in the snow-covered forest. De Maisonneuve's Monument was created by the sculptor Louis-Phillipe Hébert and was erected in 1895. Montreal's founder is shown planting the Royal Standard of France, while at each corner of the plinth is a statue of an early inhabitant of the colony. Jeanne Mance is shown nursing an Amerindian child. Lambert Closse, de Maisonneuve's military lieutenant, who died, as he had wished, fighting the Iroquois, is depicted with his dog, Pilote. Charles Le Moyne, who arrived in 1645 and whose sons became founders and governors of Louisiana, kneels on the northwest corner. Completing the quartet is an Iroquois Indian, whose tribal territory once included the island of Montreal. The bas-reliefs on the plinth depict the founding of the Society of Our Lady of Montreal; the celebration of the first mass; de Maisonneuve shooting an Iroquois; and the death of Dollard des Ormeaux, Quebec's greatest hero.

The buildings that surround the square are monuments to the religious and economic forces that shaped this city. In inspiration, they represent two thousand years of Western architecture. The domed Bank of Montreal (1845) resembles the Pantheon, an ancient Roman temple; the twin-towered Notre-Dame Basilica (1824) recalls medieval Europe. The red-stoned office tower (1889) is Montreal's first skyscraper and yet seems inspired by Scottish castles. The smallest building, the Old Seminary (1685), is Montreal's oldest structure, similar to those built in France at the same time. The styles of the other buildings range from Belle Epoque, Art Deco and Modern to International (1972).

VIOLENCE IN PLACE D'ARMES

Place d'Armes has seen more than one battle: In 1775, invading American soldiers decapitated a statue of George III (Montreal's first public monument) and threw the head down the well; in 1832 three men were shot during an election riot; in 1837 conservative British residents attacked radical French and Irish revolutionaries; and ten years later, Protestants and Catholics, the latter led by an internationally famous strongman, Jos Favre, went to battle.

Jean de St. Père, the colony's first notary, was shot by an Iroquois and fell dead from the roof of his house to the west of the square. It is said that after he was decapitated, he scolded his assassins in Iroquois and threatened them with the vengeance of Heaven.

The Old Seminary (3), which is not open to the public, has been occupied continuously by the Sulpicians, a teaching order of mission priests, for three hundred years. The order was granted the island of Montreal by Louis XIV in 1663. The large public clock on the roof was installed in 1701 and is thought to be the oldest in North America. The traditional French manor house was designed by Dollier de Casson, the first local head of the Sulpicians. He also laid out and named the first streets and made the first attempt to build the Lachine Canal.

THE SULPICIAN FATHERS

Dollier de Casson was a giant in stature and strength. He is said to have been able to hold a man seated on each of his hands. De Casson and his immediate successors strictly controlled the colony for about fifty years, establishing a nine-o'clock curfew and interdictions on swearing, dancing and even the wearing of ribbons. Their control did not go unchallenged. The Jesuits, in Quebec, were jealous of their power. As the royal administration grew, the aristocratic governors flaunted the theocracy, traders objected to the ban on selling alcohol to the Amerindians, and young men occasionally abandoned the colony, where there was a shortage of women, to live with natives.

Notre-Dame Basilica (4), despite its size, is only a parish church. Nonetheless, it is Montreal's most important building. It embodies the city's history, houses works of art by some of her best artists, and is the focal point for her collective moments of grief and joy. It is considered to have one of the most beautiful interiors in the world. Every year it hosts the December performances of Handel's *Messiah* and the summer festival Mozart Plus, performed by the Montreal Symphony Orchestra. On Sundays, at the 11:00 A.M. mass, the great organ and the mixed choir sing in polyphony and Gregorian chant—an experience not to be missed!

Open Labor Day to June 24: 7 A.M. to 6 P.M.; June 25 to Labor Day: 7 A.M. to 8 P.M. Guided tours: mid-May to June 24/Labor Day to mid-October: Monday to Friday 9 A.M. to 4 P.M.; June 24 to Labor Day: daily 9 A.M. to 4:30 P.M.

Montreal's first chapel was a hastily built structure of wood in the fort by the river. By 1657, a larger wooden chapel was erected in the compound of Jeanne Mance's hospital just to the east of this present church. Improved and enlarged, it was replaced in 1672 (under the direction of Dollier de Casson) by a steepled stone building that divided Notre-Dame Street. In 1822, when there were fifteen thousand Catholics in Montreal, it was decided that a new church, one that could hold the majority of the population, should be built and money was raised by subscription. Rejecting the Greco-Roman fashion of contemporary churches in Paris, the Sulpician Fathers decided to employ James O'Donnell, a New York architect who was inspired by English Gothic Revival. Notre-Dame was to be his last building, for soon after its completion in 1829, he converted to Catholicism, died and was buried in the crypt of this present church, his greatest creation.

The **exterior** is a chaste specimen of the perpendicular style of the Middle Ages; but unlike Westminster Abbey in London or Notre Dame in Paris, it was designed to be heated by air warmed in furnaces under the floor. The twin bell towers, Temperance and Perseverance, were added, according to O'Donnell's design, in 1842. In Temperance, the eastern tower, there is a carillon of ten bells, each blessed with a name—the largest is called Marie-Victoria. In Perseverance hangs Jean-Baptiste or, more popularly, "Le Grand Bourdon," which is the heaviest bell in the Western Hemisphere (10,900 kilograms) and can be heard twenty-one kilometers away when it rings on Easter Sunday, Corpus Christi and Christmas Eve. In 1865, Baccerini's statues of the Virgin Mary, St. Joseph and John the Baptist were hoisted into the niches over the main doors, and in 1929 the wrought-iron lamps were placed in front.

Although Montrealers were immediately proud of the exterior of their parish church, they were embarrassed by its dark, cavernous, undecorated **interior.** The huge window that was once behind the present-day altar did not light the building well, the wood pillars supporting the balconies were painted in an unsuccessful attempt to make them look like Italian marble, and the high vaulted ceiling was a dull gray. From 1856 to 1870, architects and artists proposed raising or altering the roof, installing windows in different places and even removing the balconies. Gradually, however, a consensus not to alter the basic structure of the building emerged. Inspired by the tiny Sainte-Chapelle in Paris and encouraged by historical evidence that proved that medieval cathedrals had been painted in brilliant colors, Victor Bourgeau was put in charge of the work that would take six years for painters and wood carvers to complete. The three stained-glass rose windows in the roof, the magnificent altar, the azure-blue and gold-star-studded ceiling, and the flamboyant use of color all have proved to be an enduring success, one that can be seen yearly on PBS's "Christmas Special with Luciano Pavarotti." The stations of the cross (1876), although not great art, are the fourth to be designed for Notre-Dame and are presumably better than those designed in 1833, 1838 and 1847. The last of the nineteenth-century additions to the church was the Cassavants organ on the upper gallery above the front entrance. Built between 1887 and 1891, it has 5,722 pipes and is counted among the best in North America. To listen to it played well can raise your hair, reduce you to tears or transport you into ecstasy. Finally, in 1929, to celebrate the centenary of the consecration of the church, the stained-glass windows, designed by J. B. Lagacé and executed in Limoges, France, were installed. They represent scenes from the history of the city.

The **west wall** is to your right as you enter. The first wood carving is of Sister Marie-Leonie Paradis (1840–1912), founder of the Sisters of the Holy Family, who was beatified in 1984. The oak-and-cherry statue in the chapel of St. Thérèse de l'Enfant-Jésus was sculpted by Elzéar Soucy in 1925. The baptistry dates from 1882 but did not receive its present Neogothic decoration, by Ozia Leduc, until 1927. Admire its stained-glass windows and vaulted ceiling. The two chapels before the door that leads to the Old Seminary are dedicated to the Blessed Martyrs of the French Revolution and St. Amable. The windows depict Jacques Cartier reading the Gospel of St. John to the people of Hochelaga in 1535 and the foundation of the Society of Our Lady of Montreal in 1640. The St-Joseph Chapel is followed by windows depicting the first mass at Ville-Marie in 1642, de Maison-neuve carrying a cross up Mont-Royal in 1643, and the arrival of the Sulpicians in 1657. The last chapel on the western side is dedicated to the rosary—Mary is giving a rosary to St. Dominic while the Infant Jesus places a crown of thorns on the head of Catherine of Siena. The two paintings on the inside wall are copies of Titian's *John the Baptist* and Minnocheri's *Vision of Heaven and Purgatory.*

The **altar,** in the words of its chief sculptor, Henri Bouriche, is "a lesson in theology that presents the faithful with the whole doctrine of the sacrifice that Our Lord Jesus Christ who was offered on the cross of Calvary, prophesied and symbolized by the sacrifice of the Ancient Law, and renewed everyday in the mystery of the Holy Eucharist." On either side, extending the galleries, are six recesses housing painted statues of St. Peter, St. Paul and the four Evangelists. At the bottom, the prophets David and Malachi stand on either side of a carved bas-relief, *The Last Supper.* Behind the reredos are St. John communing with Mary and St. Charles Borromeo aiding victims of the plague. A bas-relief of the Tabernacle surrounded by adoring angels is flanked by statues of Daniel and Isaiah. Statues of St. John, Mary Magdalen, the Virgin Mary, and Jesus on the cross occupy the center of the huge carved-wood composition. To the right of them, one above the other, are two figures of the Immolation: Isaac about to be slain by his father, Abraham, and Aaron offering a lamb. On the left are two figures of the Eucharist: Melchisedech before an altar and Moses offering manna. In the highest niche, above the Crucifixion, Jesus crowns Our Lady.

The **pulpit,** also designed by Bourgeau, was carved by Louis-Phillipe Hébert. Unveiled in 1885, it was immediately declared "a masterpiece of solid elegance." The prophets Ezekial and Jeremiah, almost life-size, form the base. Around the pulpit are Moses, David and John the Baptist, and facing the nave is Jesus. Above, there are small statues of Saints Paul, Peter, Francis of Sales, Francis of Assisi, Charles Borromeo and Dominic. Above the sounding board stand life-size statues of two Greek and two Roman fathers of the church: Saints Basil, Leo, Chrysostome and Augustine. Above them is a figure of a young man, Religion, leaning on a cross and pressing a chalice to his breast.

The **Sacred Heart Chapel** was built between 1888 and 1891 in order to accommodate intimate family celebrations. The original "florid Gothic" interior was destroyed by fire in 1978. The redesigned and reconstructed chapel (Jodoin, Lamarre, Pratte & Associates) was finished in 1982. It is a Postmodern blend of Roman, Gothic and Modern styles. The fifty-five-foot-tall bronze sculpture, by Charles Daudelin, represents humanity on the path to Christ, the Holy Ghost and God. To the right of the doors stands Olinda Gratton's statue *Kiss of Judas* (1892), which was spared by the fire, as was the confessional on the left.

Notre-Dame Museum is up the stairs. It houses a collection of Quebec's religious silver, sculpture and paintings. A series of paintings by Arthur Guindon (1864–1923) was inspired by Iroquois folklore. The rich embroideries are by Jeanne Le Ber.

THE SAINTLY SPINNER

Jeanne Le Ber was the daughter of a rich merchant and for almost thirty years (1695–1724) lived as a recluse in a cell behind the altar of an old church close to the river. It is said that she never once changed her bedclothes, yet smelled of sanctity. Angels inspired the designs of her embroideries and even, on one occasion, descended from Heaven to mend her broken spinning wheel. In 1711, when an English fleet from Boston threatened to attack Quebec, she broke her vow of silence and wrote a prayer to the Virgin. When a storm caused the English ships to founder in the St. Lawrence River, Montrealers prayed in thanks.

The **east wall** of the main church begins with the Little Sacre-Coeur Chapel and a simple wooden statue (Sylvia Daoust, 1958) of Montreal's first native-born saint, Marguerite d'Youville. The paintings come from the old church. The first window depicts the sacrifice of Dollard des Ormeaux in 1660; the second, de Maisonneuve's Militia of the Holy Family and Brotherhood of Good Souls (1663); and the third, dedicated to Jeanne Mance, shows the present Hôtel-Dieu Hospital. The painting in the St. Anne Chapel is attributed to Carnevali. On the wall is a bronze sculpted profile of Jeanne Mance by Alice Nolan (1942). The next chapel is dedicated to St. Marguerite Bourgeoys, Montreal's first schoolteacher, who was canonized in 1982. The painting of her teaching Amerindian girls is by Marius Dubois (1944–   ). In the window, you can see the two towers in which she started her school for Amerindians—they still stand on rue Sherbrooke. The next window is dedicated to St. Marguerite d'Youville. The icon of Our Lady of Perpetual Help is a copy of one in St. Alphonse Church in Rome. Next to it are a bronze sculpture of Peter and a magnificent wooden crucifix that was carved in 1738. The last window depicts the construction of Notre-Dame, and the last chapel is dedicated to St. Jude. The painting depicting Mary holding the Infant Jesus and a maple leaf is also by Marius Dubois. The statue by the main entrance is of Marie-Rose Durocher, the Montrealer who founded the Sisters of the Holy Names of Jesus and Mary. She was beatified in 1983.

THE DEVIL AND THE WIND

One day, the Devil and the Wind were walking down rue Notre-Dame when the Wind dared the Prince of Darkness to enter the church. "I shall wait outside for your return," said the Wind, and blew the dust up the street. The Devil disappeared inside, but he never came out. The wind that you feel on Place d'Armes today is the one that still waits for the Devil!

Rue St-Sulpice (5) is to the east of the church. Daniel Du Lhut, the founder of Duluth, Minnesota, lived at the corner of Notre-Dame. Stash Café Bazaar, a recommended Polish restaurant with moderate prices, is at 461 St-Sulpice. A little farther down is a quiet pedestrian mall flanked by buildings that were designed in 1860 as warehouses and shops. Like the interior of Notre-Dame, they were designed by Victor Bourgeau. The proto-rationalist style, with its stone frame facades and large windows, is a distant ancestor of Modern architecture. Built on the original site of Jeanne Mance's hospital, which, after 218 years, moved up to avenue des Pins, they were first used as barracks for British soldiers when it seemed that Canada was going to be dragged into the American Civil War (on the side of the South). Because of their architectural importance, they have recently been renovated and now house condominiums and the **International Design Institute,** 86 St-Paul, which frequently hosts exhibits that are open to the public.

FROM THE RED LIGHT DISTRICT TO THE BLACK MARIA

St-Sulpice Street was the site of Montreal's most lurid scandal. During the building of Notre-Dame Church, a series of tunnels connecting the hospital and a monastery of cloistered Black Nuns to the seminary and old church was revealed to the public. Precursors of Montreal's "underground city," these tunnels had been built for protection against Iroquois attacks (one ran down to the river) and the harsh winters. However, a local prostitute, Maria Monk, whose mother was a cleaning lady at the governor's residence, the Chateau Ramezay, imagined that they had a different purpose. It is thought that while she was lying in bed with one of her customers, a publisher from New York, she began to tell a story about how she had become a woman of the street. She said that she had entered the Black Nuns' convent as an innocent novice, but had soon learned that one of her duties was to descend into the tunnels and be raped by the priests of the seminary. If a nun were to get pregnant, the baby was thrown into lime pits under Notre-Dame. At the time, anti-Catholic sentiment was rife in the United States and racy Gothic novels, notably Mathew Lewis's The Monk, were selling well. The publisher encouraged Maria to write her memoir. The resulting book, Awful Disclosures, became Canada's first international best-seller, and the ensuing scandal caused public outcry in New York, Boston and London. Investigating committees were formed and other "true confessions from Montreal" appeared in print. The publisher got rich. Maria Monk was discredited in 1837 and went on to work the streets of New York and Baltimore. She died, a syphilitic alcoholic, in Cincinnati.

Rue St-Paul (6) was named, by Dollier de Casson, after Paul de Maisonneuve. At that time, it was not much more than a path that ran from Jeanne Mance's hospital past de Maisonneuve's manor house and over a small footbridge to the fort. With the development of the colony, it grew in importance and, despite repeated fires and rebuildings, it was Montreal's busiest shopping street for most of the eighteenth and nineteenth centuries. In 1815, the city's first streetlights, which were fueled by whale oil, appeared here. On the northwest corner of St-Paul and St-Sulpice was the birthplace of Pierre Le Moyne, who became the Sieur d'Iberville; fought the English on Hudson's Bay; founded Biloxi, Mississippi, and Mobile, Alabama; became Louisiana's first governor; and died in Havana, Cuba. His brother, Jean, founded New Orleans in 1722, became the Sieur de Bienville, and was thrice the governor of Louisiana.

Place-Royale (7) was first a military square in front of de Maisonneuve's house. It became a public market in 1706, and proclamations, including the nightly curfew of 9 P.M., were announced from there. As the colony's population grew and crime developed it became the place where transgressors of the law were punished. Petty criminals were placed on a wooden horse with weights attached to their feet, and felons were hung. When, in 1722, the wall around the city was built, the primary gate to the river was there. Amerindians were not allowed inside, but once a year the governor, carried on a ceremonial chair, would arrive, open the gates, smoke pipes of peace with them and declare the season's fur trade open. Much brandy and many animal pelts were exchanged on the riverbank under the walls. In the early 1800s, as the Amerindians were losing their territory and no longer came to Montreal with their furs, the French *voyageurs* would gather in Place-Royale before heading upriver and across the continent to work for the Scottish merchants who now controlled the trade. It was a matter of pride for a young man to get drunk on his initial pay and then head for Place-Royale for a fight. On an early April evening, a dozen sparring matches might provide the entertainment for an excited and betting crowd. All this activity came to an end when the Customs House was built in the middle of the square in 1837. Designed in the Neoclassic style by John Ostell, it was, at that time, no more than thirty meters from the river. A federal building until recently, it was the site where many American immigrants to Canada received their papers.

PUNISHMENT IN PLACE-ROYALE

The first Montrealer to be condemned to death was found guilty of "committing unnatural acts." Fortunately for him, the colony had no hangman at the time and the governor at Quebec condemned him to become the hangman.

In 1696, four young Iroquois warriors, all brothers, were brought to Place-Royale, tied to stakes, given last rites and tortured with fire and red-hot irons for six hours. One witness wrote: "Their strength and stamina was kept alive by brandy that passed down their throats as quickly as if it had been thrown into a hole in the ground and the brothers never ceased to chant of their deeds of war until they were dead."

In 1734, Angélique, a black slave (70 percent of all slaves in Montreal were not black but Amerindian) fell in love with Claude Thibault, a free white man. They had decided to run away to New England. Unfortunately, Angélique's mistress suddenly decided to sell her and would not allow her out. The house caught fire and a large part of St-Paul Street, including the hospital and forty-six houses, went up in flames. Angélique was blamed. She was tortured until she confessed, but she refused to implicate her lover, who had fled. She was sentenced to be burned alive, but the punishment was considered too severe. After being forced to openly repent at the altar of the church, she was carried in a cart to Place-Royale, hanged and then burned.

Pointe-à-Callière (8) was once separated from Place-Royale by the mouth of St. Peter's Brook, which now runs under d'Youville Street. It was here that de Maisonneuve, Jeanne Mance and the other colonists lived for the first few years. Because of the danger of flooding, the growing colony moved to the slightly higher ground across the stream, but the fort was not demolished until 1682, when the land became part of the grounds of Governor Callière's new mansion.

In the 1980s the skeleton of one of the original settlers was discovered here, and the area was set aside for archaeological investigation.

When the work was completed, it was decided to build Pointe-à-Callière Center, a museum that would preserve the findings, incorporate the Old Customs House in Place-Royale, and present exhibits on the earliest years of the colony. The bronze statue in front of the center is of John Young, chairman of the Port Commission, who was the prime mover behind the construction of the Victoria Bridge (the first to span the St. Lawrence River) and instrumental in turning the port of Montreal into an international center for shipping. The statue was erected in 1908 and is the work of Louis-Phillipe Hébert. Open: mid-June to mid-September: daily 10 A.M. to 4:30 P.M.; mid-September to mid-June: Tuesday through Sunday 11 A.M. to 4:30 P.M.

A **granite obelisk** (9) stands in the center of the eastern end of Place d'Youville. It bears the names of the original colonists. On the north side of the esplanade is the pumping station that keeps St. Peter's Brook flowing under the street. The buildings on the south side are on the site of Governor Callière's mansion, where the final peace between the Iroquois and French was signed in 1701.

THE LAST OF THE IROQUOIS WARS

The 1667 peace that followed the First Iroquois War was never stable. The British, because of political developments in Europe, wanted to use the Iroquois to threaten New France; and New Englanders, still loyal to the Crown, had little desire to share the continent. As Austria and England prepared to go to war against France, the Iroquois became part of a plan that envisioned the conquest of all of French North America. The Royal Navy would attack Port-Royal in Acadia (now Nova Scotia) and then go on to Quebec, where it would meet an army that had made its way up the Hudson and Richelieu rivers from New York. The role of the Iroquois was to use guerrilla attacks to soften resistance. On August 5, 1689, the Iroquois attacked and destroyed the settlement of Lachine, just a few miles to the west of Montreal. That autumn, in retaliation, the Algonquins destroyed the English colony of Schenectady, New York. The war was on! But, in the spring, both the Royal Navy and British army failed to make their objectives. The abandoned Iroquois made peace with the French, but the war in Europe continued and

Governor Frontenac, in Quebec, goaded the Iroquois into breaking the treaty. In 1697, at the head of a two-thousand-man army, he was carried in a sedan chair (he was seventy-seven years old) from Montreal and personally supervised the destruction of village after village in the Iroquois heartland south of Lake Ontario. Four years later, the Iroquois agreed to be neutral in future French-English wars.

The d'Youville stables are just to the west. They were built between 1825 and 1865. Originally warehouses, the oldest was first used for the storage of lye to be used in soap manufacturing. The most easterly was a granary for the Confederate army of the U.S. Civil War. They were restored and renovated by a group of businessmen in 1967. The Norman-style interior courtyard, which was once a common feature of Montreal buildings, is now a garden where you can eat and order a drink. **Gibby's** is considered to be one of the best restaurants in the city.

The **Montreal History Center** (10) occupies the old fire station in the middle of Place d'Youville. It houses exhibitions that describe the development of the city and give a good idea of what it was like to live in Montreal in the early 1960s. Built in 1903, the building is an inspired mixture of seventeenth-century Dutch and English styles. Open: mid-June to mid-September: daily 10 A.M. to 4:30 P.M.; mid-September to mid-May: Tuesday through Sunday 11 A.M. to 4:30 P.M.

THE TORIES BURN DOWN PARLIAMENT

It's ironic that a fire station should have been built here, for it occupies the site of one of Montreal's most spectacular blazes.

The English-speaking business community of Montreal has a history of being politically schizophrenic—it has always favored elected representation, yet feared "French Power." At no time was this more apparent than in 1849.

Quebec's first democratic assembly had been created in 1791, but executive power had remained in the hands of a small English-speaking elite. Tension between the assembly and the executive council came to a head in 1837, when a popular uprising took place. The British, fearing a second American revolution, decided to unite Upper and Lower Canada (Ontario and Quebec) and give the colony self-government. Montreal was chosen as the capital and the parliament building was built in present-day Place d'Youville.

Although no expense was spared in the construction, the gas-lit building did not last long. When Prime Minister Louis-Hippolyte Lafontaine introduced a bill that would compensate most citizens, including pardoned rebels, for their losses during the uprisings, the "loyal" British Tories saw red. When the governor, Lord Elgin, upheld the rights of the elected assembly, the Tories threw rotten vegetables at his carriage, rioted and attacked the parliament building. The militia and police did nothing, and it was not long before gas pipes were broken. In a few moments, the building was shaking with explosions. Nothing was saved except a portrait of Queen Victoria, which now hangs in the parliament buildings in Ottawa. To add further confusion to the general political consciousness of Quebec, these same "loyal" Tories, who had called the French-Canadians "rebels and aliens," were soon advocating that Canada leave the British Empire and seek statehood in the United States.

In front of the old fire station and on the northern side of Place d'Youville are examples of late-nineteenth-century commercial and industrial architecture. The building at the western end, with its colonnade and finely carved sandstone facades, is a fine example of American Beaux Arts style. The lobby, with its marble staircase and cast-iron balustrade, is worth seeing. It was built, in 1899, as the headquarters of the Grand Trunk Railway, a mismanaged and extravagant company that caused repeated Canadian governments much heartache until it was nationalized. The area behind this building was, for most of the last century, a poor Irish neighborhood that was prone to floods. On the southeast corner of the square is the huge, pillared, Neoclassic New Customs House that was built, in 1915, to replace the tiny building that we left on Place Royale.

The Grey Nuns' Convent (11) is typical of French religious architecture of the seventeenth century. The original building was built in

1694 for the Charon brothers, who operated a hospice for disabled and infirm men. Their brotherhood ran into financial trouble, and in 1747, Marguerite d'Youville took control of the hospice and opened it to women. In 1755, she founded the Sisters of Charity, which is now an international order of nuns. The complex of buildings continued to grow until 1870, when the order moved to larger quarters and the original mother house was turned into a warehouse, which generated revenue to support the charitable work of the nuns. With the secularization of Quebec after 1960, the state began to assume responsibility for social services, and with a dwindling population in Montreal, the order returned to its old buildings in 1980. Today there are four thousand Sisters of Charity, in ten countries, working with orphans, the old, refugees, runaways, the homeless, alcoholics, drug addicts, the mentally ill, AIDS patients and battered women.

MONTREAL'S FIRST NATIVE SAINT

Although a number of saints have lived in Montreal, Marguerite d'Youville is the first native to be canonized. In 1726, she was left alone to raise her two young sons when her thirty-year-old husband, François, suddenly died, leaving her deeply in debt. It had not been a happy marriage, three children had died in infancy and François had spent most of his time on a farm with his friends, where they drank, gambled, sold brandy to the Indians and avoided the strict moral code of Montreal.

Widow d'Youville, reduced to poverty, opened a tailoring shop on Place-Royale, where she must have witnessed the hanging of criminals, including the slave Angélique. The rest of her life was spent in poverty, and yet, starting with an old, blind woman who had been refused entrance to the Charon brothers' all-male hospice, she began to take care of the needy. Her example encouraged three other women, and in 1737, they took secret vows and began to give shelter to the sick, the mad, the old and the poor.

In the beginning, their generosity did not please everybody. They were nicknamed *les soeurs grises* ("the tipsy sisters") because it was rumored that they drank and got the money to support the growing number of their dependents by illegally selling brandy to the

Amerindians. On one occasion they were stoned, but gradually their work earned the respect of the Sulpician Fathers, who were losing control of the colony to the increasingly corrupt governors. When the Fathers suggested that she be made administrator of the bankrupt Charon brothers' hospice, with its bakery and brewery, the authorities objected to both her reputation and her sex. Nonetheless, word of her work had spread to France and Rome. In 1747, she gained control of the hospice and, in 1755, with letters of patent from Louis XV and authorization from the Pope, she founded the Sisters of Charity. Clearly showing that she had a sense of humor, she adopted gray (grises means gray as well as tipsy) as the color of her order's habits.

Mother d'Youville proved to be an excellent administrator. Her charitable work expanded, but controversy continued to surround her. When she sheltered "fallen women," she was said to be contributing to moral decay. During the Conquest, when a British soldier who was being chased by an Indian, rushed into her room, she hid him under a tapestry that she was making and was later accused of being a traitor. In 1761, she was again accused of contributing to moral decay when she began to adopt newly born children who were left on her door. She had found a baby, with a knife in its throat, frozen in the stream that ran in front of the hospice—from that day forth infants were anonymously and "scandalously" left with her. Controversy still surrounds her. When she became a saint in 1990, she was accused of being a slave trader. There is evidence that her husband's estate sold a slave, that she and the hospice acquired Amerindian children whom explorers brought from the West, and that some French aristocrats who returned to Europe after the Conquest gave her their slaves. However, there is no evidence that she did any more than protect unwanted people who had no legal status in the colony. At least one "slave" was given her freedom and took the name of Youville.

When Mother d'Youville died in 1771, many claimed that a luminous cross was seen hovering over her room. In this century, she was named "Mother of Universal Charity" by Pope John XXIII, beatified in 1984 and canonized in 1990.

When **rue St-Pierre** (12) was extended to the docks in 1870, the east wing of the convent was demolished. The curved wall of the apse of the chapel can still be seen. On the other side of the street is a fine row of buildings. Completed in 1874, their stone-skeleton facades reveal the principles of the Chicago School of Architecture—light, space, ventilation and solidity.

The **Marc-Aurèle Fortin Museum,** 118 St-Pierre, is the only museum in Montreal that is dedicated to one artist. A permanent exhibition of the landscape watercolors of M. Fortin (1888–1970) is augmented by temporary shows of paintings by Quebec artists. Open: Tuesday through Sunday 11 A.M. to 5 P.M.

WALKING TOUR TWO: THE WATERFRONT

Rue de la Commune (13) gets its name from the time when the strip of land between the city wall and the river was the communal grazing pasture for the colony's cattle and sheep. For many decades lost to the commercial activities of the port, it has only recently begun to be reclaimed by the ordinary Montrealer. At its junction with St-Pierre, you are treated to one of the great views of the city. The curve of the waterfront, with the dome of Bonsecours Market and Jacques Cartier Bridge in the distance, is perhaps more beautiful than it has ever been. Across the basin is Bickerdike Pier, the only part of the old harbor where oceangoing freighters still dock. Beyond that is Habitat '67, a revolutionary complex of apartments, each of which was prefabricated and then, like a jigsaw puzzle, put together so that no window or balcony invades the privacy of its neighbor. It was designed for Expo '67 by Moshe Safdie, one of Montreal's most celebrated architects, who envisioned the units being mass-produced so that comfortable, low-cost urban housing would become a reality. Across the newly rebuilt entrance to the Lachine Canal is the last of three huge grain elevators, significant examples of functionalist design that Le Corbusier admired and included in his book *Towards Modern Architecture.*

The **Allan Building,** at the corner of St-Pierre and rue de la Commune, has a small octagonal observation tower from where Sir Hugh Allan (1810–1886), Montreal's greatest shipping magnate of the last century, watched his ships dock. By the entrance you can still see the high-water mark of the great flood of 1886.

FROM RAGS TO RICHES

Born in Scotland, Hugh Allan arrived in Canada at age sixteen and by age twenty-five was a partner in a shipbuilding firm. In 1852 he founded a steamship line that received lucrative government contracts. By the 1870s, when a construction worker earned $1 a day and a woman in a factory earned fifty cents, he was pulling in $600,000 a year. A full-bearded, erect, martinet of a man, he kept his eyes out for more than ships. He was involved in iron and steel, pulp and paper, mining, banking and shoe factories. His business practices were at times questionable. He "encouraged" his workers to accept noncompetitive insurance schemes, provided substandard passage for thousand of immigrants arriving from Europe, paid newspaper editors and reporters to manipulate public opinion, sent his stevedores to bully voters during elections and, in an attempt to get the contract to build Canada's transcontinental railroad, contributed so much money to the election campaign of Prime Minister John A. Macdonald and Georges-Etienne Cartier that the government was forced to resign. His mansion, Ravenscrag, still stands on the slopes of Mont-Royal, but it now houses the Allan Memorial Institute, a psychiatric hospital where the CIA, in the 1970s, funded experiments on the brainwashing capabilities of LSD.

The **Harbour Commissioners' Building** (14), with its angular facade, dome and conspicuous weather vane, is in the popular Neo-Renaissance style of the 1870s and was designed by J. W. Hopkins. Its tower gave the commissioner a clear picture of the activities in the port. The building is presently occupied by the trading company of the People's Republic of China.

THE HISTORY OF THE OLD PORT

Until 1815, the Old Montreal waterfront was nothing more than a muddy strip of shore where riverboats were unceremoniously beached and cargoes were unloaded across a welter of barges, canoes and rotting timber rafts. Because of the powerful St. Mary's current that runs just offshore, ox teams were needed to pull sailing ships into harbor, and it was not until steamships were invented in 1807 that the development of Montreal's port became possible. After visiting Robert Fulton, John Molson, the founder of the famed brewery, established the first steam service between Montreal and Quebec, but was obliged to build his own wharf. Yet even with the inauguration of his steamships, it would take another forty years for the river below Montreal to be dredged from its original eleven feet in the shallow stretches.

The second development of the port came with the opening of a canal that runs along the pre-Columbian portage route around the violent Lachine Rapids west of the city. First envisioned by Dollier de Casson in the seventeenth century, the canal was needed to protect Upper Canada from American invasion. It was built by mostly Irish immigrants between 1821 and 1825.

In the 1830s, the first harbor commissioner, Jules Quesnel, organized the building of a river wall and a ramp for flat-bottomed boats. Even so, most oceangoing ships would unload their cargoes in Quebec and have them shipped to Montreal on barges. The most impressive river traffic consisted of giant log rafts destined for England and the Royal Navy. Complete with more than a dozen shacks for the raftsmen, sails, anchors, oars and even livestock, some were 480 feet long and 60 feet wide. They had been first assembled on the Ottawa River and then, after being broken into 40-by-60-foot sections, had come crashing down the Lachine Rapids. Reassembled west of Montreal, they then continued a leisurely voyage to Quebec, where they were again broken down and loaded into ships. Charles Dickens was astounded when he saw one float by his hotel.

The dredging of the river was begun in the 1850s and has never ceased. By 1867 the channel was 20 feet deep; twenty years later it was 27 feet deep; and by the turn of the century it had reached its present 35 feet. One man, John Young, was responsible for much of this activity and the accompanying replacement of the low stone wharves by the high-level piers of today. He realized the importance of railroads, was the prime mover in the construction of the Victoria Bridge (once considered one of the Wonders of the World) and was instrumental in turning Montreal into a great port that still rivals New York in its importance to international trade.

In 1959, when the St. Lawrence Seaway was opened by Queen Elizabeth and President Eisenhower, the Lachine Canal was closed and Montreal's port facilities began to move downriver and away from the city center. For many years, Montrealers debated what to do with the largely abandoned piers of the Old Port. The huge grain elevators, which blocked the river from the city, were demolished in the early 1980s, the passenger terminal on Alexandria Pier was retained for cruise ships and the buildings on King Edward Pier were recycled to house a flea market and an exhibition center. Finally in 1990, the federal government, which owns the area, decided to spend $70 million to rebuild the entrance to the Lachine Canal and create a park and marina out of Jacques-Cartier and Victoria piers.

Les Jardins d'Youville (15) is a series of 1842 warehouses that have recently been turned into condominiums. Opposite, **Croisières le Maxim Inc.** offers a variety of excursions and cruises that can include shows, discos, dinner or cocktail parties. Total capacity is a thousand passengers. Open: June 20 to September 1, five cruises per day. Tickets can be bought on the pier. For reservations, telephone 849-4804. The building on the corner of de Callière was, from 1870 to 1970, Joe Beef's Canteen.

THE WICKEDEST MAN OF MONTREAL

Until his death in 1889, Joe Beef enjoyed the reputation of being Montreal's wickedest man. According to one newspaper report, his tavern on the ground floor "was the resort of the most degraded men. It was the bottom of the pit, a sort of cul de sac where thieves could be corralled." No strangers, including preachers, were ever turned away. A skeleton that Joe Beef said was the remains of his father stood behind the bar—it was still there in the 1940s. A performing bear that was named after a virulent, local temperance advocate (who had been unsuccessfully sued for libel after his newspaper exposed the conditions that immigrants suffered in Sir Hugh Allan's ships) entertained the clientele. In the basement there was a menagerie of animals, including a bison, an alligator, snakes and parrots. The top floor was a flophouse. Although Joe Beef said that money was the only thing in life, he sheltered the homeless, fed striking workers free of charge and occasionally would pay some of his customers' hospital bills. The sailors gave him a reputation that spanned the world, and when he died, his funeral procession was watched from the dike along the harborfront by men, women and children standing eight deep. He would have appreciated the send-off—some years earlier, while returning from the cemetery where he had buried his wife, he had demanded that the funeral band play "The Girl I Left Behind Me."

King Edward Pier (16) is the home of a flea market (*marché aux puces*) and the **I-Max Theatre,** which presents special films on a screen seven stories tall. **The Exhibition Centre** presents annual exhibitions and workshops that usually explore new technology. Open: May 31 through September 22, daily 10 A.M. to 9 P.M. For information, call 849-1612. The International Museum of Cartoon Art, which is looking for a permanent home, also mounts exhibits.

Whitewater rides (17) are offered at 105 de la Commune. Reservations are required to take the Saute-mouton ("Frisking Lamb") jet-boats that leave from Victoria Pier to run the Lachine Rapids. The trip takes two and a half hours, but it is an experience not to be missed. No other city in the world offers first-class rapids from downtown. Raincoats, hats, boots and life jackets are supplied. Telephone: 284-9607.

---◼---

SHOOTING THE RAPIDS

Before Europeans arrived in America it was part of the rite of passage into manhood for the Algonquin to brave the turbulent, swirling waters of Lachine in a canoe. Samuel de Champlain was the first "tourist" to take the rapids and, by doing so, gained the respect of his hosts. In the nineteenth century, raftsmen steered (not without loss of life) their bound logs down the channels, and at the turn of this century, a twin-funneled paddle steamer, always piloted by a Mohawk, gave dignified Victorians the thrill. The rapids are very dangerous if you do not know the rocks, and it is a rare summer when some foolish or careless boater does not lose his life. The jet-boats are, however, perfectly safe.

---◼---

If jet-boats aren't your style, you can **rent a bicycle** in the Old Port (be ready for a large deposit if you don't have a credit card) and cycle the eleven kilometers (six miles) along special paths to the suburban city of Lachine—hyperbolically so named because it was once thought to be on the way to China. Maps of the route can be obtained in the Old Port. The outing will take an afternoon, especially if you do the whole circuit along the landscaped park on either side of the canal, stop at the **Fur Trade Museum** (just beyond the end of the bicycle path) and return via Lasalle Boulevard, which borders the rapids.

Boulevard St-Laurent (18) is the street on which new immigrants have traditionally settled. Until jet airplanes were developed, tens of thousands of Jewish, Russian, Ukrainian, Hungarian, English, Irish, Scottish, Italian, Greek, Estonian and other immigrants arrived by boat. Many took the Canadian Pacific Railway to populate the rest of Canada, but a good number of them just walked up this street and out of Old Montreal to settle between the French and English halves of the city.

On the corner, the vaults beneath the building that presently houses the spaghetti restaurant **Chez Giorgio** were built in 1690 for Louis-Thomas Chabert de Joncaire, King Louis XIV's ambassador to the Iroquois Nation. Diagonally across St-Paul Street stood the chapel where the recluse Jeanne Le Ber was visited by the angels who showed her the designs for her embroideries and mended her spinning wheel. Behind the popular Keg Bar, the rough-stone building, with the archway for carriages, was built in 1786 for Simon McTavish, Montreal's first millionaire.

THE GREAT FUR TRADER

Simon McTavish, a native of Scotland, arrived in Montreal via New England soon after the United States was recognized as an independent country. He quickly became involved in the fur trade and traveled by canoe to the Great Lakes. He was, however, more suited to city life. He became the dominant force behind the North-West Company (1780–1821), which soon controlled much of the fur trade of North America. It was this company's quest for furs that opened the continent from the Dakotas west to Oregon and north to the Arctic Ocean. When John Jacob Astor, whose warehouse still stands at the corner of Vaudreuil and Ste-Therese (to the east), was a young man, he made yearly three-month-long visits to Montreal to do business with McTavish. Simon Fraser, who gave his name to the Fraser River, was one of McTavish's partners and neighbors. McTavish played as hard as he worked. He was a bachelor most of his life and earned his nickname, Le Marquis, because of his lavish life-style. He drank to excess, ate a lot of oysters, threw many a party and said that he was never happy unless in love. When he finally married, he decided to build his young French-Canadian bride a mansion on Mont-Royal. He died during its construction and was buried nearby.

His empire did not last long after his death. John Jacob Astor broke Montreal's control of the market when he successfully lobbied Washington to have all foreigners excluded from trading furs in the United States and its territories. McTavish's nephews and heirs, the McGillivary brothers, went bankrupt and the North-West Company became part of the rival Hudson's Bay Company. Simon McTavish's ghost is said to toboggan down the slopes of Mont-Royal in its coffin.

Bonsecours Basin Park (19) was created out of the old Victoria Pier. It was built by the government of Canada to celebrate the 350th anniversary of the founding of Montreal. At the tip of the pier stands the **Sailors' Memorial Clock Tower,** which was opened in 1919 by the Prince of Wales. It honors the merchant marine and now houses a small exhibition on the harbor. Visitors can also watch the clock's mechanism in operation and climb the tower for a view of the river. Open: early June to mid-September. Free admission.

Leaving Place Jacques-Cartier for later, complete the walking tour of the waterfront by heading to the Sailors' Church. **Rasco's Hotel,** at 281–285 rue St-Paul E., was built in 1835 and renovated in 1982. For years it was considered to be one of North America's most sophisticated hotels. The old Bonsecours Hotel, at 355, is a good example of the commercial architecture of 1881.

Bonsecours Market (20) is the largest nineteenth-century structure on the waterfront. Completed in 1845, the elegant, Palladian building was designed by William Footner to house a concert hall, reception rooms, council chambers, municipal offices and police headquarters. The Doric columns of the portico on the far side are made of cast iron—a unique tribute to the Industrial Revolution. For more than a hundred years, with stalls spilling out onto the surrounding streets, the building housed Montreal's busiest fresh-produce market. After the 1849 riot and burning of the parliament buildings, it was the seat of Canada's legislature, and from 1852 to 1878 it served as Montreal's City Hall. The market closed in 1961, and in 1964 the city renovated the interior to house offices, but studies are under way to recycle the building so that it will again be open to the public.

It was on this site in 1815 that John Molson, the founder of the brewery, opened Mansion House, a luxurious hotel with a 140-foot-long ballroom, a library, a terrace facing the river, and stables for seventy horses. So that his guests could alight from his steamboats, he built Montreal's first wharf. The hotel's life was short—it burned to the ground when a musician accidentally dropped a candle while making his way to his dressing room in the basement. Mr. Molson then used the site to build Montreal's first professional theater, where Edmund Kean, Fanny Kemble and Charles Dickens performed. With its circle of galleries, two tiers of boxes and its "unrivalled" (according to a newspaper ad) illumination by gas, it was never a money-maker and was demolished to make way for the present building.

Notre-Dame-de-Bonsecours Chapel (21), affectionately known as "The Sailors' Church," echoes back to the miraculous beginnings of Montreal. It is one of the city's most loved buildings. The colony's first schoolteacher, Marguerite Bourgeoys, proposed that a sanctuary dedicated to the Virgin and open to the Amerindians be built here in 1653. The blessing of the foundation stone took place in 1657 but construction was abandoned the following year. In 1670, there was only a small wooden shelter. It faced the river and contained a picture of Our Lady. The impetus for the construction of a stone chapel came in 1673, when Marguerite Bourgeoys returned from France with a statue that was reputed to perform miracles. The first building was completed five years later and quickly became a place of pilgrimage. After it burned to the ground in 1754, the British proposed to use the site for military barracks, but the citizens of Montreal objected. The present building dates from 1772. In the 1880s, the addition of an "aerial chapel" topped by a statue of Our Lady and two towers, each bearing an angel, greatly altered the simple French design. In 1953, the steeple was lowered and covered with copper.

THE SAINTED TEACHER

Marguerite Bourgeoys was born in Troyes, France, in 1620. From her earliest years, she felt that she had a religious calling but was refused entrance to both the Carmelite and St. Clair orders of nuns. She was thirty-two years old when she dreamed that she would be visited by "a man dressed in brown," who would change her destiny. When de Maisonneuve, who was in France to find new recruits, appeared dressed in brown the next day, she believed that her dream had come true. He had heard about her from his sister, who had suggested that she would make an excellent missionary and schoolteacher. That night Marguerite prayed for guidance. The Virgin appeared to her and said, "Go, I will not forsake you."

When she arrived in the colony the following year, she began her school in an old stable not far from Jeanne Mance's hospital. She also made a pilgrimage to the cross that de Maisonneuve had carried up the mountain. Deeply dedicated to the Cult of the Virgin, it was she who convinced him to take a vow of chastity rather than get married.

For the rest of her active life, Marguerite Bourgeoys continued to direct the education of children. In 1672, she founded the Congregation of Notre-Dame, a teaching order of nuns that today operates in seven countries. In 1678, she established a school for Amerindian girls. She was the guardian of *Les Filles du Roy* ("Daughters of the King") who Louis XIV sent to marry the young men of the colony. In later life, Mother Bourgeoys became a bit of a masochist. "In order to understand suffering," one biographer has written, "she wore a little cap which was lined with sharp points that penetrated deep into her head." Yet during her life, several miracles (including an unemptiable cask of wine) were attributed to her. In 1693, after a tormented period of religious doubt, she retired as Mother Superior of the order she had founded. She died in 1700 and has been credited with miraculous cures in the twentieth century. In 1974, Pope Paul II declared her to be a saint.

―――――――――――――■―――――――――――――

The **interior** and stained-glass windows of Notre-Dame-de-Bonsecours date from 1888. To the right of the altar is a large wooden statue that was carved in 1848 and placed outside on the roof. According to legend, it first faced the city but during the night twisted itself around to face the river. Since then it has been called the Sailors' Virgin. In 1867, the Zouaves, a small army of volunteers on their way to fight for the Pope against Garibaldi, credited Notre-Dame-de-Bonsecours with their being saved from shipwreck. They gave the first model ship as an offering of thanks. The chapel began to be known as the Sailor's Church, and other grateful crews gave the other models that hang from the ceiling. The crystal chandeliers, marble floor and pews were installed in 1959. Montreal's "miracle statue" stands in its niche to the left of the main altar.

THE LITTLE STATUE

The small wooden statue of Mary with the baby Jesus has an intriguing beauty. Carved out of wood from the forest of Montaigu (now part of modern Belgium), where the Virgin had once appeared, it was already a hundred years old when the ailing Baron de Fancamp, an early patron of Montreal, gave it to Marguerite Bourgeoys. Immediately, the baron was cured. When it arrived in Montreal in 1673, it quickly was credited with "cures believed to be miraculous for both body and soul." Its very survival is considered miraculous. When the old chapel burned to the ground in 1754, the statue was found, unharmed, in the ashes. It was to survive another fire in 1768. When the statue was stolen in 1831, "confidence seemed to be shaken," and attendance at the chapel dropped. In 1844 the statue was found, and four years later, with twenty thousand people in attendance, it was paraded through the streets in order to ward off cholera. It survived a third fire in 1893, when the Mother House of the congregation was destroyed.

In a room beneath the chapel is a charming **museum** where fifty-eight showcases exhibit costumed dolls in scenes from the life of St. Marguerite Bourgeoys. Clearly the labor of love of its creator, Sister Ste-Hélène-de-la-Charité, it is charming. On the roof of the chapel, the **observatory** provides a splendid, panoramic view.

Chapel open: November to April: 10 to 11:30 A.M. and 1 to 5 P.M.; May to October: 9 A.M. to 5 P.M. Museum and observatory open: May to October: 9 A.M. to 4:30 P.M.; November to April: 10 to 11:30 A.M. and 1 to 4:30 P.M. Closed Monday.

WALKING TOUR THREE: GOVERNMENT AND GUNS

The eastern end of the old city has been the administrative center of Montreal since 1705. The French and British governors maintained their residences close to the garrison, prison and government stores. City Hall, police headquarters and the superior court are still in the area. For the background on this walking tour, read about the rebellions of 1837, pages 34–35.

Maison Calvet (22) is one of Montreal's oldest surviving residential buildings (1770). With no distance between it and the street, and with its fire walls at either end of the steeply pitched roof (dangerous after heavy snowstorms) and asymmetric windows, it is typical of French architecture of the period. It was originally owned by Pierre du Calvet, a wealthy French Protestant, who was imprisoned and then banished for having supported and supplied the American invaders who occupied Montreal in 1775. Restored in 1964 by the Ogilvy department store, it now houses a small food and coffee shop.

Up rue Bonsecours is the restaurant **Les Filles du Roy** (The King's Daughters), where costumed waitresses serve traditional Quebec cuisine in a period setting. By its name, it honors the contingents of young women who were sponsored by Louis XIV to become the wives of the numerous single men in the colony.

Farther up the street, you can see the gables and steeply pitched roof of **Maison Papineau** (23), which was built in 1785. The wooden facade of this large house was cleverly carved to resemble expensive cut stone. Once owned by Louis-Joseph Papineau, the man in whose name Canada's greatest insurrection was fought, it was owned by his descendants until 1920. It has been lovingly restored by Eric McLean, the music critic who first aroused interest in the restoration of Old Montreal when he bought the building in 1961.

------------------------------------ ■ ------------------------------------

LOUIS-JOSEPH PAPINEAU

Louis-Joseph Papineau was born in 1786. He was the son of Joseph Papineau, who had carried British dispatches through the American lines in the winter of 1775–76 and had fought for the use of French in the first assembly in 1792. Louis-Joseph Papineau was educated at the Seminary of Quebec, became a lawyer and entered the assembly in 1808. A great orator "with a touch of magic," he was elected speaker in 1812, a post he held for the greater part of the next twenty years. He was a militia staff captain during the War of 1812 and wrote, in 1820, "We should act like British subjects and free men." In the 1820s, he and John Nielson went to London, where they successfully lobbied against the union of the Canadas that the Montreal merchants desired. During the 1830s he consistently fought for the constitutional right of the assembly to control the government's purse strings.

Papineau was a constitutionalist who never advocated violence. He was highly respected by liberals in England, and his name was repeatedly invoked in Upper Canada, which was also fighting for a more democratic form of government. When debate and protest turned to violence in November 1837, he fled to Vermont and was forced to live in exile until 1845. When he returned, he was a broken man with a bleak vision for the future of French-Canada. He spent his last years on his *seigneury* at Montebello on the Ottawa River.

For an **abbreviated tour** of Old Montreal, walk directly to **Chateau Ramezay** (30). For the full tour, continue east along **St.-Paul** (24), where you can compare the differences in residential buildings built over more than two hundred years. Note the rough fieldstone walls of the eighteenth century and compare them to the smooth cut limestone of the early nineteenth century. Compare the roofs and windows. The recent (1978) cement residential building, which reflects the arches of its neighbor, indicates the sensitivity of some modern architects.

Before the British conquest, the south side of the street was the site of the Royal Stores of the Intendant, François Bigot, who embezzled from the government, swindled the merchants, held lavish balls and gambled huge amounts with his friends at a time when a pound of butter cost a soldier the equivalent of three days' wages. When Bigot returned to France in 1760, he was found guilty of corruption, had his property seized and was exiled. During the British regime, the area housed the Quebec Gate Barracks.

Rue Berri (25) marks the eastern limit of Old Montreal. Ignoring the abandoned railroad yard immediately below (reserved by the city for a future residential area), from here you have a fine panoramic view of Jacques Cartier Bridge, the modern skyscraper of Radio Canada's headquarters and television and radio studios, Buckminster Fuller's dome on St. Helen's Island and the cold-storage warehouse that Le Corbusier regarded as the most architecturally interesting building in Montreal. The Molson Brewery has occupied the same site and been owned by the same family since 1785.

MOLSON, THE BREWER

John Molson was born in Lincolnshire, England, in 1763. He was eighteen years old when he came to Montreal after doctors had suggested that an ocean voyage might cure a lengthy illness. Impressed by the opportunities in the colony, he used part of his inheritance to buy land that he abandoned when he learned that it, according to the newly signed Peace of Paris, was in the United States. He then bought into a little log brewery in Montreal. He became its sole owner in 1785 and went back to England to buy equipment. Within months of returning to Montreal, he was back in business and living with a woman named Sarah. They would not marry until 1801, eight years after the birth of their third child.

The brewery was quickly a success, and Molson began to invest in other enterprises. An innovator and visionary, he inaugurated the first steamboat service on the St. Lawrence River—just two years after Robert Fulton had started the first such service in the world. The first steamboat to cross the Atlantic was owned by John Molson. He also contributed to the development of the modern hotel, built Montreal's first theater and helped found the Montreal General Hospital. By the time he died in 1837, the family was involved in banking, Canada's first railroad, real estate and distilling.

The recently restored building at **514–522 Notre-Dame Street** was part of Dalhousie Station, which was built in 1883. It was from here that Les Fusiliers de Montréal (the Rifles and the Garrison Artillery) set out on the still-incomplete transcontinental railroad to quell the 1884 North-West Rebellion led by Louis Riel. The following year, the first train to Vancouver set out; the cry of the conductor was, "All aboard for the Pacific." The station now houses the **École National du Cirque,** North America's only school of circus arts. Introductory and professional-level courses are offered to children and adults.

Sir George-Etienne Cartier House (26), at 458 Notre-Dame, is a complex of two houses where Canada's most important French-speaking Father of Confederation lived from 1848 to 1871. Upstairs, the period-furnished dining room, bedroom, sitting room, pantry and bathroom give an accurate impression of the stuffy comfort of a rich Victorian family. Open: mid-May to October 15: daily; October 15 to mid-May: Wednesday through Sunday from 9 A.M. to 5 P.M.

Before rue Notre-Dame was extended and the land leveled, the land opposite was the site of the Citadel, where Ethan Allen and his Green Mountain Boys were held captive after the Americans' first failed invasion of Montreal in 1775.

A FOUNDER OF A NATION

George-Etienne Cartier was born in 1814, studied at the Collège de Montreal and was admitted to the bar in 1835. A radical in his youth, he fought at the Battle of St. Charles, where the patriots of 1837 repulsed a British force sent to break up the rebel forces that were organizing in the Richelieu Valley, southeast of Montreal. After more than a year of exile, he was pardoned. Cartier entered active politics in 1848 and by the mid-1850s was one of the most influential politicians in the country. He is credited with the legislation that modernized and unified Quebec's road, school, legal and land systems. He took an active part in Canada's acquisition of the Northwest Territories, the creation of the province of Manitoba and the entry of British Columbia into confederation. He died in 1873 before being implicated in the Pacific scandal that revealed Sir Hugh Allan's attempt to gain the contract for the construction of the transcontinental railroad by giving $350,000 (about $28 million today) to the election campaign of, among others, Prime Minister Macdonald. It was a sad end to the brilliant career of a well-loved politician.

On **rue du Champ-de-Mars** (27) is a tiny park, which is named after Lord Dalhousie, the British governor (1819–28) who was so disliked by the population of Quebec that Louis-Joseph Papineau and Denis-Benjamin Viger went to London and successfully had him recalled.

Viger Hotel and Station, just down the hill, was designed by Bruce Price, the American architect who brought the French-Chateau style of architecture to Canada. The 1897 building now houses municipal offices. The park in front of it is built over the Bonaventure Expressway. This attempt to revitalize a public area that had once been the most fashionable in Montreal is divided into three sections, and is the **ugliest park in Montreal.** The western third is a brick plaza scattered with what look like twenty-foot-tall card tables; the central section encloses a monolithic, but interesting, sculpture and fountain; and the eastern section (the most successful, but still alienating) is designed for children.

Rue St-Louis (28) has several buildings of architectural interest. Those at 442–50 and 464–86 are good examples of the late-Victorian "gingerbread" architecture that once dominated and still influences the residential architecture in much of the city. Note the balconies and external wrought-iron staircases—features than can be seen on tens of thousands of triplexes (three flats per building) in Montreal. One nickname for the city is Balconville, another is *La Grosse Tortière* ("The Big Meat Pie").

The two-story row houses across the street are reminiscent of hundreds of thousands of similar units that were built for workers in England. Maison Brossard-Gauvin, at 435, dates from 1755; and Maison Brossard, with its icon of the Virgin above the door, from 1840.

Looking down St-Denis Street, you will see the statue of Jean-Olivier Chenier, the young doctor who died in the church at St-Eustache (northwest of Montreal) fighting the British army in late 1837. Reports that his body had been fed to pigs raised the sympathy of Americans from Vermont to Michigan, and the following year there were repeated ragtag invasions by bands of freedom-fighters who sought to liberate Canada.

Police Headquarters (29) and the adjoining classically inspired Municipal Courts Building, where you can pay your parking tickets, take up an entire block. Rue Gosford is named after the conciliatory British governor who was unsuccessful in his attempt to avert the

Rebellion of 1837. The little slope leads back to rue Notre-Dame. The Chaussegros-de-Léry Project, on the left, is a modern, multipurpose building that complements the old facades of the neighborhood. Its underground **parking** garage has room for one-thousand cars.

Château Ramezay (30), at 280 Notre-Dame, was built in 1705 for Claude de Ramezay, the eleventh governor of Montreal. The facade is of rubble stone, with cut-stone trim. The iron S-shaped bars are the ends of rods that extend through the beams to anchor them in place. The building was enlarged to its present size in 1755 by a trading company, Compagnie des Indes. From 1764 to 1849 it served as the residence of the British governors of Canada, and during the American occupation of 1775 it was army headquarters under Generals Richard Montgomery and Benedict Arnold. Benjamin Franklin also lived there. Starting in 1850, the building began to have a variety of occupants. It was successively a courthouse, headquarters of the provincial department of instruction, a school, and a seat of government until it was acquired by the city in 1895.

The old stone mansion is now a historical museum. On the ground floor, period furniture, paintings, porcelain and other objects recreate the official and domestic life of a French governor of the 1700s. The antique mahogany paneling of one room is especially beautiful. Also of note is a portrait of Henry IV (1553–1610) of France, during whose reign Quebec was founded. In the basement are rooms that exhibit collections of utensils, furniture and tools that might have been used in the early days of the Ville-Marie colony as well as displays that illustrate the life of the Iroquois. The museum also has small collections of religious sculptures, maps and drawings by Francisco de Goya. Open: Tuesday through Sunday 10 A.M. to 4:30 P.M. Open Monday during the summer. Telephone: 861-7182.

MONTREAL'S FIRST NEWSPAPER

Benjamin Franklin suffered one of his rare diplomatic failures in Montreal. In the spring of 1776, he was sent by Congress to propagate American ideas. To this end, he encouraged Fleury Mesplet, a French printer he had met in London, to buy a press and bring it to Montreal. After the Americans retreated, Mesplet remained. He had not been paid for the presses or his work. In later years, after he had founded the *Gazette de Montreal*, he asked John Jacob Astor to help convince the U.S. Congress to pay its debts—it did not. His newspaper, the first French-language newspaper in Quebec, eventually evolved into the English-language *Gazette* of today.

■

Place Jacques-Cartier (31) is the best site in Canada for contemplating the schizophrenia of being French in North America or Canadian in a bilingual country. It is named after a French explorer and dominated by a statue of the British admiral who defeated Napoleon's fleets. It is where a twentieth-century French president, whose country had been liberated by largely English-speaking armies, advocated Quebec's independence while Canada celebrated a hundred years of unity.

During the French Regime the area was inside the gardens behind the mansion that the Marquis de Vaudreuil had built in 1723. It was here that the Mohawk chief Joseph Brant, who arrived in Montreal with three hundred warriors, allied himself with the British during the American War of Independence. After a fire destroyed the building in 1803, the area became a public market, around which hotels, restaurants and inns thrived.

At the top of the square, the **Tourist Information Center** occupies a building that was built in 1811. It long housed the Silver Dollar Saloon, which was famous for having dollar coins embedded in the floor. During the rebellions, several young men, who were later sent to the British prison colony at Botany Bay in Australia, hid in the crawl space under the floor of the building at number 458. Number 454 was built in 1855 and was, until recently, the Iroquois Hotel. Number 438 was another hotel, dating from 1828, and number 435, Vandelac House, was built in 1800 and restored in the 1960s. At number 421 is the Hotel Nelson, where *Les Fils de la Liberté* ("The Sons of Freedom") was formed in 1837. Parts of number 410, Viger House, were built before 1722, and numbers 407 and 401 are two houses that were built by Amable Amyot in 1812. Del Vecchio House, number 400, dates from 1807 and was restored in 1967; Patriots' House, at 169 St-Paul, dates from the 1770s.

Nelson's Column is Montreal's oldest public monument. Ten minutes after the news of Admiral Horatio Nelson's death at the Battle of Trafalgar reached Montreal, the business community decided to build a monument. It was paid for by public subscription and erected in 1809. When the statue on top, which is made out of artificial stone, was first cast in England, a sailor who had served under Nelson burst into tears, embraced it and declared the likeness to be exact.

In summer, Place Jacques-Cartier is a pleasant place to spend some hours dining and drinking on the patios. **La Marée,** at 404, is reputed to have the best lobster dishes in town. Three of Montreal's best restaurants—**Claude Postel,** 443 St-Vincent; **Le St-Amable,** 188 St-Amable; and **Le Fadeau,** 423 St-Claude—are on adjacent streets. Artists sell their prints and paintings in the open-air market on the southern end and a flower market has replaced the produce stalls in the center.

THE MAGICIAN'S JOKE

In 1835, Adrien the magician came to Montreal to perform in the Theatre Royal. As a joke, he and a local journalist, Ludger Duvernay (who founded the nationalist St. Jean Baptiste Society) went into the market in Place Jacques-Cartier. When they came to an old woman who was selling produce from a cart, Adrien picked up two eggs and remarked on how heavy they were. Pretending to test their freshness, he broke one against the side of the wagon and a gold coin fell to the pavement. "This is astounding," said the magician. He broke another egg. A second gold coin fell to the ground. He continued to play the joke until the old woman refused to sell any more. She drove her cart down to the bottom of the square and, close to Bonsecours Chapel, began smashing her eggs one by one. Adrien and Duvernay watched as she became more frustrated, then, admitting the joke, paid her for all the eggs she had broken.

City Hall (32) was built between 1874 and 1878 on the site of the old Jesuit church. Originally designed by Maurice Perrault in the

Second Empire style, the building was greatly altered when the Beaux Arts top floor and copper roofing were added after a fire had gutted the inside of the building in 1922. It was from the balcony of City Hall that Charles de Gaulle, perhaps challenged by Nelson's Column, launched his famous cry: "Vive le Québec libre!" This statement stimulated the nationalist movement and forced the Canadian government to ask him to return to France immediately.

MAYORS OF MONTREAL

Jacques Viger, an archaeologist, was the first mayor of Montreal. He created Montreal's motto: Concordia Salus ("Salvation in concord"). The second mayor was Peter McGill, who had organized pro-British demonstrations to counteract those of the patriots of 1837. Another early mayor was Wolfred Nelson, a bear of a man, who was distantly related to Admiral Horatio Nelson. He was both a doctor and a distiller before he publicly advocated armed confrontation with the British in 1837. In this century, Montreal has been dominated by two mayors. Camilien Houde, who could break into song during a public rally, was a populist who ran the wide-open city that was much beloved by American jazz musicians of the 1930s. He charmed King George VI and Queen Elizabeth (the present Queen Mother) on their state visit of 1939, and adopted the city's flag (a St. George's cross with the French fleur de lis, an English rose, a Scottish thistle and an Irish shamrock in each corner respectively), but was held in an internment camp for his views against military conscription during World War II. Jean Drapeau, who ran on a "clean government" platform in 1954, dominated Montreal politics until he retired in 1986. He openly admired Machiavelli and, under his guidance, the metro was built, Expo '67 was celebrated and the 1976 Olympics were held.

To the west of City Hall is a fountain and statue by Eugene Benet. Erected in 1930, it is dedicated to Jean Vauquelin (1728–72), who

commanded the French fleet that unsuccessfully defended
Louisbourg in 1758 and Quebec in 1759.

Champ-de-Mars (33), directly behind City Hall, is named after
the Roman god of war. Designed as a military parade ground and
bordered by Lombardy poplars, it was built up and leveled in 1815 by
the British army. Through most of the nineteenth century, it was a
promenade where ladies and gentlemen went to see and be seen. In a
twist of irony, it was here that modern Quebec nationalism (against
Ottawa as opposed to London) first manifested itself. The largest
popular demonstration in Canada was held in Champ-de-Mars in
1885. Tens of thousands came to protest the hanging of Louis Riel,
who had been condemned for leading the Métis, French-speaking
descendants of mixed marriages, in present-day Manitoba. The park
was allowed to deteriorate for most of the twentieth century, and
eventually became nothing more than a parking lot for City Hall
employees. Its renaissance as a park (excuse me—a "greenspace")
began in 1990, when the remains of the old city walls were revealed.

Continuing west along rue Notre-Dame, you will pass the **Maison
des Arts de la Sauvegarde,** at 152, which was built between 1795
and 1805 and restored in 1912. It was the birthplace of the first
archbishop of Montreal, Edouard-Charles Fabre (1827), and was
home to Jean-Louis Beaudry, three times mayor of Montreal (1862–
84) and his brother Prudent, who was mayor of Los Angeles during
the same period. St-Vincent Street was first opened in 1689. Over
the years, many famous men, including Simon Fraser and George-
Etienne Cartier, have lived here. Maison Beaudoin, number 427,
dates from 1690, was reconstructed in 1750 and restored in 1972.
The house at the southern corner of St-Thérèse dates from 1759, and
the old Richelieu Hotel (number 443) dates from 1861. At the corner
of Vaudreuil is an old warehouse that was built in 1759 and was the
property of John Jacob Astor, ancestor of the rich and celebrated
American family. In the nineteenth century the street was a nerve
center for lawyers and journalists.

Three courthouses (34) on Notre-Dame reflect three very different attitudes toward the law. The oldest, which was designed by
John Ostell in 1849, is the most humane. In the Classic-Revival style
(the dome was added in 1890), it was the headquarters of Montreal's
Olympic Committee and now houses municipal offices. The bronze
sculpture-fountain outside is by Jules Lasalle (1988) and consists of
life-size statues of St. Marguerite Bourgeoys and three children.

Maison Ernest Cormier (1926), which is now a music school, is the most imposing. Its Doric colonnade, concave portico, magnificent bronze doors (the six bas-reliefs depict the history of criminal law) and Art Deco hall (Montreal's most majestic interior space) reflect the Latin inscription over the portico, which translates as "He who transgresses the law shall seek the help of the law in vain." Built on the site of Montreal's first synagogue (1777), it was designed by Montreal's greatest architect of the first half of the twentieth century, Ernest Cormier, who also designed the Université de Montréal and the bronze doors to the United Nations Building in New York. **Le Palais de Justice,** the new courthouse, is the modern dark-glass skyscraper diagonally across the street from Cormier's building. The most alienating of the three, it was built in 1971 (David, Barrett & Boulva, architects) and contains the provincial, superior, appeal and criminal courts as well as the bar archives and library. It is always possible for a visitor to witness the justice system in action by simply going to any courtroom as an observer. On the plaza is a modern sculpture by the Quebec artist Charles Daudelin.

On the northwest corner of St-Laurent and Notre-Dame stood the house of Antoine Laument de Lamothe, sieur de Cadillac, who founded Detroit in 1701, was made governor of Louisiana in 1710 and gave his name to America's most prestigious car. On the corner of St-Jacques, the red-stone building (1900) is the home of Montreal's biggest newspaper, *La Presse*. Heading west along St-Jacques, number 54 was built in 1729 and has been a restaurant since the beginning of this century. Across the street (at number 55), the gargoyles around the entrance were sculpted in 1892 to protect the money of La Banque du Peuple. They were not very effective—the bank went bankrupt two years later, when it was the sixth biggest in Canada.

WALKING TOUR FOUR: THE FINANCIAL CAPITAL OF CANADA

The Bank of Montreal (35) has occupied its templelike building on the north side of the Place d'Armes since 1845. Since the bank's founding in 1817, it has been one of the world's most stable and wealthiest institutions, and still today, when the graffiti "Jesus Saves" goes up on a wall, it is likely to be added to with the words "the

Bank of Montreal." This domed and pillared structure was designed by John Wells. The sculpture over the portico is by the Scottish artist John Steele. It shows a sailor, a colonist, the muses of music and literature and two Amerindians (one of whom is refusing "civilization") on either side of the bank's coat of arms. The awe-inspiring interior dates from 1905. The basilica-shaped hall is graced with Corinthian columns of dark green syenite. A Roman goddess protects the lobby. In a small room just to the right is a small museum that houses a collection of coins, bills and piggy banks.

THE COLLECTION PLATE CHANGES HANDS

Place d'Armes and rue St-Jacques were once the financial center of Canada. For those who bemoan the fact that banks are now our churches and their head-office towers dwarf the old cathedrals, there is one event in Montreal's history that has been declared to be a manifestation of God's displeasure with our worship of mammon.

On November 3, 1819, just two years after the Bank of Montreal was founded, the clouds over the city turned a strange yellow color. When rain fell, it was black and contained much ash. The skies cleared, but, the next day, the strange clouds and dirty rain returned. On the fifth, they left a filthy foam over the city. Then, on the sixth, ominous, huge storm clouds began to gather. Suddenly, there was a crash of thunder that one newspaper reported "the likes of which had never in living memory been heard before," and those who were in Place d'Armes saw a bolt of lightning shoot out of the clouds and strike the cross on top of the old parish church. Immediately, the metal ball at the cross's socket was illuminated, the electricity traveled down the lightning rod and then crackled over the cobblestones. No one was hurt, but the cross came down and the steeple broke into flames that were quickly extinguished by rain. Much speculation was given to what the phenomenon was. Scientists in Edinburgh, Scotland, later suggested that the strange clouds had been created by a volcanic eruption in some distant land, but there has been no evidence to support this theory. The superstitious have said that the instant the cross fell marks the moment from which the Church lost its power to the banks.

———————————————■———————————————

The New York Insurance Company Building (1889), also on Place d'Armes, is considered to be Montreal's first skyscraper. Now owned by the Société de Fiducie du Québec, it was designed by the American firm of Babb, Cook and Willard. The sculptures on the facade are by Henry Beaumont. The red stone, which was for some years quite a common building material in Montreal, was inexpensively imported from Scotland because it served as ballast in the timber ships that returned to Canada empty. It is said that when the large, ornate clock on this insurance company's building started ticking, the one on the Sulpician Seminary stopped. The Aldred Building next door was built in 1928. The Art Deco lobby and elevator doors are worth a brief look.

The Banque Canadienne Nationale built its headquarters on the western side of the square in 1975, a time when Montrealers (but not the city's administrators and bankers) were aware of the need to save their architectural heritage. Designed by David and Boulva, the black-glass skyscraper is inexcusably insensitive to its surroundings. The post office, at 155 St-Jacques, dates from 1959, when office towers were recessed from the street.

Hôtel Le Palais, across St-François-Xavier from the post office, is a new development (1986–91) that has incorporated the facades of the 1910 Dominion Express Building and the 1907 head office of the Royal Bank. The four monumental statues on the portico of the latter represent four of Canada's natural resources and have been recently restored. This is not the first hotel to build on this site—during the American Civil War, both Confederate secret agents and British officers stayed in the rooms of the St. Lawrence Hall. While playing billiards here, John Wilkes Booth, who was acting in a play in town and was said to have possessed "considerable personal beauty and grace," dropped veiled hints of his plans to assassinate Abraham Lincoln. Ten days later, the president was dead.

For those who want an **abbreviated tour,** continue along St-Jacques to the **Montreal Gazette Building** (41). If you are interested in nineteenth-century architecture, follow the route to the old stock exchanges. As you walk down St-François-Xavier, in the shadow of the Banque Nationale, you pass the site of the Sulpician Fathers' school for boys. The restaurant, **Chez Delmo,** at 211 Notre-Dame, has been considered one of the best in Montreal for forty years. The bar room, with its two long counters, is considered to be one of the most beautiful in the city and is a favorite meeting place for financiers.

Centaur Theatre (36), at 453 St-François-Xavier, is housed in another old temple of finance—the 1903 Stock Exchange Building. George B. Post based his design of the facade on the temple of Vesta in Tivoli, which he regarded as "the finest and most beautiful specimen of architecture in the world." Farther down the street, on the corner of St-Sacrement, is a recently renovated office building that dates from 1874. It was the headquarters of the Montreal Telegraph Company, one of Canada's first joint-stock enterprises, which was capitalized to build the telegraph lines that linked Quebec City to Toronto in 1847. **Casa de Mateo II,** 440 St-François-Xavier, is considered to be Montreal's best Mexican restaurant.

The building at **211 St-Sacrement** (37) was built in 1866. In 1883, it housed Montreal's stock exchange, which was controlled by a group of men who called themselves "the forty thieves." To be accepted as a new "thief" on the exchange, a man was obliged to buy every member a crate of champagne. The building is now the home of *Le Devoir,* French-Canada's most influential newspaper. It was founded in 1910 by Henri Bourassa.

THE INFLUENTIAL EDITOR

Henri Bourassa (1868–1952) was the grandson of Louis-Joseph Papineau. He is the father of modern Québecois nationalism. He realized that culture and national identity were rooted in language, criticized Ontario for dismantling its Catholic (mostly French) school system, denounced the power of the clergy in politics, saw the British Empire as a bulwark against Canada's cultural assimilation by the materialism of the United States, denounced Canadian participation in the British "imperial war" against the Boers in South Africa, pointed out that British institutions were not as democratic or as liberal as they claimed (Quebec had given Jews the right to vote before Catholics had been given similar rights in England), opposed military conscription during World War I, and advocated a bilingual Canada that would stretch from the Atlantic to the Pacific. His sophisticated ideas made him the darling of French university students and, according to one newspaper, "the most hated man in Canada."

Rue St-Pierre (38) has a fine ensemble of Victorian commercial architecture. The buildings at 420–34 and 438–46 were built for warehouse businesses in 1856 and 1860 respectively. When Jefferson Davis, the exiled president of the Confederate States, came to live in Montreal after the Civil War, buildings like these made him say that the city looked "well paid for."

The Exchange Coffee Shop, Montreal's first stock exchange, was located at the corner of St-Pierre and St-Paul. It was a casual affair. You entered the hotel, run by a Mr. Goodenough, by two passages that led to the coffeehouse. There, in 1832, a flour merchant might sell you shares in the Champlain and St. Lawrence Railway and then return to selling flour in Place Royale. The building opposite, at 320–26 St-Paul was built in 1849. Numbers 374–84 and 400–02 were built as factories in 1855 and 1888 respectively.

Rue McGill (39) marks the western end of the old walled city. It is named after Peter McGill, the second mayor of Montreal. The Dominion Block, at 400, was designed to look like a series of European villas one above the other. The sculpted facade dates from 1867. Turn back into Old Montreal on rue LeMoyne and walk up rue Ste-Hélène. The entire western side of the street was built between 1858 and 1871.

Before the city's wall was torn down, rue des Recollets led to a gate. It was here, in 1760, that the British army, under General Amherst, marched into the city to demand its surrender. In 1812, the American general, Hull, who had surrendered Michigan to the British, was greeted like a hero as his carriage entered the city. When Hull returned to the United States, he was condemned to death for treason, but his sentence was commuted.

The Sun Life Insurance Building (40), at 266 Notre-Dame, was recently described as having as many architectural and sculptured details as an insurance policy has restrictive clauses. The St-Jean side was built in 1883 and the others in 1889. The decorations are by Henry Beaumont, who did those on the New York Life Insurance Building on Place d'Armes. Fiesta Tapas, 479 rue St-Alexis, is considered Montreal's best Spanish restaurant. The block running from St-Jean down rue de l'Hôpital (so named because it was the route that the Algonquins and Hurons took to get to Jeanne Mance's hospital of the 1600s) gives you an idea as to the state of decay into which Old Montreal had fallen by the mid-1960s. The Cunard Building (to the south), is interesting for its brown, metal-work facing. Samuel Cunard, the founder of the great shipping line, was a Nova Scotian.

Crossing Notre-Dame and continuing up St-Jean, we are now back on St-Jacques, which, when it was the financial capital of Canada, was known by its English name, St. James.

The Montreal Gazette Building (41), at 245 St-Jacques, contains the paper's offices and presses. The building was originally built in 1900 for the *Montreal Star,* an evening newspaper that was, at the time, a strong supporter of British Imperial designs in South Africa.

NEWSPAPER RIVALRIES

By 1979, when the *Star* folded after a protracted strike, Canada's English-language newspapers were pretty much controlled by two chains, who were accused of colluding to eliminate competition by dividing the country into monopolistic urban territories. The *Montreal Gazette* bought the building and presses soon after its competitor closed.

Montreal's most dramatic closure of a newspaper also happened on St-Jacques. In 1837, two paramilitary groups, one radical and one conservative, had decided to hold meetings on the same evening. The meeting of the Doric Club, which had been founded by Adam Thom, the editor of the *Montreal Herald,* broke up earlier than that of *Les Fils de la Liberté,* a group that had been founded by T. S. Brown, the editor of the *Vindicator.* The Doric Club headed down St-Jacques to harass the radicals. Fighting raged up and down the street, and, in the process, the offices and presses of the *Vindicator* were destroyed. This event, as much as any other, sparked the Rebellions of 1837–38.

Tatersall, at 244 St-Jacques, was built in 1889 for the London and Lancashire Insurance Company. Designed by Edward Maxwell, the French Renaissance building is admired for its sculptured entrance and richly detailed eaves and roof. From here, Max Aitkin, who was born in New Brunswick, controlled his ever-growing empire of steel, cement and power companies. He later moved to London, England, where he became one of Fleet Street's great press magnates, Lord Beaverbrook. The Jones Heward Building, at 249, was built in 1850 and is the second oldest on the street. The Lincoln Mansion Building, at 255, has a magnificent Art Deco entrance hall from the 1920s. Across the street, the opulent facade of the City and District Savings Bank, at 262, was built in 1870 according to the designs of Michel Laurent. **The Canadian Imperial Bank of Commerce** (1908), at 265, was designed by Darling and Pearson of Toronto. Its six Corinthian columns and portico put it in the same "bank-as-temple" tradition of design as the Bank of Montreal and the Old Stock Exchange. Inside, the prows of ships emerge from the walls just below the ceiling. The central painting shows one of the huge log rafts sailing by Montreal. Number 275 St-Jacques was built for Canada Life in 1897. The figures of peace and industry guard the entrance and the coat of arms, like corner figures in Europe, blesses the passersby. The old wrought-iron elevator, which still works, reminds one of Paris in the 1930s.

Molson's Bank (42), at 288 St-Jacques, was built in 1866 in the Second Empire style. The building, now owned by the Bank of Montreal, was designed by one of Montreal's most prolific architects, George Browne. The plaster work and doors to the manager's office are worth admiring. The Merchants' Bank, at 355, was founded by Sir Hugh Allan, the shipping merchant who, unlike the Molson family, regarded corruption and bribery as normal business practices. The building was built between 1871 and 1872, with designs by Hopkins & Wily; it was enlarged in 1899 by Edward Maxwell. It now houses Nesbitt, Thomson et Cie, Montreal's leading stockbrokers.

The Royal Bank Building (43), at 360 St-Jacques, was completed in 1928. It was the first building in Montreal to be taller than the spires of Notre-Dame Basilica. Designed by the New York architects York and Sawyer, it is a palace, not a temple, of finance. Its facade is Florentine in inspiration, and its lobby, with its wide flight of stairs, detailed plaster work and distinctive grilling, is lit by huge chandeliers. It is as ostentatious and magnificent as the oversized coins on the huge bronze doors.

On the south side of the street, 384 St-Jacques is a well-preserved example of the Second Empire style. Number 408 was designed by George Browne, who was also responsible for Molson's Bank. It was formerly the Ottawa Hotel, where Harriet Beecher Stowe, the author of *Uncle Tom's Cabin*, stayed in 1862.

The World Trade Center and **Inter-Continental Hotel** (44) occupy almost the entire north side of this block. This $241 million complex has incorporated Nordheimer's Hall, number 363, an 1888 lecture and concert hall where Sarah Bernhardt used to come in the afternoon and play piano. The lobby has been beautifully restored and is well worth a visit. The trade center also incorporates the facades of number 371, the oldest wall in the area, number 377, which is truly Canadian in style, and the Wilson Building on rue St-Antoine. One of the most interesting features of the new building is that it has turned des Fortifications Alley, which before was nothing more than a dirty alley, into a naturally lit, enclosed pedestrian mall. The 367-room hotel is located in a Postmodern tower that seems to have been inspired by the chateau-style hotels of Canadian Pacific Railways.

Victoria Square (45) provides one of the best vistas of downtown. It's quite a shock to come out of Old Montreal and look across this open space to the huge modern buildings. Beaver Hall Hill, an old Amerindian trail, is to the north. South on rue McGill is the Wilson Chambers Building (1869), a rare example of Gothic-commercial architecture.

First called Haymarket, Victoria Square was named when Marshall Wood's statue was unveiled in 1872 by Lord Dufferin, the governor-general, who was instrumental in preserving the walls of Quebec City. The occasion was a public holiday and celebration, including a ball at which Dufferin continued dancing, "never flagging until four in the morning," as one newspaper of the day reported. Once a very fashionable shopping area, the square fell into economic decline when the larger shops began to move up to rue Ste-Catherine at the turn of the century.

Today, there is no sign of the old fenced square with its park benches; Queen Victoria has been moved across the street so that she now stands surrounded by trees that grow on top of the covered Ville-Marie Expressway. The distinctive Art Nouveau metro entrance was designed by Hector Guimard in 1900 and given by the city of Paris to celebrate the 1966 opening of Montreal's subway system. New York City was also given such an entrance, but there it is preserved in the Museum of Modern Art.

Tour de la Bourse (The Stock Exchange Tower) (46) was designed in 1966 by Luigi Moretti and Pier Luigi Nervi. The forty-seven-floor tower is considered Montreal's most elegant skyscraper. The office building also houses shops and restaurants around a four-story glass sculpture. The Grand Hotel, which has a revolving restaurant on top, occupies the building behind the tower. **The Stock Exchange Visitors' Gallery** is open Monday through Friday, 9:30 A.M. to 4 P.M. One-hour guided tours are at 9:30, 11:00, 1:30 and 3:00—by appointment only; telephone: 871-2424.

—— ❧ **4** ❧ ——

Three Walking Tours in Downtown Montreal

INTRODUCTION TO DOWNTOWN MONTREAL

Although Old Montreal was built with money that was earned in the fur trade, the downtown core owes much of its development to finance and industry. The area covered by the three walking tours in this chapter is only two kilometers long and one wide. The first walking tour is titled "In the Shadow of Lord Strathcona" because Donald Smith (later Lord Strathcona) left a greater mark on the city than any other Victorian. It is the area that has been most influenced by international finance. The second tour, "Culture and Nationalism," covers the eastern end of downtown—it has been largely developed by the French. "The English Quarter," walking tour three, covers the western end of downtown. This area was once known as the Golden Square Mile because the families in the old mansions controlled 70 percent of Canada's wealth.

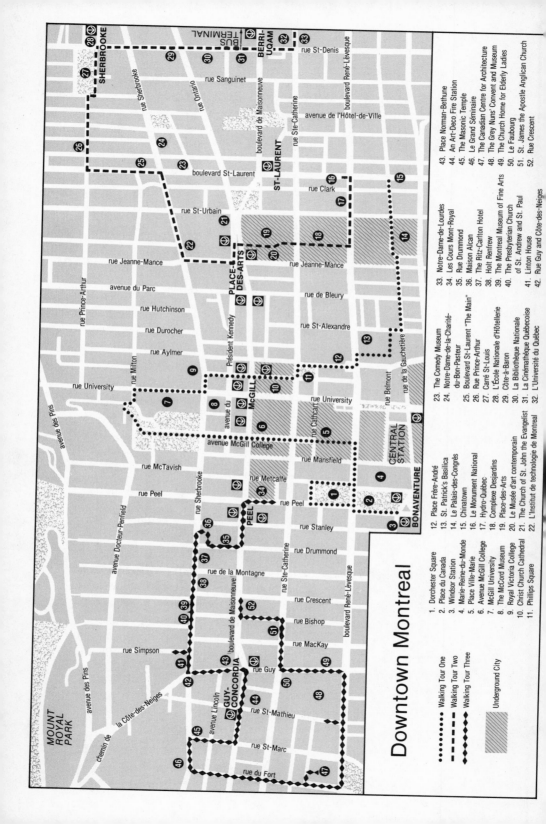

Downtown Montreal

Legend:
- Walking Tour One
- Walking Tour Two
- Walking Tour Three
- Underground City

1. Dorchester Square
2. Place du Canada
3. Windsor Station
4. Marie-Reine-du-Monde
5. Place Ville-Marie
6. Avenue McGill College
7. McGill University
8. The McCord Museum
9. Royal Victoria College
10. Christ Church Cathedral
11. Phillips Square
12. The Comedy Museum
13. St. Patrick's Basilica
14. Le Palais-des-Congrès
15. Chinatown
16. Le Monument National
17. Hydro-Québec
18. Complexe Desjardins
19. Place-des-Arts
20. Le Musée d'art contemporain
21. The Church of St. John the Evangelist
22. L'Institut de technologie de Montréal
23. The Comedy Museum
24. Notre-Dame-de-la-Charité-du-Bon-Pasteur
25. Boulevard St-Laurent "The Main"
26. Rue Prince-Arthur
27. Carré St-Louis
28. L'École Nationale d'Hôtellerie
29. Côte-à-Baron
30. La Bibliothèque Nationale
31. La Cinémathèque Québécoise
32. L'Université du Québec
33. Notre-Dame-de-Lourdes
34. Les Cours Mont-Royal
35. Rue Drummond
36. Maison Alcan
37. The Ritz-Carlton Hotel
38. Holt Renfrew
39. The Montreal Museum of Fine Arts
40. The Presbyterian Church of St. Andrew and St. Paul
41. Linton House
42. Rue Guy and Côte-des-Neiges
43. Place Norman-Bethune
44. An Art-Deco Fire Station
45. The Masonic Temple
46. Le Grand Séminaire
47. The Canadian Centre for Architecture
48. The Grey Nuns' Convent and Museum
49. The Church Home for Elderly Ladies
50. Le Faubourg
51. St. James the Apostle Anglican Church
52. Rue Crescent

DOWNTOWN MONTREAL AT A GLANCE

Downtown restaurants are listed on pages 167 to 175. They are divided into the separate areas covered by each of the three walking tours in this chapter. A separate section on shopping in Montreal begins on page 175.

Churches: The Church of St. John the Evangelist (21). **Christ Church Cathedral** (10). **The Erskine American Church** (38). **Le Grand Séminaire** (46). **Marie-Reine-du-Monde Basilica** (4). **Notre-Dame-de-Lourdes** (33). **The Presbyterian Church of St. Andrew and St. Paul** (40). **St. James the Apostle Anglican Church** (51). **St. Patrick's Basilica** (13).

Concert Halls: **Notre-Dame-de-la-Charité-du-Bon-Pasteur** (24). **Pollack Hall** (9). **Place-des-Arts** (19). **Spectrum** (18). **Théâtre St-Denis** (30).

Interiors: **Complexe Desjardins** (18). **Les Cours Mont-Royal** (34). **Maison Alcan** (36). **Place-des-Arts** (19). **The Ritz-Carlton Hotel** (37). **The Sun Life Building** (1). **Le Windsor** (1). **Windsor Station** (3).

Museums: **The Canadian Centre for Architecture** (47). **The Comedy Museum** (23). **The Grey Nuns' Convent and Museum** (48). **The McCord Museum**—Canadiana (8). **The Redpath Museum,** McGill University—natural history (7). **The Museum of Contemporary Art** (20). **The Montreal Museum of Fine Arts** (39).

Parks and Squares: **The Canadian Centre for Architecture**—sculpture garden (47). **Dorchester Square** (1) and **Place du Canada** (2). **McGill University** (7). **Carré St-Louis** (27). **Phillips Square** (11).

Pedestrian Malls: **rue Prince-Arthur** (26).

Sidewalk Cafés: **rue Crescent** (52). **rue Prince-Arthur** (26). **rue St-Denis** (30).

WALKING TOUR ONE: IN THE SHADOW OF LORD STRATHCONA

Dorchester Square (1) and **Place du Canada** (2) are two parks on either side of boulevard René-Lévesque. To get there, take the metro to Bonaventure, which is considered to be the most impressive station in the subway system. Designed in 1964 by Victor Prus, its high vaulted ceilings and deep brown tiles feel like an underground basilica. Take the exit to Gare Windsor.

Dorchester Square (1) was built on the site of the old Catholic cemetery (1799), and is still the resting place of some of the victims of the cholera epidemic of 1832. The present public park, under the name of Dominion Square, opened in 1869. During the last decades of the last century, it was surrounded by five Protestant churches and the Catholic cathedral. This prompted Mark Twain (who in 1881 lived for six months in Montreal to protect his copyrights in the British Empire) to say: "This is the first time I was ever in a city where you couldn't throw a brick without breaking a church window!" The square assumed its present name in 1989, when boulevard Dorchester was renamed René-Lévesque.

On the southwest corner, the slender slate-and-glass-sheathed CIBC Building was opened in 1963. It is in the International style (the glass box) of Modern architecture. One of Henry Moore's Reclining Women, Montreal's first nonrepresentational public statue, lies in the lobby. Next door is what remains of the Second Empire–style **Windsor Hotel.** Once "the largest in the British Empire," this hotel was the epitome of luxury until after World War II. Oscar Wilde stayed here, and in 1939 King George VI and Queen Elizabeth (the present Queen Mother) appeared on the balcony, giving rise to Montreal's only modern outburst of spontaneous royalist emotion. Most of the hotel was demolished after a succession of fires in the 1950s. This remaining wing was built in 1906, and although it was converted into offices in 1987, the lobby, grand hall (with Montreal's most magnificent chandelier) and ballroom have been beautifully renovated. Open to visitors during business hours.

The Tourist Information Center is housed in the Neo-Florentine Dominion Building at the northern end of the square. Built in 1927, it is the work of the architects Ross and MacDonald. The carefully renovated lobby is like a short indoor street with entrances on both Peel and Metcalfe streets. Outside are the stands for the horse-drawn *calèches* that will take you on a tour of the city and up Mont-Royal.

The huge, pillared, Beaux Arts **Sun Life Building** was erected over three periods from 1913 to 1933. Rising twenty-six floors, it was once the tallest and largest building in the British Empire. During World War II, the gold reserves of the British government were kept in its vaults. The marble-and-bronze interior (especially the spacious resource center, with its dark Corinthian columns and stained-glass ceiling) is worth visiting. Open during business hours.

The Sun Life Insurance Company, one of Montreal's first multinational corporations, contributed greatly to the development of the city for a hundred years. However, when it moved its head office to Toronto during the independence movement of the 1970s, it insulted many of its loyal Quebec policyholders and became the symbol of English Montreal's lack of faith in Quebec. It is said that when René Lévesque came to power in 1976, a long convoy of bullion trucks fled down Highway 401 to Toronto. Whether or not this story is true, the flight of capital (and anglophone families) was evident, but the eventual result has been that Montreal avoided some of the worst excesses of land developers, and the Québecois gained control of the economic levers of the province.

The **monuments** in Dorchester Square are varied. At the northern end, the small octagonal building is one of Montreal's retired *vespasiennes* (street urinals) that were built as "make-work projects" during the Great Depression of the 1930s. It now serves as a ticket office for bus tours. Robbie Burns (1759–96), the Scottish poet who wrote *Auld Lang Syne*, stands facing Le Windsor. The statue is a duplicate of one in London and was erected in 1930. The stone lion above the dogs' drinking fountain (the east side) was sculpted by George W. Hill. It was erected to celebrate Queen Victoria's diamond jubilee in 1897. The dramatic statue of the soldier and his horse is a monument to the soldiers who fell during the Boer War (1899–1902). It was designed by Edward and William Maxwell, sculpted by George W. Hill and erected in 1907.

THE BOER WAR IN MONTREAL

The Boer War deeply divided Montreal. The French did not see why they should fight for British imperialism in Africa, while many English rallied to the call—Lord Strathcona raised and equipped horse regiments at his own expense. The antagonism reached fever pitch after the Battle of Ladysmith, when McGill University students marched down to Old Montreal demanding the Union Jack be flown in celebration. When, the next day, the French students from Laval demanded that the flag be taken down, the young English scholars attacked the Laval campus. The brawling went on for several days.

Windsor Station's interior (3) is worth a visit. Completed in 1913, the concourse has a glass roof that is architecturally important—it traces its roots to London's Crystal Palace of 1851 and is the antecedent of many a modern shopping mall. Although the station serves only as a terminal for today's commuter trains, it has great historical significance. Many of the immigrants who developed the Canadian West passed through its doors. During both world wars thousands of troops made their way from here to the ships in the port. The statue in the entrance of the station is of George Stephen, later Lord Mount Stephen, who was the first president of the Canadian Pacific Railway. The bronze monument of an angel holding up a soldier is a war memorial that was donated by the MacCarthy Foundation in 1921.

From Place du Canada you can see the **exterior** of the building, which was designed in 1886 by the New Yorker Bruce Price. Price had a lasting influence on Canadian architecture. Windsor Station, with its solid bulk and rounded arches, is in the Romanesque-Revival style, but Price is also remembered for introducing Canada to the romantic Chateau style of Viger Station and the Chateau Frontenac in Quebec City. His work marks the ascendance of American architectural influences in Canada.

FROM SEA TO SEA

The Canadian Pacific Railway (CPR) was Canada's greatest achievement in the nineteenth century. After the Pacific Scandal toppled the Conservative government of Sir John A. Macdonald, Sir Hugh Allan lost his bid to build the transcontinental railway and a consortium led by George Stephen, the president of the Bank of Montreal, moved into the picture. Discreetly in the background was Donald Smith, later Lord Strathcona. While Smith used his position as a member of parliament for Manitoba (Canadian MPs are not obliged to live in the constituency that elects them), Stephen and other members of the consortium engaged in a series of very questionable financial maneuvers to gain very profitable contracts and land concessions from the Canadian government. According to one estimate, the railway received $206 million of subsidies, over 20 million acres of land, and even made a $10 million profit during construction. This was at a time when the population of Canada totaled less than 5 million. Nonetheless, the CPR was a tremendous achievement. Linking Montreal to Vancouver in 1885, it ensured the participation of British Columbia in confederation, opened the Canadian prairies to settlement and was, for almost a hundred years, the thread that joined the country together.

Many Québecois, however, still resent how western Canada was populated. While Europeans were being sold cheap tickets on the CPR that took them to 160-acre farms (often freely given), Quebec was suffering from economic hardship that forced almost a million of its citizens to emigrate and work in the textile mills of New England. Canada would be a very different country today if they had been encouraged to settle in the West.

Canada's most famous photograph shows Lord Strathcona hammering in the last spike of the CPR.

St. George's Anglican Church stands in front of the station. Built in 1870, it is the oldest building on the squares. Its English-Gothic design is by William Thomas. Inside, where the smell of lemon oil prevails, the open timber roof marks the evolution toward greater authenticity in Neo-Gothic architecture. The stained-glass windows, the pulpit (1842) and the oak-wood carvings in the sanctuary (including a bas-relief of St. George slaying the dragon) are elegant examples of the style. The tapestry and pulpit in the chapel came from Westminster Abbey and were used in the coronation of Elizabeth II. Although the automatic mechanism that enables the famous carillon of ten Harrington's tubular bells (1901) to play twenty-eight tunes is broken, it can still be played by hand. Visitors are welcome.

Towering over St. George's Church is a critically acclaimed Postmodern tower (1991) designed by Kohn, Pederson and Fox of New York. The green plate-glass **Edifice Laurentienne** (1988), to the rear of the church, is occupied by an insurance company and Quebec's largest engineering firm, Lavelin. As you enter the lobby to visit the small sculpture garden in the back, you get a feeling of lightness.

The **Château Champlain** is a thirty-eight-floor hotel on the south end of the park. It was designed by Roger d'Astous, a student of Frank Lloyd Wright, and was built by Canadian Pacific in 1966. Montrealers were quick to nickname it the Great Cheese Grater because of its half-moon-shaped windows, which purposefully complement the Romanesque arches of Windsor Station and pay tribute to Wright, who favored convex arched windows in his last period. From the bar on the top floor, one gets some of the best views of Montreal.

From the pedestrian flyover that leads to the hotel, you can look down rue de la Gauchetière past a Postmodern tower (1991), which has a nickname reflecting its phallic design, and see **Place Bonaventure** (1966), a huge (six-acre) concrete block that is Montreal's most outstanding example of brutalism, a short-lived movement in modern architecture. The vine-covered, blind outer walls have been called an "ingenious sculptural work."

In summer, brass bands frequently play in the bandstand of **Place du Canada,** and (most years) on Wednesday evenings there is square dancing. Telephone the **Montreal Square Dancing Association:** 747-2669. On November 11, wreaths are laid on the Cenotaph.

A statue of **Sir John A. Macdonald,** Canada's first prime minister (1867–73 and 1878–91) looks across to one of **Sir Wilfrid Laurier,** Canada's first French-Canadian prime minister (1896–1911), which stands in Square Dorchester—named after Canada's longest-ruling governor. The street that separates them is named after **René Léves-que,** Quebec's "separatist" premier (1976–84). The Neo-Gothic Macdonald monument was designed by George Hill in 1894. Be sure to look at the canopy—it is an allegorical representation of the provinces of Canada. The Laurier monument was created by Emile Brunet in 1953.

A GOVERNOR, TWO PRIME MINISTERS AND A PREMIER

Sir John A. Macdonald (1815–91), a Scottish lawyer from Kingston, Ontario, was first elected to parliament in 1844. By 1856, he had forged a powerful alliance with a French-Canadian, George-Etienne Cartier, that would dominate Canadian politics for more than three decades. Together they united the eastern colonies of British North America, gained the new country of Canada greater independence from London and negotiated the inclusion of the Northwest Territories and British Columbia into confederation. An astute politician who always saw himself as British, he is also remembered for his love of alcohol. Macdonald is quoted as saying, "The perfect political cabinet would be twelve men, each of whom, if you liked, you could put in the penitentiary." His portrait appears on the $10 bill.

If Sir John A. Macdonald is credited with being the father of present-day Canada, Sir Wilfrid Laurier (1841–1919) nursed the country through its childhood. After the death of Macdonald's ally, Cartier, it did not take long for English-French antagonism to come to the surface. Although the hanging of Louis Riel defined the differences, it was the advent of the Boer War in 1899 that gave rise to the opposing philosophies of imperialism and nationalism. Over the next twelve years, Laurier evolved the concept of the nation of Canada inside the British Empire. His creative compromises eventually resulted in his being called a traitor by both English and French. Canada did not gain control of its own foreign affairs until 1931, twelve years after Laurier's death. Nonetheless, Sir Wilfrid's ideas made possible the devolution of the British Empire and creation of the Commonwealth. His portrait appears on the $5 bill.

Sir Guy Carleton, the first Lord Dorchester, was governor of

Quebec for most of the period between 1766 and 1796. He is credited with the Quebec Act, which granted francophones their religion, language and civil laws. This act, because it included present-day Ohio, Indiana, Illinois, Michigan, and southern Ontario in the colony of Quebec, angered the Thirteen Colonies and contributed to the American Revolution. Dorchester's life was not without drama— he was wounded on the Plains of Abraham when the British seized Quebec from France in 1759; and when the Americans invaded in 1775, he was forced to flee Montreal disguised as a peasant.

René Lévesque was born in 1922 in New Carlisle, Quebec. A war correspondent with the American forces in World War II, he became a popular interviewer on TV before entering politics in the 1960s. A populist who was well aware of the growing dissatisfaction with the position of Quebec inside Canada, he founded the Parti Québecois in 1968, advocated "sovereignty-association" with the rest of the country and led his party to power in 1976. A true democrat, he accepted the 1980 results of a referendum that indicated that 60 percent of the people of Quebec wished to remain inside Canada and was elected premier of the province for a second term. He retired in 1985. His death in 1988 was deeply mourned.

Marie-Reine-du-Monde Basilica or **St. Joseph's Cathedral** (4) was built after the old cathedral, on rue St-Denis, burned to the ground in 1853. Bishop Bourget (1799–1885), who had recognized that Montreal was being divided into French and English halves, caused a furor when he decided that the new Catholic cathedral should be built in the middle of what was then English Montreal. When he decided that the building should be a scaled-down replica of St. Peter's in Rome, Victor Bourgeau, the designer of the interior of Notre-Dame Church on Place d'Armes, at first refused to work on the design. He became the architect only after the amateur priest-architect, Father Michaud, proved inept.

Like many of Montreal's most important buildings, the cathedral took decades to complete. Construction was begun in 1870, was interrupted eight years later and restarted in 1885. It was not completed until 1894, nine years after Bishop Bourget had died.

Only one-third the volume of St. Peter's, Marie-Reine-du-Monde is still large—the cross on the top of the copper dome is 230 feet above the street. The statues on the pediment represent the patron saints of the parishes of the city of Montreal. The monument outside the basilica depicts Bishop Bourget flanked by "Religion" and "Charity."

The **interior** of the cathedral is spacious, light, airy and populated by a collection of marble statues of saints. The paintings, by Georges Delfosse, depict events in the history of Montreal. The canopy under the dome is a replica of St. Peter's *baldachino* by Bernini. Donated by the Sulpician Fathers, it is made of red copper, was fashioned by hand and was later decorated with gold leaf. On entering through the main door, there is a chapel on the left-hand side containing the relics of saints, including the remains of St. Zotique. The artifacts come from the small crusading army that was raised by Bishop Bourget to defend the Papal States from Garibaldi, who was unifying Italy for the king of Piedmont. The silver boat, made into a sanctuary lamp, is a facsimile of the votive offering that the grateful soldiers hung from the ceiling of Notre-Dame-de-Bonsecours after they were saved from being shipwrecked. The Bishops' Mortuary Chapel, built between 1931 and 1933, is the last resting place of the bishops and archbishops of Montreal.

THE BISHOPS OF MONTREAL

The bishops of Montreal have had a powerful influence in Quebec. The see was created in 1837. During the rebellions of that year, Bishop Latrigue was seen to have sided with the British when he cited Pope Gregory XVI's 1832 encyclical, which had instructed the Poles to abandon their revolt and accept the Tsar of Russia as their sovereign.

Bishop Bourget, who replaced Latrigue in 1855, held deeply conservative views, yet was widely believed to be a Quebec nationalist. He believed in the absolute supremacy of Rome and the infallibility of popes, feared the influence of Protestantism, saw the secularizing dangers of city life and industrialization, advocated censorship, launched a battle against liberal political thought and encouraged the colonization of the Ottawa Valley, Laurentians and Lac St-Jean regions of the province.

Bishop Charbonneau is perhaps the most interesting prelate of this century. In the 1950s, he was a supporter of the dignity of the working man and incurred the displeasure of Premier Duplessis when he supported a strike in the asbestos mines southeast of Montreal. In later years, after he had resigned from the see, he became so angered by the conservativism of his fellow bishops that he refused to attend their meetings. Today, he is considered to have been ahead of his time—many of his beliefs were enshrined during Vatican II.

Cardinal Leger was Montreal's first archbishop to become a cardinal. Highly respected in Rome and considered saintly by many, he resigned the see to dedicate himself to helping lepers in Africa. He died in 1991.

Place-Ville-Marie (5), to the east of the Sun Life Building and opposite the Queen Elizabeth Hotel (opened in 1958), is the only edifice in Montreal that has influenced world architecture. In the late 1950s, William Zeckendorf engaged I. M. Pei to build office blocks over a huge, ugly hole that had been left from a rail tunnel bored under Mont-Royal in 1930. They chose a cruciform shape that not only reflected the heritage of the Cross in Montreal but also allowed a maximum amount of natural light into the offices. There was nothing radically new in the concept until one of Pei's assistants suggested that an underground shopping mall be added. The success of the mall led to the development of Montreal's underground city and the downtown malls, including Trump Tower in New York City, throughout the world. On the top of PVM is a restaurant and bar. At night, the Royal Bank's four searchlights, whose beams can be seen fifty miles away, rotate on its roof. On the plaza above the shops there is a fountain and an impressionistic sculpture of a reclining woman.

Avenue McGill College (6) leads from the plaza to the gates of McGill University, behind which rises the wooded parkland of Mont-Royal. We owe this vista to Donald Gordon, the president of Canadian National Railways, who had his offices at the top of the Queen Elizabeth Hotel. When he saw the original plans for PVM and noted that the central tower would be directly in front of his window, he demanded that the building be moved to the east. Thirty years later, the view was again threatened when Place Montreal Trust was first planned. After a public outcry, this development was also redesigned so that the street could be widened.

Place Montreal Trust (1988), with its distinctive shaping and red-granite facade, is considered to be a Postmodern building. Just to the north, the gray-stone facade of the Industrial Life Tower (1987) is a Modern tower with Postmodern influences. In front of it, the bronze children, *Secret Bench—Lost Paradise,* is by Lea Vivot. (A more controversial statue of hers, *The Lovers' Bench,* sits in the Botanical Gardens.) Opposite, the blue-glass, multifaceted Banque Nationale de Paris (1986) plays with the Modern style. In front, *Illuminated Crowd,* by Raymond Mason, is a large, complicated and arresting sculpture made of yellow polyester-resin. Some Montrealers consider it the worst of the city's new sculptures; some consider it to be the best.

On the corners of rue Sherbrooke, two new buildings, Place Mercantile (1986) and Maison Ultramar (1991), incorporate older buildings into new structures. Maison Ultramar is more successful because its modest scale wraps itself around the old stone mansion (built for one of the Molson family) and the early high-rise apartment building. Place Mercantile, on the other hand, dwarfs Strathcona Hall (given to McGill University by Lord Strathcona) and has truncated the old gray stones on rue Sherbrooke.

McGill University (7) has enjoyed an international reputation for over a hundred years.

THE HISTORY OF MCGILL

Some people believe that McGill's campus occupies the site of Hochelaga, the Amerindian town that Jacques Cartier visited in 1535. Other people say that Hochelaga was on land that is now on the campus of the Université de Montréal, on the other side of Mont-Royal. Yet others say that it occupied the crater in the middle of the mountain. Since nobody knows where Cartier beached his boats, none of the claims can be proved.

When the Scottish-born fur trader James McGill died in 1813, he left ten thousand pounds and his farm, Burnside, for the endowment of a college, which would bear his name and be established within ten years of his death. The university received its charter in 1821 but would have no students until 1829. As a result, François Desrivières, a nephew of McGill's wife, continued to live in the farmhouse and refused to release the money. Yet even after winning the legal battle in 1838, the young college wallowed in bad management for another seventeen years and the campus and its half-built buildings had been all but abandoned to a herd of cattle. It was not until William Dawson of Pictou, Nova Scotia, arrived in 1855 that the institution, which is today famous throughout the world, came into its own.

It is ironic that the eastern wing of the Arts Building is named after Dawson. He was a deeply religious man who believed that since human beings were "fallen creatures," only the study of practical learning, like medicine, engineering and science, was justified. He felt that all study of the humanities would be tainted by the Fall and that any exploration of the arts would stand in the way of the development of civilization. So strong was his belief in the tainted nature of the arts that when his church, the Erskine Presbyterian, installed an organ, he publicly led half the congregation down the street to worship in a more austere establishment.

Nonetheless, within five years of his arrival, Dawson had increased enrollment to fifty, reoccupied the single building and encouraged William Molson to build a west wing. By the time he retired, in 1893, the university was being generously supported by the wealthiest of Montreal's families and was already beginning to earn an international reputation in medicine, physics, chemistry and engineering.

It is the Faculty of Medicine, and the associated Royal Victoria Hospital and Montreal Neurological Institute, that has garnered McGill the most fame. Sir William Osler, whose ideas on diseases and hospitals revolutionized North American medicine, was intimately connected to the university for most of his life. Babkin's work on digestive glands, Bethune's approach to the terminally ill, Collip's understanding of the pituitary hormones, Hebb's experiments in perception and Penfield's exploration of the brain's electrical impulses have all been major steps in the understanding of the human mind and body.

Many would argue that McGill's greatest contribution to the world is the invention of ice hockey. On March 3, 1875, two nine-man teams of students began knocking an old hard rubber ball over the ice of Victoria Skating Rink, which was situated on rue Stanley, just below Ste-Catherine. Over the next decade, the rules of the game were developed. Because the bouncing ball often struck the spectators, it was replaced by "a flat piece of board." (A puck is a wood-sprite that materializes out of nowhere.) In 1884, the Victoria Rink Carnival Committee officially reduced the size of the teams to six.

The university's most peculiar graduate is said to have been a twenty-year-old pedigree cow, who never attended a class and died just after her graduation in absentia. She had been sponsored by a fraternity, the brothers of which wrote all her exams.

Although McGill has long been considered a bastion of English wealth and power, francophones now make up 30 percent of the approximately 28,000 students.

As you enter the campus through the **Roddick Gates,** which were given by Lady Roddick in 1924 to honor her husband, Sir Thomas, you walk up a tree-lined road. Across the playing field on the western side of the campus are the **MacLennan** and **Redpath libraries.** These are both extensions of the original library building (designed in the Neo-Romanesque style by Sir William Taylor) that was donated by the sugar magnate John Redpath in 1894. The old reading room, with its timber ceiling, is open to the public. It now houses a fine organ and is used for receptions, ceremonies and concerts.

On the eastern side and close to rue Sherbrooke are the 1967 Otto Maass Chemistry Building and the tower of Burnside Hall, the university's computer center. The **Macdonald Physics Building** (1894) is just north of them. It was built entirely of wood and stone so that experiments on magnetism would not be distorted. It was here that a young New Zealander, Ernest Rutherford, ushered in the atomic age when he made his early radium experiments that provided the basis of his theory of the radioactive disintegration of atoms. It was also here that Foster made the transition from spectrometry to nuclear physics.

The **Macdonald Chemistry Building** was built in 1896. It was here that Maass did his work on "the critical state," Steacie made his contributions to photo-chemistry and Hibbert did his research on cellulose. The green dye that is still used for the manufacture of American "greenbacks" was first created at McGill.

The **Macdonald Engineering Building** (1908) was designed by Percy E. Nobbs in the English Baroque Revival style. Note the phoenix sculpture on the south side to indicate the resurrection of the building after the first was destroyed by fire.

SIR WILLIAM MACDONALD

Although the Molson family has supported McGill for 150 years, the university's greatest single benefactor was Sir William Macdonald. Although he disliked smokers and smoking, he built Canada's greatest tobacco company. He not only paid for the three buildings just mentioned but also gave the university an entire agricultural college (with farmlands) at the west end of the island of Montreal. A bachelor, he was generous to the poor and clearly a bit of a wag: When someone asked him what his hobby was, he replied, "Collecting string." When he died, he left his fortune to the Stewart family, which, through the Macdonald-Stewart Foundation, continues his philanthropic work.

Midway up the McGill campus, the driveway splits in three. The westward prong leads past the basilica-shaped **Redpath Museum** (1880–82), the first building in Canada to be built solely as a museum. Behind its Greek and Renaissance facade are housed anthropological and natural history exhibits, including two mummies, shrunken heads and dinosaur bones. The fountain, in the hollow beside it, is called the Three Bares—when you see the figures, you'll understand why. Museum open: September to June: Monday to Friday 9 A.M. to 5 P.M.; June to September: Monday to Thursday 9 A.M. to 5 P.M.

Adjacent to the museum is **Morrice Hall,** one of Montreal's most fanciful buildings. Built in 1875, its tower and polygonal annex, a miniature of the library of the Houses of Parliament in Ottawa, are in the Neo-Gothic style. The gates beside the building lead directly to the Students' Union on rue McTavish.

THE GHOST OF SIMON MCTAVISH

When the fur baron Simon McTavish died, in 1805, he was having a mansion built on Mont-Royal. He was buried in a mausoleum (the blocked entrance is inside the park beyond the end of rue McTavish) just behind the unfinished house. It was not long before rumors of supernatural events began to circulate. Some people said that the abandoned building was inhabited by a colony of fairies who would dance on the tin roof. According to others, McTavish had died after seeing the ghost of his Scottish wife hanging from the rafters of his unfinished mansion. This could not have been true because McTavish married a French-Canadian who outlived him. The "haunted house" stimulated the imagination of Montrealers for over a century. Even in this century, some students claim that they have seen McTavish tobogganing down the mountain in his coffin. This last story may have had some basis in reality: In the 1870s, when corpses for medical studies were hard to acquire, there was an anatomy professor who lived close by—he may have employed grave robbers to raid the new cemeteries on Mont-Royal.

The Modern (1963) building behind Morrice Hall is named for Stephen Leacock, the internationally known humorist who was a history professor at McGill. He said of the university: "A great center of medicine, a fair center of engineering, but no one can ever pretend that it is a center of thought." The Leacock Building is on the site of the old McGill Observatory at "60 degrees, 54 minutes, 18.67 seconds west of Greenwich." It is connected to the Molson Wing (1855) of the **Arts Building,** the central portion of which was designed in 1839 by John Ostell. It is said that Stephen Leacock would stand on the portico of this Neoclassic building and grade his students' papers by throwing them down the steps—the one that went the farthest got the highest grade! The monument in front of the portico is a replica of James McGill's tombstone.

The Chateau-style building above and behind the Arts Building is the pumping station for a water reservoir. The sculpture in the rose garden to the east is by Barbara Hepworth.

When the new Engineering Building (just inside the Milton Gates) was opened in the 1950s, J. W. McConnell, who owned the *Montreal Star*, was given a tour of the new facilities. After he had seen them, he asked how much they had cost. Three million dollars, he was told. McConnell took out his checkbook and paid the entire amount.

Over the years, McGill has expanded up the mountain and to the west, where a great number of the mansions of the Golden Mile have been given to the university. Directly behind the central campus is the Elizabethan-style **Strathcona Medical Building,** which was built in 1907 and now houses the departments of anatomy and dentistry. Behind it, across avenue des Pins (Pine Avenue), is the solid, copper-roofed **Royal Victoria Hospital,** which was founded in 1890 with a gift of $500,000 by Lord Mount Stephen and Lord Strathcona. With its gables, turrets and high-pitched roof, it is in the Scottish-Chateau style; it is remarkably similar to the Royal Edinburgh Infirmary in Scotland. As you look up rue University, you will see the walkway that connects the hospital with the Montreal Neurological Institute, which was founded by Dr. Wilder Penfield.

The residential neighborhood to the east of the campus is known as the Student Ghetto. The majority of the university's fraternities occupy converted houses on rue University, to the north of the **Milton Gates.** At the corner of Milton and University is the Presbyterian College. Compare the simple lines of this Modern (1963) structure to the ornate, carved stone of its Victorian neighbor, the Montreal Diocesan Theological College.

Walking back to Sherbrooke, you will pass the immense classical facade of the High School of Montreal. It was designed in 1914 by Edward and William Maxwell.

The McCord Museum (8), at 690 Sherbrooke and owned by McGill, houses paintings, drawings and engravings that the McCord family started collecting in the 1830s, and has one of Canada's largest collections of Amerindian and Inuit art. The decorative arts, toy and costume collections are also important—as is the Notman Photographic Archives, which houses 700,000 glass negatives and proofs of the world-famous Montreal photographer William Notman. The building, another of Sir William Macdonald's gifts to McGill, dates from 1907 and was, until 1965, the Student Union. The modern extension is a gift from the McConnell Foundation. Open: Wednesday through Sunday 11 A.M. to 5 P.M.

Royal Victoria College (9) was designed by Bruce Price, who also designed Windsor Station. It is in the Romanesque tradition. Outside, the bronze statue of a seated Queen Victoria was sculpted by Princess Louise, Victoria's daughter. Nicknamed Her Royal Shyness, she was the wife of the Marquess of Lorne, governor-general of Canada, 1878–83.

McGill University was an exclusively male college until Lord Strathcona decided to endow it with a college for women. Although both sexes attended the same classes and were awarded the same degrees, the women were technically members of Royal Victoria College and the men members of McGill College. In the 1970s, the original women's dormitory was converted and given to the Faculty of Music. Pollock Hall, where there are almost nightly free student concerts during the school year, was built over the swimming pool.

Maison des Cooperants is the bronze-colored, glass-sheathed tower down rue Union. The 1986 Postmodern design is inspired by the Neo-Gothic Anglican cathedral just in front of it. Because its double-peaked roof reminds some people of bat wings, it has been nicknamed the Batman Building. The scaffold-looking construction on the top is an automatic snow-melting device. Underneath is the shopping mall, Les Promenades de la Cathédrale.

Christ Church Cathedral (10) looks as if it belongs on an old-fashioned Christmas card. This Neo-Gothic church was designed in 1857 by Frank Wills, who was inspired by Salisbury Cathedral in England. It replaced the previous Anglican cathedral, which had burned to the ground, in Old Montreal.

Built on the site of a pond, the cathedral began to sink shortly after it was completed. By 1927, the stone spire had to be removed. In 1940, it was replaced by an exact copy in acid-treated aluminum, but the cathedral continued to sink. Finally, in the early 1980s, the diocese was forced to find a way to save it. The result is the Maison des Cooperants and the shopping mall beneath the sacred ground. During construction, the cathedral never closed its doors and never missed a service. While it was being placed on its new concrete pillars, it seemed as if the whole Gothic structure were about to levitate. The church may now be solidly supported, but the soft sandstone facing, which was chosen for ease in sculpting, is now threatened by acid rain.

The present cathedral's most notable features are the carved triple portico and the stained-glass windows from William Morris Studios. The reredos (back walls of the high altar) are a 1923 war memorial and depict seven scenes from the life of Christ. In the grounds, the spired monument is modeled after the fourteenth-century Martyrs' Memorial in Oxford, England, and honors the memory of Bishop Fulford, Montreal's first Anglican archbishop. Open: daily 8 A.M. to 6 P.M. Free organ concerts at noon.

Phillips Square (11) was given to the city by Thomas Phillips, who grew Montreal's first peach trees here. In the center is a statue of King Edward VII that was executed, in 1914, by Phillipe Hébert, a descendant of Canada's first farmer, Louis Hébert. It is coincidental that Edward stands between two statues of his mother, Victoria—one in Victoria Square to the south and one outside Royal Victoria College. That the three statues are not in sight of each other reminds me of the story of how Edward, even at the age of fifty, would hide behind pillars so that his mother would not see him smoking.

The Bay, a department store, occupies the red-sandstone building to the north of the square. It was opened in 1891 when Henry Morgan moved his shop up from Victoria Square. Considered at the time to be one of the world's great emporiums, it continued to expand until it was bought by the Hudson's Bay Company, one of the oldest companies in the world, in 1960.

THE HUDSON'S BAY COMPANY

The Hudson's Bay Company was founded in 1670 after two Montreal *voyageurs*, Radisson and Grosseillers, had gone to London to interest the British in the fur trade. They never owned shares and never saw any of the vast profits, but the company went on to control all the land that drains into Hudson's Bay and to build trading posts from Labrador to Oregon.

Donald Smith, Lord Strathcona, began his career in 1838 with the Hudson's Bay Company. He traded furs in Labrador for thirteen years. By the time he left, according to a witness at the British Parliamentary Committee of 1857, the Inuit population had been reduced to starvation and cannibalism. He, however, was worth an estimated $50,000 when he arrived in Montreal in 1856 and assumed the duties of the Hudson's Bay Company's chief executive officer in North America. When the British government recommended that the company's control of its vast territories be given to the newly formed confederation of Canada, the rights of the Métis and Amerindian people who lived on the land were unclear. Stock prices fell. Donald Smith began inside trading—he knew not only how to manipulate both the Métis and the Canadian government but was also aware of the value of the settlement the Hudson's Bay Company would receive. Although Lord Strathcona was, in later life, a great philanthropist, the means that he used to acquire his fortune were criticized by both British and Canadian parliaments in an age when laissez-faire capitalism was standard business practice. Whenever his motivation and conduct were questioned, he claimed that his ability to remember events had been severely impaired ever since he had suffered from "snow blindness" in his early years in Labrador.

The Hudson's Bay Company, now owned by the Thompson family of Toronto, is still the dominant trading force in much of Canada's north but no longer sells furs in its department stores.

Henry Birks et Fils, opposite the cathedral, is Montreal's Tiffany's. Henry Birks opened his first shop on rue St-Jacques in 1879 and was the company's active president until he died, aged eighty-eight, in 1928. The store, which still employs its own designers, is noted for its gems, jewelry, silver, crystal and fine china. Some middle-class Montrealers will save Birks boxes so that they can use them for gifts that they have purchased elsewhere.

The Canada Cement Building, on the south side of the square, was erected in 1922. It houses one of Montreal's oldest underground parking garages.

Place Frère-André (12) is down côte Beaver Hall, diagonally across from the cathedral. The statue is of Brother André, the Miracle Man of Montreal, who founded St. Joseph's Oratory (see page 149). He looks down a slope, once an Indian trail, that leads to Victoria

Square and the western edge of Old Montreal. Behind the statue stands Dow House, which was built for a Scottish brewer in 1860. It is in the Renaissance-Revival style and draws its inspiration from the urban palaces of Venice. A private club from 1912 to 1979, it is now a restaurant in which the original 1860 decor can be seen in the bar. The decoration of other rooms dates from 1912.

St. Patrick's Basilica (13) is the largest of Montreal's English-language Catholic churches. It was built by Montreal's Irish community between 1843 and 1847. Designed by P. L. Morin and Father Felix Martin, it is considered to be one of North America's purest and grandest specimens of fifteenth-century Gothic Revival. The steeple is 228 feet tall, and the carillon, which rings the Angelus each noon, includes Charlotte, a bell cast in 1774 and once hung in the old Notre-Dame Church in place d'Armes.

To enter the door on the east side, cross the grounds and circle around the front of the church, which because of the modern development of the city seems to be facing backward. The interior, with its decorations of shamrocks and *fleurs de lis*, is quite magnificent. Integrated into the oak wainscoting that lines the walls of the nave, the Gothic panels contain 150 oil-painted figures of saints and one of Montreal's most pleasing Stations of the Way of the Cross, which are by the Italian artist Patriglia. The pews are made of red Indiana oak and were installed in 1894; the wooden floor underneath dates from 1847. Each of the pillars is a single length of pine, over eighty feet (twenty-five meters) long. St. Pat's, which is nicknamed the Irish cathedral, is also proud of its Neo-Gothic stained-glass windows, which are the work of Alex Locke of Brooklyn, New York. The two Renaissance-style windows at the rear are of a later date and were made in Innsbruck, Austria. On the walls and ceilings of the sanctuary is a mural of gold, cut to represent a Venetian mosaic. The choir loft, with its beautiful carved stairways, was added in 1894 and can accommodate one hundred singers. The organ was built in 1852. The lamps are the most magnificent in Montreal. Each of the six angels on the larger one are six and a half feet tall. Purchased in 1896, the lamp weighs 1,800 pounds.

THE IRISH IN MONTREAL

The Irish began to arrive in Montreal in the early 1820s. They were employed as dock and construction workers and settled in Griffintown, just west of Old Montreal, an area that had a tendency to flood when ice jams formed on the river. Since their arrival, the Irish have often found their loyalties split between the Protestant British and the Catholic French. Many were sympathetic to the Rebellions of 1837, but others, during elections, were employed as thugs who influenced French voters. The community was powerful enough in the 1860s for Irish-Americans (Fenians) to imagine invading and conquering Montreal so that they could either trade it for the independence of Ireland or make it part of the United States. Their objectives were unclear and their plans came to nothing. Montreal did fear invasion, but the Irish of the city, led by Darcy McGee, favored the confederation of British North America into the country of Canada. In 1868, McGee, who had received many anonymous death threats (mostly from residents of the United States) wrongly accusing him of being a traitor to the Fenian cause, was killed by an unknown assassin. His funeral was one of the most impressive that Montreal has seen.

Through the first half of the twentieth century, the Irish community remained large but poor. They have the dubious honor of having been the majority of the inhabitants in Canada's first large slum, an area called Little Burgundy, which is below the bluffs to the west of downtown. By the 1980s the Irish community was shrinking in size and losing much of its distinctiveness. In the 1970s, it was noted by some separatists that the poorly paid and poorly educated descendants of Irish immigrants were three times more likely to speak French than a McGill graduate. Montreal still has the second largest St. Patrick's Day Parade in North America. On Victoria Day, which celebrates the Queen's birthday, Pointe St. Charles, an old Irish neighborhood, can erupt in street violence. Such violence is no longer politically motivated, yet its roots are buried in the tradition of resentment against the British that some Irish people still feel.

The eleven-floor Unity Building, directly in front of St. Pat's, was built in 1913. With its Art Nouveau cornice, it has been compared to the Wainright Building of St. Louis (1890) and the Guaranty Trust Building of Buffalo (1894), both designed by Louis Sullivan, the dominant force in the Chicago school of architecture.

Walking east along rue de la Gauchetière (down from the main entrance of St. Pat's), you are in an old, but mostly demolished, residential area, once called Little Dublin. Allowed by speculators to fall into disrepair, the remaining buildings and land have been bought by the city, which plans to revive the area as a residential neighborhood.

After crossing rue de Bleury, on which the terra-cotta facade and sculptures of the Southam Building are worth looking at, you come to the Chinese Catholic Church (1835), which was only recently saved from demolition. In front of it is the open plaza of Montreal's convention center.

Le Palais-des-Congrès (14) was officially inaugurated in 1983. Designed by Victor Prus, who is also responsible for the design of the Bonaventure metro station, it rests on eighty-three layers of concrete that straddle the Ville-Marie Expressway. Its most interesting facade is its main entrance, where an immense glass wall descends to an open plaza. It faces Complexe Guy-Favreau, which was built on the site of the Spanish and Portuguese Synagogue (1838). This federal office building, in deference to the neighborhood that it destroyed, includes residential units.

Chinatown (15) is an old neighborhood where the majority of buildings were built in the mid-nineteenth century. In the 1970s, the area was threatened by modern, urban development and the Chinese population began to disperse throughout Montreal. Community leaders protested until the city was convinced that it was economically important to have a Chinese quarter that tourists could visit. A cultural center was built and rue de la Gauchetière was turned into a pedestrian street decorated with Chinese-style arches and designs in the pavement. Although the number of residents is small, the neighborhood is still lively. Chinese families and those who love good food are willing to travel in order to shop and eat in the multitude of stores and restaurants. On Chinese holidays, fireworks and winding dragons provide entertainment in the streets. The Lee,

Tam, Chan and Wong family associations, which will provide help to new immigrants with the same name, maintain their respective offices at 94, 90, 88 and 76 rue de la Gauchetière.

THE CHINESE IN CANADA

Although Lord Strathcona had nothing to do with the building of Montreal's Chinatown, he is indirectly responsible for its creation. When the Canadian Pacific Railway was being built in the 1880s, Chinese laborers were imported and employed, for seventy-five cents a day, to do the work that was considered too dangerous for whites. One particularly difficult stretch of track in the Rockies is said to have cost one Chinese life per mile. Although Chinese labor was appreciated, the Canadian government imposed a head tax on those "oriental" immigrants who were considered unable to earn a living (that is, women and children). With the completion of the railroad, some Chinese men headed east to Montreal to set up businesses and earn enough money to pay the tax on their families. As in many North American and European cities, the growing population of single Chinese men attracted an adjacent red-light district. In Montreal, rue de Bullion was known by sailors all over the world. Harpo Marx said that he spent a week in an opium den in Montreal's Chinatown.

The Canadian government did not end blatant discrimination against Chinese immigrants until the 1930s. It is only in recent decades that Asian minorities have started to become integrated into Quebec society.

For those who do not wish to eat oriental cuisine, two of Montreal's best Italian restaurants are close to Chinatown. **Le Latini** is at 1130 Jeanne Mance. **Le Piémontais** is at 1145A rue de Bullion.

WALKING TOUR TWO: CULTURE AND NATIONALISM

Le Monument National (16) is at 1182 St-Laurent, just north of Chinatown. There is no better place to begin a tour that focuses on Quebec's culture than here. This large multipurpose cultural center was built in 1891 for the Société St-Jean-Baptiste, an organization dedicated to the preservation of Quebec's heritage. The architects, Perrault, Mesnard and Venne, chose a highly original facade that mixes Romanesque and Baroque details—note the pediments inside the arched windows. The workshops, conference rooms, classrooms and Canada's oldest surviving theater have recently been restored.

This building was the focal point for Quebec's dissatisfaction with its position inside Canada almost as soon as it opened. It was here that Henri Bourassa and others vocalized their opposition to British Imperial policy during the Boer War and Canadian conscription during World War I. It was also in this building that Quebec playwrights, starting with Gratien Gélinas in the late 1930s, began to express the unique position of being francophone in North America.

QUEBEC PLAYWRIGHTS

It is hard to believe, but Quebec did not have a popular dramatic hit by one of its own writers until *Ti-Coq* in 1948, when Gratien Gélinas wrote about an ordinary soldier who had no wish to go to war. In the 1950s, the number of theater companies began to multiply, and television enabled actors to earn a living; but plays written by Quebecers were rarely produced. Then, in the 1960s (as with the rest of society), there was an explosion of theater that began to reflect the reality of living in Montreal. Nonetheless, critics believed that Quebec culture was still laboring with a sense of alienation and a colonial mentality until 1968, when Michel Tremblay wrote *Les Belles-Soeurs,* a play in which the characters spoke in *joual,* the language of the streets. Since then, the number of playwrights, directors and productions of

Quebec plays has multiplied; and it is now a rare year when a home-grown product is not the hit of the season.

Just to the north, the corner of Ste-Catherine and St-Laurent can be best described as the midpoint of Montreal's Forty-second Street. The city plans to redevelop the area and create a park opposite Le Monument, but plans have lately been shelved.

West on René-Lévesque, you will see a rather dull, late-1950s skyscraper with a giant *Q* on its facade near the top. This is the headquarters of **Hydro-Québec** (17), the nationalized hydro-electric company that is the center of the province's economic plans for the future.

HYDRO-QUÉBEC

If the Canadian Pacific Railway was the motor that drove Montreal into the twentieth century, Hydro-Québec is the one that will carry her into the twenty-first. Perhaps more important than the fact that it is one of the greatest power companies in the world and is harnessing the extensive river systems that flow into James Bay, more than 800 kilometers (500 miles) north of Montreal, it has given the Quebec people the confidence in their economic management to believe that they can, if necessary, survive as an independent country. To indicate how closely this power company and the government are intertwined, you only have to state that Quebec's premier has his Montreal office in this building.

Complexe Desjardins (18) is Montreal's most humane shopping mall, where there are often free concerts or television shows being shot. This complex of buildings, with its huge atrium, cascades, plants and balconies, was opened in 1975. It is especially loved by the

Québecois, not only because Santa Claus takes up his seasonal residence in a children's village on the lowest level, but also because it was the first major downtown development to be financed solely by French-Canadians.

QUÉBECOIS CAPITAL

The development of Québecois capital has been slow. During the French Regime, when the appointed intendant controlled the economy of the colony, there was little chance to accumulate wealth. Modern capitalism began to develop in Holland and slowly spread to England in the early 1700s, but would not make its way to Canada until after the British conquest in 1758. John Molson arrived from England and started his brewery in 1786, but small domestic industries were the order of the day. Throughout the nineteenth century, Quebec's educational system produced priests, lawyers, notaries, journalists and politicians, while industrial development was left in British, American and English-Canadian hands. J.-E.-A. Dubuc of Chicoutimi, Sir Rodolphe Forget of Montreal, and G.-E. Amyot of Quebec were almost the only great French-Canadian industrialists in a century of tremendous economic growth.

Québecois capitalism grew out of the rural, cooperative movement of cheese and butter manufacturers. In 1901, Alphonse Desjardins founded a *caisse populaire* (credit union) in Lévis, opposite Quebec City. The movement spread quickly, was supported by Henri Bourassa and other nationalists and even won (in 1912) the support of Earl Grey, the British governor-general of Canada. Desjardins introduced, through the large French-Canadian population of New England, credit unions into the United States.

Yet even with the steady growth of "the movement," the small savings of farmers and workers could not compete with international financiers. As industrialization progressed in Quebec, rural traditions were threatened, Montreal grew and Quebec's native, creative energy continued to go into politics and religious institutions. As a rising belief in ethnic discrimination grew, a powerful union movement surfaced. By 1934, 394 American companies controlled 35 percent of Quebec's industrial capital. Both the British and English-

Canadians were almost as powerful. That immigrants were becoming rich and successful confused many Québecois. A sense of isolation and even xenophobia blanketed the province, and new immigrants, even Catholic Italians, tended to identify with the more outward-looking English. Yet, Le Mouvement Desjardins continued to expand, and by the time the Québecois awoke to the "Quiet Revolution," it controlled a substantial part of the provincial banking system.

Since the secularization of Quebec, and because of changes in the educational system, the French-Canadian distaste for business has entirely disappeared. Paul Desmarais is, today, one of the richest men in Canada. The Bombardier family, which began by building snowmobiles, now controls a multinational consortium that manufactures airplanes, subway cars and railroad rolling stock. Today, 80 percent of Quebec's investment capital is owned by people who live in the province.

The **Spectrum de Montreal,** where many of Quebec's entertainers and musicians establish their reputations, is just to the west, at 318 Ste-Catherine O. The Théâtre du Nouveau Monde, Quebec's most important theater, is to the east, at number 84.

Place-des-Arts (19) is directly opposite Complexe Desjardins. This ensemble of buildings was Mayor Jean Drapeau's first major project for the city. The large central building houses the 3,000-seat Salle Wilfred Pelletier. Opened in 1963, it is the home of the Orchestre Symphonique de Montréal, which, since it has been under the direction of Charles Dutoit, has earned an excellent international reputation. It is also used by Les Grands Ballets Canadiens, the Opéra de Montréal and local impressarios. From the Peking Opera and the Royal Ballet to Lily Tomlin and Bob Dylan, hundreds of others have played this house.

The works of art that decorate it are a distillation of the Montreal School. In the foyer, a tapestry designed by Robert Lapalme represents Orpheus meeting Dionysius on the banks of the River Styx; another, by Micheline Beauchemin, was inspired by the fatal flight of Icarus. The metal sculpture on the west side of the foyer is by Anne Kehane, while Louis Archambault's *Agnes Radieux* dominates the main stairway. The large aluminum mural in the lower foyer is by

Julien Hébert, while the ceramic tympana that adorns the corridors leading to the orchestra seats are by Jordi Bonnet. A large marble swan by Hans Schleeh and a work by the Inuit sculptor Innukpuk are in the upper part of the lobby. Two important paintings, *La Bolduc* by Jean-Claude Riopelle, and *Hochelaga* by Fernard Toupin, were donated to the concert hall in 1976.

The **Théâtre de Maisonneuve,** with 1,300 seats, and **Théâtre Port-Royal**, with 800, were completed in 1967. In the Maisonneuve, a painting by Louis Feito decorates the entrance. The mural is by Peter Gnass and the mezzanine tapestry by Helene Baranyna. On the upper level is a sculpture by Charles Daudelin. The acrylic curtain is by Micheline Beauchemin. In the Port-Royal, the terra-cotta mural is by Jean Chartier and the two paintings are by Jean McEwen and Paul Beaulieu. The two enormous photographic murals are by Michel Saint-Jean. For a guided tour of the complex, telephone 285-4270.

Le Musée d'art contemporain de Montréal (20) was founded in 1984 "to preserve contemporary Quebec art and to ensure a place for international contemporary art through acquisitions, exhibitions and other cultural activities." This new building, which opened in 1991, houses a permanent collection of over three thousand works and a documentation center. Open: Tuesday through Sunday 10 A.M. to 6 P.M.

THE FINE ARTS IN QUEBEC

The history of the fine arts of Quebec begins with the tradition of embroidery that Marie de l'Incarnation brought from France in the seventeenth century. Jeanne Le Ber, the religious recluse, was Montreal's first artist. There is no record of any male artist until 1700, when Bishop Laval founded a school for artisans at St-Joachim, a village just outside Quebec City. For 150 years, the Church was the only significant patron of painters and sculptors, who were employed to decorate places of worship. The French and British aristocratic governors, the only other people able to afford luxury, tended to bring their furniture and paintings with them and then carry them back home.

It was not until the 1800s that businessmen and landowners began having their portraits painted by traveling artists from London and Paris. Antoine Plamondon (1802–95) became the first Quebec artist able to establish himself as a portrait painter. During the same period, Cornelius Krieghoff (1815–72) began to record the rustic life in the villages and country, but his approach was anecdotal and, in part, satiric, and to the embarrassment of the educated French-Canadians, tended to satisfy the wealthy English businessmen's desire to believe in the "happy *habitant.*"

Churches continued to be the major patrons of both sculpture and painting, but by the 1880s local sculptors, notably Henry Beaumont (a British immigrant), were employed to decorate the facades of buildings, and by the turn of the century, Henri Julien was a popular (if sentimental) illustrator and painter. Then, as public monuments to figures in history became fashionable, Phillipe Hébert became the first Quebec sculptor of secular subjects to be widely employed. Alfred Laliberté, in the 1920s, was able to follow in his path.

In the first decades of the twentieth century, Fauvism and Impressionism arrived with the European-trained artists, Maurice Cullen (1866–1934), James W. Morrice (1865–1924) and Aurèle Suzor-Côté (1869–1937); but the tradition of representing rural Quebec was still dominant and brought to new heights by Clarence Gagnon (1881–1942) and Marc-Aurèle Fortin (1888–1970).

In the late 1940s and 1950s, under the leadership of Pellan, who taught at the Ecole des Beaux Arts, the Montreal School of painting and sculpture began to develop. But the most important event in the fine arts of Quebec came in 1948 when a group of artists, led by Paul-Emile Borduas, published a manifesto, *Refus Global,* which not only denied the relevance of the classical traditions but also proposed that if society were to develop, then it must make an absolute break with the past. This call for revolution, which was inspired by Marxist-Leninism, may seem, to a European, to have come rather late, but it must be remembered that the clergy of Quebec were still threatening their congregations with Hell if they went to the movies. The combination of the influences of Pellan, a surrealist, and *Refus Global* created a dynamic environment for Quebec artists and critics to accept modernism and abstraction. Riopelle, de Tonnancour, Mousseau and Archambault actively embraced the ideas of the twentieth century, and by the 1970s, the variety and depth of contemporary Quebec art had expanded to include performance and installations.

─────────────■─────────────

The Church of St. John the Evangelist (21) is behind Place-des-Arts. This Neo-Gothic church was founded in 1905 by Father Edmund Wood (1829–1909). Believing that "the holiness of beauty is part of the beauty of holiness," he favored the highly ritualized, "bells-and-smells" ceremonies of the Church of England's High Church. A musician and the founder of English Montreal's most prestigious boys' school, he was generous to the point of abstraction and would literally give away the clothes on his back. In 1859, he had thrilled Montrealers when he climbed to the top of the newly completed steeple of Christ Church Cathedral. His funeral was one of the largest that the city has witnessed. It is said that his ghost still haunts the church that he founded.

Up the slope of **rue Jeanne-Mance** is a beautiful row of houses that were saved from demolition in 1975. Opposite, **l'Institut de technologie de Montréal** (22), now part of the Université du Québec, was designed, in 1910, by Archibald and Perrault. The entrance on rue Sherbrooke is patterned after the New York Public Library. It is another example of Montreal's imitative architecture. On the next block east is the old École des Beaux Arts, which was built in 1907 and from 1922 until recently housed Montreal's most respected school for painters and sculptors. Its graduates include many of Quebec's best-known artists, including Jean-Paul Riopelle, Jacques de Tonnancour, Guido Molinari, Armand Vaillancourt and Yves Gaucher. Behind it is the former School of Architecture, which was designed in 1922 by Ernest Cormier (the Old Courthouse, Université de Montréal) and J. Omer Marchand (City Hall, Bibliothèque Nationale).

On the next block there are some fine examples of nineteenth-century residential architecture. **Notman House** (number 51) was built in 1852 for Alexander Molson. This beautiful, simple-lined, Neoclassical building is named after William Notman, Montreal's great Victorian photographer, who lived in the house. His collection of photographic plates, which is now housed in the McCord Museum, left an extensive record of the city. Beside Notman House is a good example of the tower-and-turreted Chateau style, and across rue Clark is a large, classically inspired home that dates from the 1830s and was saved from demolition in 1975. On the south side of Sherbrooke, the steep gables of the apartment building opposite betray the influence of the Queen Anne style. The Second Empire building with its false mansard roof is the headquarters of the Société St-Jean-Baptiste.

CHANGING NAMES

La Société St-Jean-Baptiste was founded in 1834 by Ludger Duvernay. This self-proclaimed guardian of French culture in North America was responsible for organizing the festivities of Quebec's national holiday on June 24. It has often represented the most nationalist sentiments of Quebec, and because of its continued agitation for the language laws that have made outdoor signs in English illegal, it is resented by the anglophone minority. It advocates changing the names of major streets that honor English speakers.

Rue Sherbrooke is named after Sir John Sherbrooke, a British governor who in 1816 encouraged Louis-Joseph Papineau and John Nielson to lobby the British parliament to counteract the influence of wealthy Montreal businessmen who wanted to pass a series of laws that would lead to the total assimilation of the French within fifteen years.

The Comedy Museum (23) is housed in the solid, Richardsonian edifice at 2115 St-Laurent (just south of Sherbrooke). It was built as a brewery in 1894 for Henry Ekers, Mayor of Montreal (1906–08). This new museum, described as a "meat plant of humor," is an outgrowth of the annual Just for Laughs Comedy Festival.

In 1819, the northwest corner of Sherbrooke and St-Laurent marked the edge of the Molson estate. On the southwest corner is a reinforced-concrete, Art Nouveau (1910) building by J. A. Godin. The convent of **Notre-Dame-de-la-Charité-du-Bon-Pasteur**

(24) was built, starting in 1846, when the area was still mostly farmland. The design for the complex of buildings and courtyard was based on seventeenth-century French monasteries. The nuns operated a boarding school for orphans ("the sheltered") and a rehabilitation and training center for delinquent girls ("the protected"), many of whom were addicted to alcohol and morphine. The convent grew until the turn of the century, but as the state began to assume the administration of the social services the community diminished in size. In 1982, a municipal agency supervised the recycling of the building to house condominiums in the workshops, washhouse and outbuildings in the back along with subsidized housing for low-income families in the old school, which had been in the east wing, and offices and a cultural center in the central block. The restored 1878 chapel by Victor Bourgeau is now a concert hall, and a home for the elderly occupies the former School of Industry. A day-care center is now in the rectory, and the courtyard is a pleasant park.

Farther east, the old Collège Mont-Saint-Louis, with its mansard roofs, dates from the turn of the century. This very prestigious boys' school was run by Les Frères des Écoles Chrétiennes. The building, which takes its design from Tuileries Palace (a seventeenth-century royal residence in Paris), has also been recycled to house condominiums.

Boulevard St-Laurent (25) is nicknamed The Main, because it was once the main street of a suburb, St-Laurent. It's worth walking north if you wish to shop for food, clothes and antiques.

THE HISTORY OF THE MAIN

When Old Montreal was still surrounded by a wall, there was only one gate, Port St-Laurent, that led north. By the early eighteenth century, St. Lawrence Street was an established road, passing through many fertile farms and orchards, which, starting in the 1850s, began to be replaced by the suburb of St-Laurent, where a few English-speaking merchants, businessmen and tradesmen began to build their homes. Separated from Old Montreal by the steep slope between today's boulevard de Maisonneuve and rue Sherbrooke, it was not until the Montreal City Passenger Railway Company opened a line of horse-drawn tramways, extending as far north as boulevard Mont-Royal, that the street began to assume the economic and cultural importance that it maintains to this day.

In the 1880s, as a result of the pogroms in Russia, a wave of working-class Jewish immigrants began to arrive in Montreal and settle in the newly developing suburb. The wealthy ones established textile factories, while the poorer ones worked in them. The community flourished and Yiddish was as common as English and French. In the first half of the twentieth century, as more and more immigrants from numerous countries arrived, they tended to move into this area that had grown up between the English community to the west and the French to the east. During the 1940s, the more successful began to move northward, past boulevard Mont-Royal, and then around and up the slopes of Mont-Royal itself to bigger and sturdier houses. Mordecai Richler's novels *The Apprenticeship of Duddy Kravitz* and *St. Urbain's Horseman* give vivid descriptions of life in this old Jewish community.

After World War II, new immigrants from many different European countries began to settle and work in the light-manufacturing industries. Large Italian, Greek and Portuguese communities first established themselves close to The Main. According to the last census, French is the mother tongue of 58 percent of the population of Montreal. English-speakers make up 19 percent. But 23 percent speak other languages.

In the 1960s the factories began to move away from The Main. The abandoned lofts were gradually inhabited by many young anglophone artists, writers and film directors. Immigrants from Latin America, Vietnam and Africa continue to arrive, but gradually boulevard St-Laurent has become the territory of the young and bohemian. Although many of the old European food shops still remain, the street is now the fastest developing (and already one of the busiest) centers for restaurants, avant-garde boutiques, bars and nightclubs.

Rue Prince-Arthur (26), named after Queen Victoria's third son, is a popular pedestrian mall that teems with life all summer. Artisans, portrait artists, painters, musicians and jugglers sell their wares and entertain the throngs that head for the multitude of restaurants and bars that spill out onto the street. Although none of the restaurants is rated as the very best in Montreal, you can choose from a wide variety of cuisines and eat very well. For those on a tight budget, Mazurka, at 64 Prince-Arthur E., offers hearty Polish cooking at very reasonable prices. Bal St-Louis is the most popular bar.

POWERFUL DREAMS

In the early 1980s, there was a very popular bar, Le Prince-Arthur, that suddenly and surprisingly fell down in the middle of the night, when no one was there. A number of the employees went on to open their own bars and restaurants. A number of them swear that the Prince-Arthur collapsed because their dreams and those of the customers were too powerful for the building to contain.

Carré St-Louis (27) is a popular square where bohemian types pass the day. A Victorian fountain graces the center of the park. It is surrounded by trees, benches and Victorian residences that have been described as "frozen music." To the east, there are sculptures by Armand Vaillancourt; to the west, a flower stall in a converted *vespasienne*. In winter, there is a circuitous skating path, and lights decorate tree branches.

The square has long been associated with Quebec nationalism. In the summer of 1837, Les Fils de la Liberté practiced their military drills there in preparation for the uprisings of November. In the 1850s, the site was a small reservoir, but in 1879, as the growing bourgeoisie began developing the area, it was turned into a public park. In the 1890s, Quebec's "national poet," Émile Nelligan, lived just to the north, on rue Laval. For the first few decades of the twentieth century, the area prospered, but with the development of suburban housing, it was allowed to deteriorate in the 1950s. It has been lately revitalized and is now the favored neighborhood for some of Quebec's most successful artists. The poem *Lettre à Jean Drapeau* by

Michel Bujold, which is written on the side of the house at number 336, expresses modern nationalist sentiments.

LITERATURE IN QUEBEC

Although Quebec's literary fiction dates from 1837, when Aubert de Gaspé's novel *L'Influence d'un livre* appeared, Pierre Chauveau's 1846 novel, *Charles Guérin* (which describes the plight of classical college graduates whose training is good only for professions that are already overcrowded) was the first to be deeply rooted in Québecois concerns. During the second half of the nineteenth century, literary reviews and societies sprouted, but development was seriously hampered by the Church's conservative fears and active attempts to suppress liberalism. Writers, notably Octave Crémazie, explored the legends and rural life of Quebec. Antoine Gerin-Lajoie's *Jean Rivard, le défricheur* (1862) gives an epic quality to the hero's struggle with the wilderness. In the early 1890s Emile Nelligan (1872–1941), Quebec's greatest poet, burst onto the scene. Influenced by Baudelaire, Verlaine, Rimbaud and Mallarmé, his *Le Vaisseau d'Or* and *La Romance du Vin* border on genius. His career, however, was short—at the age of twenty, he was placed in a hospital for the insane, where he lived until his death. The next major literary achievement was Louis Hémon's *Maria Chapdelaine* (1914), a critical portrayal of pioneer life in the Lac St-Jean area. It was not until the 1920s and 1930s that Quebec's literature began to diversify into the schools of the fantastic (Desrosiers' *Nord-Sud* of 1931), the psychological (de Roquebrune's *Les Dames Les Marchand* of 1937), and the socially critical (J.-C. Harvey's *Les Demi-Civilisées*). With World War II, the urban environment began to be reflected in fiction, with the publication of Gabrielle Roy's *Bonheur d'occasion* and Roger Lemelin's *Les Plouffes*. Ann Hebert began to experiment with symbolism in *Le Torrent*.

But there was one more barrier to break in the 1960s—language. French in Quebec, because of the two-hundred-year separation, had developed differently from that in France—it had retained many words that had died in Europe and had accepted many anglicisms. In 1964, Jacques Renaud's *Le Casse* finally made it possible to write in *joual*, the patois of the street. Today, the works of Marie-Claire Blais,

Rejean Ducharme, Michel Tremblay, Antoinine Maillet and Yves Beauchemin are internationally published and eagerly awaited by the public.

L'École Nationale d'Hôtellerie (28) is located in the tall gray-and-black building across rue St-Denis from Carré St-Louis. It is one of the few professional hotel and restaurant schools in the world. Tourists are invited to stay in the forty-two-room hotel, and during the term, anyone can experience the cuisine of Montreal's newest chefs (telephone: 866-4611). The Montreal Society of Architecture awarded the building the 1974 Prix Citron (Lemon Award) for being the ugliest building built that year.

This tour turns down St-Denis, but for those who wish to do some clothes shopping, it is worth walking a few blocks up the street to rue Duluth. The restaurant **Citronlime,** at 4669 St-Denis, is recommended for its innovative French cuisine that incorporates South American and Asian influences.

Just north of Sherbrooke, **Café Cherrier** is a fashionable bistro. **Witloof**, at 3619 St-Denis, is highly recommended for its mussels, soups, salads and Belgian stew.

The old name of the slope south of Sherbrooke is **Côte à Baron** (29). **Les Mignardises,** at 2037 rue St-Denis, is considered to be one of the best restaurants in the city. Although prices are expensive, the cuisine of J. P. Monnet is described as "formidable." The area started to become known as the Latin (or Student) Quarter in 1878, when Laval University (of Quebec City) opened its Montreal campus for medicine, theology and law. Bars and cafés began to thrive around the campus, and writers, actors, painters, musicians and other artists began to gather and define the modern cultural expressions of the Québecois.

La Bibliothèque Nationale (30) was designed in 1914 by Eugène Payette in the Beaux Arts style. The library not only receives a copy of every new book published in the province, but it also houses the extensive collection of Canadiana (begun in 1844) that the Sulpician Fathers gave to the government of Quebec in the 1960s. The stained-glass windows, which can be seen from the street at night, represent Art, Science and Religion. Next door, at 1704 St-Denis, is an early

(1914) reinforced concrete apartment building with Art Nouveau touches. It was designed by Joseph-Arthur Godin.

Le Théâtre St-Denis was built in 1908. Montreal's largest theater for more than fifty years, it seats 2,500. The building has been renovated twice since Sarah Bernhardt performed there. The latest renovation, in 1990, was in the Art Moderne style, which draws its inspiration from the great passenger liners of the first half of the twentieth century.

POPULAR MUSIC IN QUEBEC

Quebec's popular music was largely ignored until the 1960s. Fiddlers and singers were well appreciated in many of the rural regions and city neighborhoods, but they lived hand-to-mouth. La Bolduc, a folksinger of the 1930s, was the first star to be truly appreciated by her own people, but like many a musician of the period she was obliged to continually travel from small town to small town. In the early 1950s, Felix Leclerc, still drawing on the tradition of folklore, was received well enough in Paris to be taken seriously by Montrealers, but until the early 1960s the greater number of Quebec's popular singers made a living by translating American hits into French. Then, in the forefront of the Quiet Revolution, artists like Louise Forrestier, Gilles Vigneault and Robert Charlebois, expressing themselves in original compositions, burst onto the scene. As rock concerts got larger, so did the status of Quebec singers. In the mid-1980s, Diane Dufresne could ask her audience to dress all in pink and come to the Olympic Stadium to see her sing her own unique songs—and they would. Today, although much of the music played on the airwaves is American or British, there is a continual parade of local stars and groups who are idolized. Beau Dommage, Ginette Reno, René and Natalie Simard, Céline Dion, Harmonium, Daniel Lavoie and Mitsou are all *vedettes* (stars). The McGarrigle Sisters and Leonard Cohen are English Montreal's best-known singers. Kashtin is a popular rock group that sings in the Montagnis language.

La Cinémathèque Québecoise (31), at 335 de Maisonneuve East, is dedicated to "defending and illustrating Quebec's cinema." It has a small museum and operates a repertory cinema. Screenings: Tuesday through Sunday 6:30 and 8:30 P.M.

FILM IN QUEBEC

Although Montreal's first French cinema was opened in 1906 by Ernest Ouimet, it was not until 1939 that the Catholic church stopped threatening audiences with the fires of Hell. There were, of course, many great movie palaces built to screen the English-language films of Hollywood, but filmmaking in Canada did not really start until the National Film Board of Canada was founded, in Montreal, in 1938. This organization is still mostly dedicated to the production of documentary and educational films, but it did prove to be the training ground for a dynamic team of dramatic directors that began to emerge in the 1960s. To date, Montreal's most famous director is Denys Arcand, whose *Le Déclin de l'Empire Américain* (1988) and *Jésus de Montréal* (1989) were both nominated for Best Foreign Film at the Academy Awards.

The Université du Québec (32) like many American state universities, has several campuses that serve different areas of the province. The Modern (1974) brick Montreal campus was built close to the old campus of the Université de Montréal, which had moved to an entirely new site on the northern slopes of Mont-Royal in 1943. The building on the east side of St-Denis incorporates the dismembered facade (designed in 1860 by Victor Bourgeau) and elegant steeple of the parish church, St-Jacques. It is not without its architectural critics. According to one, "Montreal's tallest steeple now looks like a 'folly' of an eccentric, European aristocrat." Nonetheless, the building does provide a metaphor for the secularization of Quebec. Across the street, the Postmodern (1991) building wraps itself around J. E. Vanier's Neoclassic École Polytechnique (1905). As a whole, the complex of buildings is a lesson in the development of the Postmodern school of architecture, which incorporates styles from the past.

Notre-Dame-de-Lourdes (33) is on rue Ste-Catherine. It was designed by Napoleon Bourassa (the son-in-law of Louis-Joseph Papineau and father of Henri Bourassa), who also painted the murals. With its model of the grotto at Lourdes, Byzantine dome and Romanesque details, this church has been popular with tourists since its consecration in 1876. One of the most active churches in the city, it is run by the Sulpician Fathers, who preach conservative Catholic doctrines. Beneath the altar, the statue of the Virgin Mary is by Louis-Phillipe Hébert.

WALKING TOUR THREE: THE ENGLISH QUARTER

At the turn of the century, 70 percent of the wealth of Canada was owned by families who lived in this area, which was known as the Golden Square Mile. Most of the mansions along Sherbrooke and René-Lévesque are gone, but many of those above Sherbrooke are now the property of McGill University, and a good number of the row houses, built for the upper-middle class, have become shops, offices, restaurants and bars. It is the neighborhood where *les anglos* go to eat, drink and be merry.

When the **Mount Royal Hotel** (34) opened in 1922, it was the largest in the British Empire. Converted into an elegant shopping mall (1986–88), the Neo-Georgian exterior, designed by Ross and Macdonald, has been preserved, and one hardly notices the offices and condominiums that were built above the original structure. Inside, the ornate ceilings and huge chandeliers (the central one came from the old casino in Monte Carlo) have been preserved, and the four light wells have become ten-story interior courts. During the reconstruction and building of the underground garage, huge pillars had to be installed to stop the building from collapsing—some have been cleverly incorporated into the exotic decor of the Egyptian Cinema. Considering the extent of the modifications and complete change of activities in this building, I can only applaud ARCOP and Associates, the designers.

Opposite, at 1430 rue Peel, the castlelike Seagram's Building, complete with portcullis, is the headquarters of the Bronfman family, one of Montreal's wealthiest.

Boulevard de Maisonneuve, with its march of modern office towers on either side, has become Montreal's urban canyon. One block east you will see a new Postmodern building with a stone facade on the lower floors and a glass-sheathed tower above—it has been nicknamed the Half-Peeled Banana.

Rue Drummond (35) was named after Jane Drummond, the daughter of John Redpath, the sugar refiner who ceded the street to the city in 1842. George Stephen House, just down from Boulevard de Maisonneuve, was designed by William T. Thomas, who did the exterior of the British Houses of Parliament. Built (in 1880–83) as a private home for George Stephen, a wool and cotton trader who became president of the Bank of Montreal and founder of the Canadian Pacific Railway, it is an opulent mix of Renaissance and Baroque styles. No expense was spared in the interior design—marble, onyx and gold were generously used, and rooms were paneled in Cuban mahogany, Ceylonese satinwood and ebony. Stephen resided in the house for only a few years—he retired to London in 1888. His mansion has been a private club since 1925.

Up the street is the Neoclassic Salvation Army Building (1906). Walk into the park on its northern side and you will come to a small, whimsical sculpture garden that takes its inspiration from the classical ruins of Greece.

Enter **Maison Alcan** (36) from the garden. Considered to be the city's best example of recycling old buildings and integrating them into the new, this complex was the brainchild of David Culver, the president of Alcan, the Aluminum Company of Canada. Designed by ARCOP and Associates, the spacious glass-covered atrium, which incorporates the backs of the older buildings, often hosts free classical music concerts. Open: 9 A.M. to 10 P.M.

The buildings on this block of rue Sherbrooke give an idea of what the street was like at the turn of the century. Maison Corby and its neighbor, Maison Forget, were built in 1882, and the more classically inspired Mount Royal Club was built in 1904. Lord Atholstan House, the Beaux Arts mansion now incorporated into Maison Alcan, dates from 1894.

SAVING MONTREAL

Montrealers became aware of the destruction of their city's architectural heritage in 1973, when the Van Horne Mansion, on the northeast corner of Sherbrooke and Stanley, suddenly fell to the wrecker's ball. Almost immediately, citizens began to take a stand against indiscriminate modern urban development. When artists were invited to celebrate the Olympic Games of 1976, they were asked to display their works along Sherbrooke, but instead of only creating original works, they also put up huge plastic hands with fingers that pointed to the sites of beautiful old buildings that had been destroyed. A photograph and a history of each building was displayed under each of the many fingers. Mayor Drapeau, late one night before the games opened, drove along the street, and by dawn the next morning the whole exhibition, including the "legitimate" sculptures, had been carted away. The artists eventually were successful in suing the city for damages. Since then, a citizen's group, Save Montreal, keeps a watchful eye on the plans of developers and the building permits the city issues. As a result, Windsor Station, Le Monument National, Shaughnessy House, the Grey Nuns' Convent and a number of other important buildings have been saved. Save Montreal also gives out a yearly Prix Orange and Prix Citron (Orange and Lemon prizes) to the best restoration project and the worst new construction.

The Ritz-Carlton Hotel (37) was designed in 1911 by the New York architects Warren and Whetmore (Grand Central Station). The Belle-Epoque entrance, elegant lobby and ground-floor lounge—complete with huge classical paintings—have been beautifully preserved and still evoke Edwardian opulence. First under the management of Cesar Ritz, who introduced the concept of chain hotels, the Ritz has been an "upper-class institution," and is still considered to be the best hotel in Canada. A number of the rooms have their own fireplaces, and in the courtyard, where a luxurious, traditional English tea is served, twelve ducklings paddle around in a pond. Since the ducklings are replaced every two to three weeks, I calculate that about twenty thousand ducks have stayed at the Ritz. Elizabeth Taylor and Richard Burton were first married in the Ritz. John Lennon and Yoko Ono held their publicized nude "love-in" in the modern Four Seasons Hotel, just down the street.

On the next block, **Holt Renfrew** (38) is an expensive clothing store. The building was designed in 1937 by the architects Ross and Macdonald. Recipients of a medal from the Royal Architectural Institute of Canada, the Art Moderne–style windows get their inspiration from the great passenger liners of the period. Opposite, the huge chateaulike apartment building, complete with carriage entrances and gargoyles, was designed in 1924 by H. L. Featherstonehaugh, Ross and Macdonald for Pamphile du Tremblay, the owner of the newspaper *La Presse*. The Erskine American Church, built in 1883, is in the solid Romanesque style of H. H. Richardson, the great American architect. The interior, which resembles an amphitheater, was designed by Nobbs and Hyde in 1938. Its stained-glass windows are by Tiffany of New York.

The Montreal Museum of Fine Arts (39), Canada's oldest art museum, was founded in 1860. It first occupied the Neoclassical building on the north side of the street in 1912. Its facade, in Vermont marble, was designed by Edward and William Maxwell. The museum has recently expanded south of Sherbrooke, where Moshe Safdie's design incorporates the 1888 facade of an apartment building.

Because the Montreal Museum of Fine Arts was long controlled by the families of the Golden Square Mile, its collections are diversified, even eclectic. It has Egyptian, Greek, Roman, Chinese, Islamic, pre-Columbian, Inuit and Amerindian art. It has classical and modern European and North American sculptures, paintings and drawings, as well as furniture, porcelain, textiles, silver and gold. In short, it is not famous for having an especially good collection of anything, but has a bit of everything and is quite fascinating. Currently it hosts many of the world's major traveling exhibitions and often provides the facilities for musicians and dancers who come from the more exotic cultural traditions. Open: Tuesday through Sunday 10 A.M. to 5 P.M. Temporary exhibitions: 10 A.M. to 7 P.M.

The Gothic-Revival **Presbyterian Church of St. Andrew and St. Paul** (40) was designed by the same architect as Le Château Apartments down the street. It is clear that H. L. Featherstonehaugh was as comfortable in English Gothic style as he was in Loire Château. The primary place of worship for the Scottish families who dominated the Golden Square Mile, the church does not lack decoration. The huge stained-glass window above the altar dates from 1900 and, like the lower tier of memorial windows, comes originally from the old St. Paul's Church that had been on Dorchester Square. Sir Edward Burne-Jones designed the windows at the back of the building. William Morris is responsible for the two that use garlands of leaves to frame the subjects. The upper windows were designed by Lawrence Lee and were installed in the 1960s. The church is open only during services.

The converted graystones on the opposite side of Sherbrooke house the most exclusive of Montreal's private art galleries, antiques and objet d'art shops. The sculpture outside the Dominion Art Gallery at 1438 is of Jean d'Aire, Burgher of Calais, who was one of the men who offered their lives to England's Edward III if he would save the city from the siege being mounted by the French. The statue was produced by Auguste Rodin in 1885. The gallery is one of the largest on the continent.

The Linton, at the corner of rue Simpson, is an apartment block in which the residents shared the servants and the ground-floor dining hall but could have their meals served in their apartments. Built in the Beaux Arts tradition of 1907, the ornamented, terra-cotta facade was made in molds. Behind the apartment block stands the Second Empire–style **Linton House** (41), built in 1867. Amazingly, the interior, down to the embossed wallpaper, is entirely in place. Still privately owned, it may one day become a museum.

Rue Guy and **Chemin de la Côte-des-Neiges** (42) were once an Amerindian trail. It is probable that de Maisonneuve, after the tiny colony had been saved from floods in 1642, carried the heavy cross up this slope. It is still the best route for driving from downtown to Mount Royal Park. Under the junction with Sherbrooke lies the body of Amery Girod, a patriot of 1837. He was buried under the crossroads because he commited suicide rather than be captured. The classical Bank of Montreal was built in 1928 and is a replica of the J. P. Morgan Bank of New York City. The Grosvenor Apartments opposite date from 1905; their design was inspired by the English Renaissance.

Place Norman-Bethune (43) is a tiny triangular park that was created in 1978 when the People's Republic of China gave Montreal the statue.

A HERO OF CHINA

Norman Bethune was born in Gravenhurst, Ontario, went to medical school in Edinburgh, Scotland, and settled in Montreal. While on the staff of the Royal Victoria Hospital, he pioneered many medical techniques and established the world's first palliative-care unit for the terminally ill. He led a bohemian life-style, was a painter of some talent and was clearly courageous—after learning that he was suffering from tuberculosis, he cured himself by piercing his own lung. A political radical, he practiced medicine during the Spanish Civil War and the Communist Revolution in China. A highly respected comrade of Mao Tse-tung, he died of gangrene poisoning after he cut himself while operating on a Chinese soldier. Because of Bethune's love of Montreal, the People's Republic of China continues to honor the city. The largest Chinese garden outside China is in Montreal's botanical gardens, and whenever the Peking Opera tours North America, it gives a free concert at Royal Victoria Hospital.

On the corner of **rue St-Mathieu and boulevard de Maison-neuve** (44) is a wonderful Art Deco firehouse and police station. Designed by Shorey and Ritchie and built in 1931, the fire hose tower, doors and windows have interesting details. The Victoria School, 1822 de Maisonneuve, was built in 1888. The Royal Montreal Curling Club, founded in 1807, has its present home at number 1850.

The **Masonic Temple** (45) is up rue St-Marc. The Neoclassical building was designed by Saxe and Archibald in 1928. Note the decorative lamps at the entrance. The Latin inscription on the pediment reads: "Faith, Hope, Charity, Truth, Liberty."

THE FREEMASONS

The Freemasons are a fraternal, charitable organization that some claim was founded by Hiram Abiff, the architect of King Solomon's Temple. Most historians trace its modern roots to eighteenth-century Scotland, from which it spread rapidly to Europe. Its secrecy and practice of quasi-religious rituals have at times, notably in the eighteenth and early nineteenth centuries, caused it to be the feared center of an international conspiracy that has been blamed for historical events as diverse as the French Revolution and international communism.

Le Grand Séminaire (46) is set in extensive grounds on the north side of Sherbrooke. The two towers by the street were built no later than 1695, when they were part of a fort in which Margeurite Bourgeoys had a school for Amerindian girls. Her nuns lived in the westerly tower; the easterly tower was a classroom.

Throughout the eighteenth century, the fort and its buildings were used as a summer residence for the Sulpician Fathers. In 1758, it was here that the British Army of ten thousand men camped while the surrender of Montreal, which had a population of five thousand, was negotiated.

The present seminary was begun in 1854. The main rectangular building, with its five projections of different sizes, was designed in the Classic Revival style by John Ostell, who also designed the old courthouse in Old Montreal. His work on this building was continued by Maurice Perrault. The chapel was designed by Joseph-Omer Marchand in 1905. The exterior is not remarkable, but, on request, you can see the impressive, rigorously symmetrical, Romanesque interior. The nave is eighty meters long, the exposed ceiling beams are of British Columbian cedar and the three hundred stalls are all hand carved. In the grounds to the west is a reflecting pool, a place of meditation, flanked by trees.

Since the secularization of Quebec, many parish vicarages have been turned into community centers. As the number of seminarians has dropped (there were only five graduates in 1989), many priests have moved to this building. The eastern wing is a private school for boys. /

The Canadian Centre for Architecture (CCA) (47) wraps itself around Shaughnessy House (1874), a Second Empire–style mansion that was designed, by William Thomas, as two semidetached houses. Lord Strathcona, whose mansion was next door, used the western side as a guest house. Converted into one dwelling in 1877, it was owned by successive general managers of the Canadian Pacific Railway, Sir William Van Horne and Lord Shaughnessy. In 1941, the building was converted into a Catholic residence for working women. Allowed to deteriorate and threatened with demolition, the mansion was bought by Bronfman heir Phyllis Lambert, a Montreal architect who began to create the CCA. In 1989, the world's largest and probably best museum devoted solely to architecture opened to international praise.

The rue Baile side of the new building, which was designed by Montrealer Peter Rose, is severe, even forbidding, and does not prepare one for the intimate play of shapes, light and textures of the interior. Housing a library, public exhibition galleries, a book shop and a lecture hall, the building has been called a "magnificent architectural present" by the London *Financial Times.* And, according to the *New York Times,* it "beautifully integrates classicism and modernism." The small permanent exhibition that describes the ideas behind the design is an excellent lesson in architecture and will help you appreciate other buildings in the city. The mahogany-paneled smoking room in the restored Shaughnessy House is also worth a visit.

Across boulevard René-Lévesque is the **CCA's sculpture garden.** Loved by some and hated by others, it sits on a bluff that overlooks the old working-class suburb of Little Burgundy. Designed by Melvin Charney, it is composed of four parts: a meadow (the site had been a meadow in the seventeenth and eighteenth centuries), an apple orchard (nineteenth century), an arcade that mirrors Shaughnessy House, and an esplanade of allegorical column-sculptures that explore the history of architecture.

The Mother House of the Grey Nuns (48) was built from 1869 to 1898, mostly according to the plans of Victor Bourgeau. It housed a convent, a hospice for the old, an asylum, an orphanage and a chapel. The western wing alone once housed seven hundred people. Threatened by demolition in 1975, it was bought by the Ministry of Cultural Affairs but has not found a new use since most of the nuns have moved back to their old mother house in Old Montreal. The entrance to the Marguerite d'Youville Museum is on rue St-Mathieu. It exhibits the tomb and religious objects of the order's founder (see more about this on page 55) and furniture and objects from the eighteenth century. Open: Wednesday to Sunday 1:30 to 4:30 P.M. Guided tours: 1:30 and 3 P.M. Admission is free.

The red cross at the corner of Guy and René-Lévesque, according to legend, marks the grave of Belisle, Montreal's most notorious highwayman and murderer. Behind the main complex is a row of *habitant*-style cottages, the only examples of traditional Quebec architecture (which has its roots in Brittany, France), in the western part of Montreal.

The Church Home for Elderly Ladies (49) is at 1221 rue Guy. It was built in 1859 for Edward Major, a city inspector. Since 1890 it has been owned by the Anglican diocese of Montreal, and the two wings (1919 and 1957) do little to change the tranquility of the house and its yard. **Chez la Mère Michel,** at 1209 Guy, offers the best French regional cooking. **Woodlands,** at 1241 Guy, is an excellent Indian restaurant.

Le Faubourg (50) is a new shopping center that is dedicated to food. The building is a converted garage and car showroom from the 1920s. The open spaces, light and gourmet foods make this an ideal place to rest. If you want a more intimate atmosphere, Montreal's top-rated tearoom, **Toman's Pastry,** is at 1421 MacKay, just a block east.

On the corner of Ste-Catherine and Bishop is the Neo-Gothic **St. James the Apostle Anglican Church** (51). It was built in 1863 and nicknamed St. Cricket in the Fields, because of its proximity to the old cricket field. Opposite, the **Coronation Building** (1911), with its terra-cotta facade and projecting cornice, is considered to be one of the best examples of the Chicago School of architecture. Its name commemorates the coronation of George V.

Peter Lyall House, at 1455 Bishop, was one of the first Montreal buildings to be built with imported Scottish red sandstone. Its fine exterior sculptures (by Henry Beaumont), towers and Romanesque entrance make it one of the most attractive mansions in Montreal. Built in 1889 for a developer, and now housing shops, it has a curious mantlepiece (also by Henry Beaumont) and an elegant staircase that can be seen during business hours. Opposite, the white terra-cotta facade of an old (1912) apartment building has been preserved as part of the new library of Concordia University. North America's first Y was built in Montreal. Its program of night courses led to the founding of Concordia University.

Les Chenets, at number 2075, produces some of the finest classic French cuisine. It has one of the largest wine cellars in the city. Feel like spending $20,000 for a bottle of Moët & Chandon Imperial Champagne? **Le Mas des Oliviers,** at 1216 Bishop, offers excellent Provençal dishes.

The buildings on **rue Crescent** (52) mostly date from 1890 to 1914. The elegant old row houses are now occupied by boutiques, bars and restaurants. **Troika,** 2171 Crescent, offers the best Russian cuisine in Montreal. **La Vigna,** at 2045, is said to have the best pasta. **Les Halles**, at 1450, is French and is considered to be the very best restaurant in town. **Le Chrysanthème,** at 1208, is said to offer the best Chinese cuisine.

❖ 5 ❖

Three Great Parks in Montreal

ÎLE STE-HÉLÈNE AND ÎLE NOTRE-DAME

Introduction

Situated in the middle of the St. Lawrence River, the two connected islands of île Ste-Hélène and île Notre-Dame, with the skyline of Montreal on one side and the seaway on the other, are municipal parks that are excellent places for families and friends of all ages to spend a day or longer. Without feeling crowded, their facilities include an amusement park, an aqua park, barbecue pits, bicycle paths, a freshwater beach, canals, an exhibition center, formal flower gardens, a Grand Prix circuit, rolling parklands, a historical museum, a marina, a military fort, restaurants, a rowing basin, sailboards, swimming pools, a tranquil pond and a theater. In winter there is ice-skating, cross-country skiing and snowshoeing.

How to Get There

Take the yellow metro line to île Ste-Hélène or the green line to Papineau, where Bus 169 leaves for the islands via the Jacques-Cartier Bridge. In summer, a bus route connects the cultural center on the westerly end of île Notre-Dame to La Ronde, where daytime mooring for one hundred small boats is available. Drivers can get to île Notre-Dame via Cité du Hâvre (turn off just after rue Université becomes the Autoroute Bonaventure) and to île Ste-Hélène by the Jacques-Cartier Bridge.

History

In 1611 Samuel de Champlain, aged forty, named île Ste-Hélène after his twelve-year-old fiancée, Hélène Boulle. She came to New

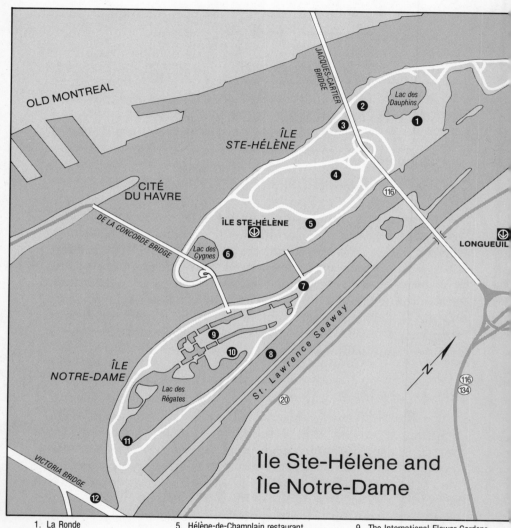

Île Ste-Hélène and Île Notre-Dame

1. La Ronde
2. Aqua-Parc
3. Le Musée David M. Stewart
4. Parkland
5. Hélène-de-Champlain restaurant
6. Man sculpture
7. The Gilles Villeneuve Grand-Prix Circuit
8. The Olympic Rowing Basin
9. The International Flower Gardens
10. Le Palais de la Civilisation
11. La Plage
12. Victoria Bridge

France in 1620 to live in Quebec with her new husband, but after only three years, she returned to France, never having seen the island named after her. During the early Iroquois wars, the island was used as a defensive base by the French but was never settled, and by the time Montreal was firmly established, it had been granted, by the king of France, as part of the *seigneury* of Longueuil (the name of the town across the river on the south shore), to the Lemoyne family, who had been instrumental in founding Louisiana and New Orleans. During the French Regime, apple trees were grown on the island and a cider press was constructed, but there was little development. When the British invaded in 1760, it became the last stronghold for the French troops; they burned their regimental flags here rather than surrender them in Montreal. Fifteen years later, the British retreated here when the Americans occupied the city. The governor, Sir Guy Carleton, dressed as a *habitant*, fled in a canoe from St. Helen's Island to Quebec City.

The American conquest only lasted a winter, but in 1807, because of renewed threats by the United States, the island was fortified. By 1817 it had become a major military establishment, and by 1820 it was the primary munitions depot for the entire British army in North America. Except for a brief period in 1830, when the barracks became a hospital for cholera victims, and another in 1837, when they became a temporary prison for Canadian rebels, the island was mostly a military base. This was not entirely to the liking of the citizens of Montreal, and they insisted on the right to visit the island at leisure.

When the British withdrew their armies in 1870, they gave the island to the Canadian government, which officially declared part of it a public park in 1875. In 1900, the city took possession of the park, but it still remained wild and wooded. During World War I, the fort was used as a major munitions depot. It took the Depression and the building of Jacques-Cartier Bridge to change île Ste-Hélène. As a make-work project, the federal and provincial governments combined forces and employed Frederick Todd, a student of Olmsted, the man who had designed Mount Royal Park, to draw up plans that would realize the recreational potential of the island. The old fort was restored, the road and swimming pool were built and trees were planted on the rolling landscape. During World War II, 250 German prisoners of war were held in the fort. Not a bad place to spend a war!

Frederick Todd, who also designed Stanley Park in Vancouver and

Battlefields Park in Quebec City, had envisioned that the low-lying islands and shoals around île Ste-Hélène should be incorporated into the park. He envisioned lagoons, bridges, a marina and even a public beach. It would take sixty years for his dream to become a reality. In 1967, Canada threw herself a hundredth-anniversary party. The center of that party was the International Exposition, which was built on the man-made île Notre-Dame and the extensions at either end of île Ste-Hélène. The landfill came from the excavation for Montreal's subway.

Expo '67 changed Montreal forever. Not only did Charles de Gaulle poke his long nose into Canada's internal affairs by saying "Vive le Québec libre!" but Montrealers found themselves to be popular hosts of one of the most successful World's Fairs of all time. The province that had, for so long, looked in on itself now looked suddenly at the world. But development of the park did not stop after that. When Montreal hosted the Olympics, a rowing basin was built. A racetrack was added to host Le Grand-Prix du Canada. In 1980 the Floralies International, a flower garden competition, led to the creation of almost a dozen formal gardens, designed by landscape artists from countries with climates as different as Mexico and Austria, Israel and England. The beach that Todd had envisioned was finally opened in 1990.

La Ronde (1), Montreal's amusement park, was opened as part of Expo '67. With its own overhead minirail for transportation, it has been designed for children of all ages. For tots there is Chnouguiville, a children's village with organized activities, games and shows. For small children there are specially designed rides in Le Monde des Petits. For children over 3'8" but less than 4'4," there are eight different rides. For thrill-seeking adults and adolescents there are thirty-one rides, including one of the highest roller coasters in the world. Most years, there is a circus in residence, and three times daily, on Lac des Dauphins (Lake Dolphin), Ronald McDonald and fifteen water-skiers perform amusing acrobatics. At Jardin des Etoiles there is a daily musical review. In the evening, there is dancing at the Terrasse du Dixieland, a show at Fort Edmonton and rock concerts on the floating stage. In all, during the summer, there are almost 2,500 shows staged here every year. Oh, yes, there's also a beer garden for when you get thirsty. Open: May weekends: 11 A.M. to 1 A.M.; May 20 to September 3 (except August 27 to 30): Sunday to Thursday 11 A.M. to midnight, Friday and Saturday 11 A.M. to 1 A.M. Visitors can buy simple entrance tickets, individual unlimited passes for all rides, family passes and passes that include entrance to the neighboring Aqua-Parc. Seniors are admitted free of charge, Monday through Thursday. Telephone: 872-6222.

Aqua-Parc (2) has sixteen waterslides, an Olympic-size heated swimming pool, three restaurants, a bar-terrace and changing rooms. One slide starts eighty-two feet up in the air and drops at a sixty-seven-degree slope before gradually delivering a gentle landing in the pool below. As your speed approaches seventy-five kilometers per hour, you feel that you are dropping straight down. Open: June 1 to August 13: 10 A.M. to 8 P.M.; reduced entrance price after 6 P.M. in August.

Le Musée David M. Stewart (3) is housed in the old British fort near the Jacques-Cartier Bridge. This museum, dedicated to Canada's history up to 1837, is large enough to exhibit only 5 percent of its collection at one time. It boasts the largest collection of seventeenth- and eighteenth-century kitchen utensils in the world, a fine and very large gun collection, documents, an excellent map collection and scientific instruments. Outside in the summer, highly disciplined, costumed students, using real guns, daily reenact the military drills (including a mock battle, which is quite noisy) of the seventeenth century. The Compagnie Franche de La Marine, which had, in the eighteenth century, the responsibility of protecting all French territory from the mouth of the Mississippi to the Great Lakes and the St. Lawrence River, performs the battle. The Scottish Frazer Highlanders, a regiment that participated in the 1759 conquest of Quebec, performs saber dances and plays the bagpipes. There are also guided tours of the fort, the museum and demonstrations of military uniforms. Open: Tuesday through Sunday 10 A.M. to 5 P.M. Performances are at 11 A.M. and 2:30 and 5:00 P.M.

A GREAT PHILANTHROPIST

David M. Stewart, heir to the Macdonald Tobacco Company and avid amateur historian, was refused membership in the Montreal Numismatic and Antiquarian Society in the early 1950s. As a result, he founded the Lake St. Louis Historical Society and opened a small museum to exhibit his quickly growing private collection of artifacts, books, maps and costumes that related to Canadian history. He was also responsible for restoring the Château Dufresnes, near the Olympic Stadium, creating a museum of design, endowing universities with professorships, encouraging the sport of curling, leading the movement to save Old Montreal and revitalizing the Château de Ramezay Museum, which was run by the society that had snubbed him. His posthumous gift to Montreal will be a full-scale replica of Pierre Le Moyne d'Iberville's 47-meter, 1,300-ton, seventeenth-century flagship, *Pelican.*

━━━━━━━━━━━━━━━━━━━ ■ ━━━━━━━━━━━━━━━━━━━

Every evening, inside a building of the old fort, **Le Festin du Gouverneur,** a banquet and dinner show, re-creates the humor and joie de vivre of a seventeenth-century governor. Costumed waiters serve while, between courses, troubadours, musicians and even a village fool encourage the audience to clap hands, stomp feet and join in the singing of traditional Quebec songs, Irish ballads and arias from operettas. Two services: June through October, 6:00 and 8:30 P.M. Reservations: telephone 879-1141.

The **parkland** (4) that was designed by Frederick Todd has not been altered. Nestled by an idyllic stream in the woods near the Jacques-Cartier Bridge is a small theater in an old, converted powder magazine. The blockhouse (rebuilt in 1990) was the first defensive building on the island. The Martello Tower hides an elevated water tank. There are swings, teeter-totters, picnic tables and barbecue pits under the trees close to the subway station. Behind the station are large, outdoor, municipal swimming pools. The view across the river to Montreal is splendid, and the whole park has a sense of tranquility that makes one forget that "soldiers" are fighting battles in the fort, teenagers are screaming with fear and delight at La Ronde, and people are splashing into pools at the Aqua-Parc.

The **Hélène-de-Champlain** (5) is a luxurious restaurant that hosted the kings, queens, presidents and prime ministers that visited Expo '67. Today, managed by Shirley and Pierre Marcotte, it offers lunches from 11:30 A.M. to 2:30 P.M., dinner from 5:30 to 11:00 P.M. and facilities for banquets and press conferences. It is expensive but has one of the better wine lists in town. According to some

Montrealers this is the best place to get engaged to be married. Scare the living daylights out of them at La Ronde and then declare everlasting love here!

Buckminster Fuller's **geodesic dome** was built to house the American Pavilion in 1967. During the exposition, a monorail ran about halfway up the building, and two large photographs, one of Charlie Chaplin and one of Paul Robeson, dominated the entrance. This caused some comment—both men had been suspected of "un-American" activities by Senator McCarthy. Chaplin left for Switzerland and Robeson was blacklisted and denied an American passport. For several summers in the 1970s, the plastic-covered dome housed an aviary. Fortunately, it was deserted when the covering burst into spectacular flames on a still winter's night in 1980. The lightweight aluminum frame remains intact, and the city plans to use the building to house a permanent exhibition on the environment.

Man (6) is a huge sculpture that was created by Alexander Calder to celebrate Expo '67 and Canada's one-hundredth anniversary. At the western tip of île Ste-Hélène is a huge amphitheater that was built for Montreal's three-hundred-and-fiftieth anniversary.

The Gilles Villeneuve Grand-Prix Circuit (7) and the **Olympic Rowing Basin** (8) are on île Notre-Dame. The tarmac on the racetrack is of a quality that you will see only on formula-one tracks—the slightest bump can cause an accident. Gilles Villeneuve was Quebec's most famous driver. Part of the Ferrari team, he died while racing. After the annual car race, the winning team and hangers-on follow the tradition of jumping, fully clothed, into the Olympic Rowing Basin.

The International Flower Gardens (9) were created in 1980. The French and English gardens are usually considered the best, but the Canadian garden is my favorite—it not only incorporates Montreal's single outdoor totem pole, but has the world's only *taiga* (northern forest) garden. I also like the Austrian garden, and I am surprised that both the Mexican and Israeli gardens manage to survive in a climate as severe as Montreal's.

Le Palais de la Civilisation (10) was formerly the French Pavilion. This architecturally unique building houses yearly exhibits on anything from Hollywood to ancient Egypt. Montrealers, depending on the show, either come or stay away in droves. In either case, the exhibition is discussed. Open: June 21 to September 3: Wednesday through Monday 10 A.M. to 10 P.M.; September 4 to October 21:

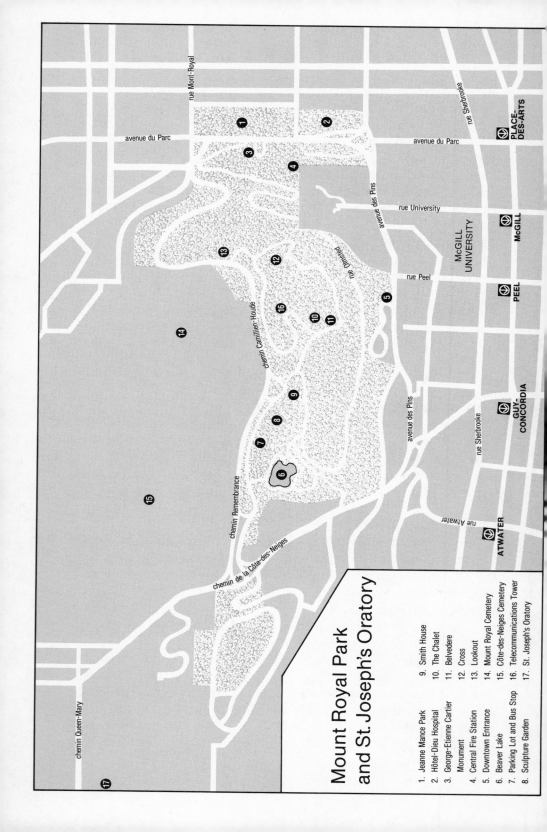

Mount Royal Park
and St. Joseph's Oratory

1. Jeanne Mance Park
2. Hôtel-Dieu Hospital
3. George-Etienne Cartier
   Monument
4. Central Fire Station
5. Downtown Entrance
6. Beaver Lake
7. Parking Lot and Bus Stop
8. Sculpture Garden

9. Smith House
10. The Chalet
11. Belvedere
12. Cross
13. Lookout
14. Mount Royal Cemetery
15. Côte-des-Neiges Cemetery
16. Telecommunications Tower
17. St. Joseph's Oratory

Monday through Friday noon to 10 P.M.; weekends 10 A.M. to 10 P.M. Admission prices vary with the exhibit. Adult, student, senior, children (five through seventeen) and family rates. The handicapped and children under five enter free. Telephone: 872-6093.

La Plage (11) is one of the most popular daytime retreats for Montrealers of all ages. The sand for the six-hundred-meter-wide beach was carried in by trucks in 1989. The water in the lake has been treated. Sailboards, canoes and kayaks can be rented.

Victoria Bridge (12) was considered to be one of the Wonders of the World when it was officially opened on August 24, 1860, by the eighteen-year-old Prince of Wales. Not only was it the longest bridge in the world, it could withstand, and break, huge accumulations of ice that came downriver. Nicknamed the Iron Box, it was a covered bridge until 1901, when the tubular metal tunnel was taken away.

MOUNT ROYAL PARK AND ST. JOSEPH'S ORATORY

How to Get There

The most romantic and most expensive way to get to the summit of Mont-Royal is to hire a horse-drawn *calèche* from Dorchester Square. The most invigorating way is to climb the steep path and steps that lead up from the top of rue Peel (number 5 on the map). Bicyclists, joggers and cross-country skiers will usually take the winding road (closed to motorized traffic) that starts near the Cartier monument (3) just off avenue du Parc—take the 80 or 129 bus from the Place-des-Arts metro station. Those who wish to do as little walking as possible can either take the 11 bus from the Mont-Royal metro station to the parking lot (7) or drive up chemin Camilien-Houde to Beaver Lake (6).

History

Mont-Royal, with the illuminated cross on the most easterly of its three peaks, is the symbol of the city. There is an old myth that says that when the dormant volcano erupts, the whole island of Montreal will sink into the St. Lawrence River. Geologists disagree—they say that "the mountain," which rises 739 feet, is a nonvolcanic igneous "intrusion" that appeared on the surface of the Earth only after the glaciers of the last ice age had eroded the soil that had covered it. In 1535, Jacques Cartier named Mont-Royal to honor Francis I, king of France.

Until the mid-nineteenth century, Mont-Royal remained wild and relatively untouched. Some people believed that it was inhabited only by a couple of ghosts, a colony of fairies and an old hermit who would tell you stories of betrayed love, murder and revenge. Then, in 1852, the crater, formed by the three peaks of Montreal, Westmount and Outremont, was designated to become two large cemeteries—one for Catholics and one for Protestants. It was not until ten years later that the city fathers debated turning most of the remaining land, which was then owned by eighteen proprietors, into a public park.

Some councillors said that the land was too rugged to be popular. However, the commander of the Montreal Field Battery, a man by the name of Stevenson, was not convinced and decided to celebrate the birthday of the Prince of Wales (later Edward VII) by transporting heavy guns up the slope and shooting the twenty-one-gun salute from the top of the mountain. It was November and a foot of snow had fallen during the night. His militia soldiers were forced to put the guns on sleighs, and their horses struggled for many hours to drag the heavy equipment over the old tree stumps, across ravines and up the steep slope to a plateau near the summit. Precisely at noon, the first salvo was fired. In the city below, some paranoid citizens began to fear that Irish Fenians from the United States had invaded to liberate Canada and trade it for Ireland's independence. There was a sense of relief when Stevenson and his men began their descent and the truth was made known. The argument that the mountain was too inaccessible was dismissed and the city bought the land.

Frederick Law Olmsted, an American visionary who thought that "the therapeutic value of nature could regenerate a soul overpowered by the sordid temptations of the city" and who had designed Central Park in New York City, was employed to landscape the park. His network of access roads and paths was laid out along the lines of least resistance, linking the different panoramic views and emphasizing the natural topography. Since then, Montrealers have skied, tobog- ganed, skated, flown kites, fed ducks, sunbathed, danced, partied and made love on their "volcano."

In **Jeanne Mance Park** (1), there are public tennis courts, two soccer fields, two softball diamonds and volleyball nets. With its enclosed wading ponds, children's park with swings, jungle gym, teeter-totters and other attractions, it's a good place for a young family to pass some hours. To the southeast is the **Hôtel-Dieu Hospital** (2), which was founded by Jeanne Mance in 1644 and moved to this site in 1860. The complex of buildings and a large garden is dominated by its domed chapel, which was designed by Victor Borgeau in 1858. The building to the west is a residence for retired priests and the one on the east is the convent. The other buildings house hospital wards and some of the most up-to-date medical facilities in North America.

The sloping lawns (Fletcher's Field) on the western side of avenue du Parc are, in summer, a favorite place for sunbathing and kite flying. In winter, there is a popular toboggan run here. Rue Olmsted, an unmarked dirt road, begins just to the north of a huge, **angel-topped monument** (3), which was erected to honor Sir George-Etienne Cartier, a father of confederation and Montreal's most influential politician of the nineteenth century. With four bronze lions (on which children like to sit) guarding him, Cartier stands over nine larger-than-life bronze statues of women, each representing a Canadian province. In recent years, the plaza behind the monument has become the gathering place for African drummers, and on most summer weekends there is spontaneous dancing here. If you're young at heart, go—it's lively and fun!

The control center of Montreal's fire department (4) is to the south of the Cartier monument. Behind it, there is a footpath that runs up behind McGill University's modern student residences. It leads to a flight of steps that takes you to rue Olmsted, which has been winding its way up from the monument. As you walk along this gravel road, you will get glimpses, between the trees, of Royal Victoria Hospital, where Norman Bethune introduced radically new techniques in surgery, and the Allan Memorial Institute, a psychiatric hospital.

Five minutes further on, you will come to a long (and I mean long) flight of steps that leads up to the **Belvedere** (11), an observation plaza that looks over downtown. The path and steps that lead down take you to rue Peel and the **downtown entrance of the park** (5). For a more leisurely walk, continue along the road until the woods open to reveal the lawns that lead down to **Lac aux Castors** (Beaver Lake) (6), a man-made pond where there are no beavers, but where children sail their toys. In winter, there is a skating rink in front of the snack bar and chalet at the far end of the pond. In summer there is twice-weekly (Monday and Thursday at 8:00 P.M.) under-the-stars folk dancing. Generally, the expert dancers occupy the center of the large dance space. If you don't know the steps, there are always enough people around the edges to find someone with whom you can learn. The romantic setting, friendly atmosphere, international music and public display of talent make it a great place to meet the unattached.

After walking around Beaver Lake and up the grassy slope near the **parking lot and bus stop** (7), you will come to **sculpture garden** (8), which was built in 1964 for the First International Symposium on Habitable Sculpture in North America. In winter, a short ski lift runs through the sculptures and down the slope. Also beside the parking lot is **Smith House** (9), which was built as a private residence in 1858. It is architecturally of a solid British style and is the only nonnatural remnant of Mont-Royal's prepark days. It now houses a small museum of hunting and nature. If you come to the park very early in the morning, you may see wild pheasants; if you come in the early evening, you may run into unperturbed skunks and raccoons.

Continuing along rue Olmsted and past a sculpted tree trunk (*Le Sentinal* by Yves Morin), within ten minutes you will come to **The Chalet** (10). Inspired by Swiss mountain lodges, it is a large, open building in which a small exhibition on the park and its wildlife is mounted. The paintings above the doors depict some of the events of Montreal's history. In front of the chalet is the large, semicircular and balustraded **Belvedere** (11). Although the skyline of Montreal is more impressive from île Ste-Hélène, the view of the river sweeping around the island is magnificent. In order to preserve the view, the city allows no skyscraper to be taller than Mont-Royal.

Rue Olmsted runs behind the chalet, past a second carved tree trunk and up to the top of Mont-Royal, where you get panoramic views to the east and north. After about ten minutes, you will come to the **Cross** (12), which is one hundred feet tall and illuminated at night. It was erected in 1924, paid for mostly by the donations of children, and honors the cross that de Maisonneuve carried up the mountain in 1643 to give thanks for the miraculous retreat of the flood on Christmas Day. From this point you can see, through the trees, the Olympic Stadium with its immense leaning tower.

Just beyond the Cross is a pathway that leads down to a **second lookout** (13), which has been designed for those people who prefer not to leave their cars. At night, young lovers park here and, in tight embraces, contemplate the glittering lights below.

Rue Olmsted continues to sweep around the northern side of Mont-Royal, providing you with a bird's-eye view of the huge **Mount Royal** (14) and **Côte-des-Neiges** (15) **cemeteries** that occupy the old "volcanic crater," where almost 1½ million people are buried. Immigrants to Montreal have historically first settled near boulevard St-Laurent to the southeast, and then, as they achieved greater financial success, moved north and, house by house, around the back of the mountain to its western side. Only the most successful make it to the top of Westmount Summit (the most westerly of the three peaks), but eventually, successful or not, they are all buried or cremated in the cemeteries in the center.

The tower that rises from the peak opposite is part of the Université de Montréal. The huge dome on the third peak, Westmount Summit, is that of St. Joseph's Oratory, Montreal's shrine. Continuing along the road, you will pass the **telecommunications tower** (16), from which Montrealers receive their radio and television signals, and begin a winding descent that will, after about fifteen minutes, lead you back to the parking lot and bus stop.

If you are in a car, it is a simple matter to make your way to **St. Joseph's Oratory** (17), on chemin Queen-Mary, but if you are on foot, it is a good half hour's walk through the cemeteries. The 11 bus turns off Côte-des-Neiges at Ridgewood.

THE MIRACLE MAN OF MONTREAL

St. Joseph's Oratory was founded by Brother André, the Miracle Man of Montreal, who was born on August 9, 1845. At age twelve, orphaned, uneducated and without money, he was forced to emigrate and work in the textile mills of New England. He returned to Canada in 1867 and three years later joined the Congregation of the Holy Cross, where he became the doorman for the teaching order's Collège Notre-Dame, which faces the oratory. He was about thirty years old when attention was drawn to some miraculous cures that he had performed by invoking the help of St. Joseph, husband of Mary.

His reputation as a healer spread quickly and he began to dream of building a chapel, dedicated to St. Joseph, on the mountain that faced the window of his tiny doorman's room. In 1904, he and a colleague, Brother Abundius, built a tiny chapel, only fifteen by eighteen feet, where he could meet the ever-increasing number of pilgrims who were asking for his help. In 1906 Brother Abundius sculpted the altar and in 1910 Brother André's room and the spire were added. From this humble building, the reputation of the healer spread around the world, and by 1915, financed by the donations of grateful pilgrims, plans for a huge Italian Renaissance—style oratory were drawn up by the Montreal architects Viau and Venne. Construction on the crypt-church was begun almost immediately and, nine years later, the foundations for the oratory were built. After the stock market crash of 1929, construction came to a halt.

Brother André, aged ninety-one, died in 1937. His funeral was the greatest that Montreal has ever witnessed—more than a million people filed past his bier. That same year, after the Benedictine monk Dom Paul Bellot had adapted the original plans, the huge outer dome (it is second in size only to that of St. Peter's in Rome, while that of St. Paul's in London would fit entirely inside) was poured. It would take another twenty-nine years to complete the whole complex. Brother André was beatified by Pope John Paul II in 1982 and is expected to soon become a saint.

At **the entrance** to the oratory grounds is a bronze statue of St. Joseph. To the right is the Pilgrim's Hostel. Between the driveways that curve up the hill to the church are three flights of over a hundred stairs each. The central one is reserved for pilgrims who say a prayer on each step as they climb on their knees.

To the right of the church is a **fifty-six-bell carillon** that was built by Paccard Frères, of Annecy-le-Vieux, France. Originally intended for the Eiffel Tower, it came to Montreal in 1955. It is one of the largest carillons in North America and is noted for its rich sound.

The entrance to the **Votive Chapel,** one of Montreal's most impressive interior spaces, is by the carillon. Inside, eight large banks of vigil lights give off a subtle light and the comforting smell of burning wax. The main lamp rack, which rises to a statue of St. Joseph and has small cascades of water on either side, alone carries 3,500 candles.

Sculpted-wood scenes depict the functions that are attributed to St. Joseph. Hundreds of canes and crutches left by pilgrims unobtrusively hang between the tall pillars.

Brother André's tomb is behind the chapel. Pope John Paul II prayed here. The fresco that illustrates the devotion to the Passion of Christ is by Henri Charlier. A bust of Brother André is on the opposite wall.

The Crypt-Church, where twelve masses are celebrated daily, is in front of the chapel. The nine-foot statue of St. Joseph was sculpted out of Carrara marble by A. Giacomini and installed in 1917. The stained-glass windows, completed in 1919, depict events in the life of St. Joseph and come from the workshops of Pedriau and O'Shea. The marble altar, tabernacle, oak chairs, crucifix and chandeliers are the work of Montreal artist Jean-Charles Charuest.

St. Joseph's oil burns before the small wooden statue just outside the Votive Chapel. Brother André humbly credited the oil with miraculous cures that were attributed to him. The room beyond contains a scale model of the oratory and a fresco (executed by Canon Provost in 1954) that represents St. Joseph as "the model of laborers, mainstay of families and protector of the Universal Church."

The escalator leads to **Concourse Hall** and a terrace, which offers a panoramic view. Straight ahead is Collège-Notre-Dame, where Brother André acted as a doorkeeper for forty years. In the distance are Rivière-des-Prairies and the Laurentian Mountains. To the left is Lac St-Louis, where the Ottawa River flows into the St. Lawrence. To the right is the Université de Montréal, which was designed in 1929 in a heroic, Art Deco style by Ernest Cormier, one of Montreal's most celebrated architects. With its yellow-brick tower and steep, copper roof (which recalls the university's Jesuit roots) over one wing, it is a unique and architecturally satisfying complex.

Behind Concourse Hall is a **museum dedicated to Brother André.** When one looks at the life-size wax statues of him in the "Doorkeeper's Cell," where he worked from 1872 to 1909; the "Office," where he greeted pilgrims; and the "Hospital Room," where he died, one realizes how confined his material world was. After a French and Italian tradition, his heart is preserved and on display.

Outside and to the right of Concourse Hall is a beautiful multilevel **sculpture garden.** It had been one of Brother André's fondest dreams to offer pilgrims an open-air setting conducive to meditation on the mystery of the Passion of Christ. The highly praised statues were designed between 1943 and 1953 by a Montreal artist, Louis Parent. The one of Christ being nailed to the cross is especially forceful. During July and August an open-air passion play is presented here. Many of Quebec's leading actors started their careers in this play, which recently inspired Denis Arcand to make the Academy Award–nominated film *Jésus de Montréal.*

The Exhibition on St. Joseph is at the top of the escalator that leads from Concourse Hall. This museum includes wax figures in tableaus depicting the life of the Holy Family, and collections of paintings, statues, statuettes and artifacts that date from the Renaissance to the present day. It's worth a visit. Voluntary contributions are expected.

Yet a third escalator carries you to the **main portico,** where sixtyfoot Corinthian columns rise above you. From there, 283 steps lead down to the lawn at street level.

The **interior of the main church** has been unflatteringly compared to a blimp hangar, but I enjoy the mid-twentieth-century Modern style that contrasts with the Italian Renaissance–inspired exterior. The altar, crucifix and twelve apostles were executed between 1955 and 1959 by the French master Henri Charlier. The Way of the Cross was created between 1957 and 1959 by Roger de Villers. The mosaic comes from the workshops of A. Labouret, and the bronze work was created by Robert Prevost. The stained-glass windows are by Marius Plamondon (1958–61) and depict ten episodes when St. Joseph, the patron saint of Canada, interceded in the history of the country. The organ was built by Rudolf von Beckerath of Hamburg, West Germany. It has 5,811 pipes and five keyboards.

The Blessed Sacrament Chapel, located in the apse, is the most richly decorated part of the oratory. The columns are of green marble from Vermont and the hemicycle ceiling is covered with gold leaf.

The exit to the right leads outside to the tiny chapel that Brothers André and Abundius built from 1904 to 1910. Brother André's room is above it.

Before making the long descent to the Pilgrim's Pavilion, where there is a cafeteria and a shop that sells a variety of religious articles— including vials of St. Joseph's oil—a visitor may wish to pass through the gate at the back of the oratory and wander along the roads of Westmount Summit, Montreal's most exclusive residential area. Summit Park is a flower and bird sanctuary—Montreal's best site for bird-watchers.

St. Joseph's Oratory is open from 6:30 A.M. to 9:30 P.M. Carillon concerts: Saturday and Sunday, noon and 2:30 P.M.; Wednesday through Friday noon and 3:00 P.M. Organ recitals: January through December: Sunday 3:30 P.M.; July and August: Wednesday 8:00 P.M. Tickets are available at the door. Passion play: English, Tuesday and Friday; French, Monday, Wednesday and Thursday; all performances at 8:30 P.M. For reservations to stay at the Pilgrim's Hostel and John XXIII Pavilion, where the sick and handicapped of all races and creeds are welcome to spend from two to ten days, write to Father Rector, St. Joseph's Oratory, 3800 Queen Mary, Montreal, Quebec H3V 1H6. Telephone: 733-8211.

THE OLYMPIC PARK AND BOTANICAL GARDENS

The Olympic Park

The Olympic Park is south of rue Sherbrooke at the east end of the city. Metro station Pie IX gives direct access to the stadium. The fountain on the plaza behind the station is by Jean-Paul Riopelle.

The Olympic Stadium (1) is the most amazing structure in Montreal. It was designed by the French architect Roger Tallibert. From a distance, its mollusclike shape, immense leaning tower and retractable roof, which descends on wires, have a great beauty; from Sherbrooke, the building looks like a huge, hovering spaceship; from the windswept plaza, it feels cold and alien; and from inside you appreciate its vastness and elegant shape. It is, however, perhaps more successful as a work of art than as a stadium. It is reputed to be the most expensive building ever erected. The entire complex cost almost $1 billion. Its nickname? The Big O, or alternatively, because of the cost, the Big Ow!

The stadium is home to the Montreal Expos baseball club (for tickets, telephone 253-0070). The statue at the entrance is of Jackie Robinson—the first black to play major-league ball—who started his career with the Montreal Royals, then a farm team of the Brooklyn Dodgers.

The Olympic-size **swimming and diving pools** are located in the base of the tower and are open to the public. Telephone: 242-4737.

A guided tour of the Olympic Park is heaven for anyone who likes

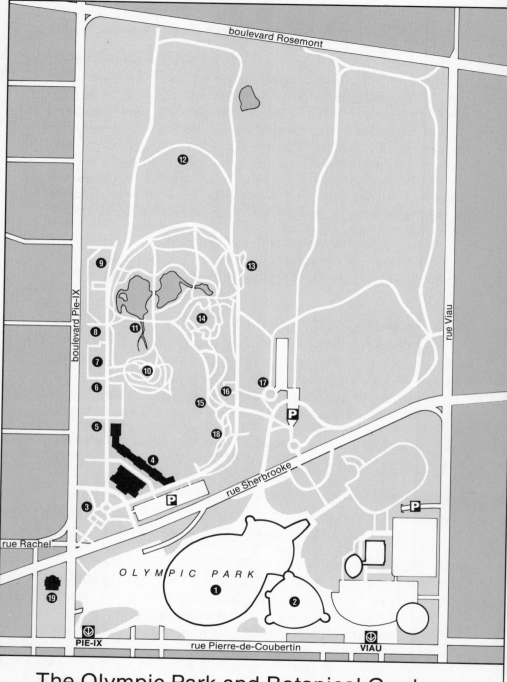

The Olympic Park and Botanical Gardens

1. The Olympic Stadium
2. The Biodome
3. The Entrance Gardens
4. The Greenhouses
5. The Perennial Gardens
6. The Economic Garden
7. The Annuals Garden
8. The Monastery Garden
9. The Shrub Garden
10. The Alpine Garden
11. The Flowery Brook
12. The Arboretum
13. The Shade Garden
14. The Japanese Garden
15. The Chinese Garden
16. The Marsh and Bog Garden
17. The Montreal Insectarium
18. The Rose Garden
19. Château Dufresne and Musée des Arts Decoratifs

boulevard Rosemont

boulevard Pie-IX

rue Viau

rue Sherbrooke

rue Rachel

OLYMPIC PARK

PIE-IX

rue Pierre-de-Coubertin

VIAU

superlatives. It includes a two-minute ride, in the largest and fastest funicular in the world, up the tallest leaning tower (270 meters, or 890 feet) in the world. Michelin gives the complex its highest rating—"But then the architect *was* French," say Montrealers. Guided tours: September to May: daily 11 A.M. and 2 P.M.; June through August: daily 9 A.M. to 5 P.M.

THE TROUBLED HISTORY OF THE BIG O

Construction of the stadium was a huge headache for almost fifteen years. European prefabricated-concrete technology had to be adapted to the severe Montreal climate. Modifications became so serious that it was thought that the building would not be ready for the opening ceremonies of the Olympic Games, and Bob Hope, who headed a benefit show for American athletes, made the crack, "I'm glad to be in Montreal, where the women are well made, the men are well made, and the Olympics almost made." Round-the-clock construction, at huge cost, enabled the stadium (without its tower and roof) to be ready on time; the games, which were opened by Queen Elizabeth II, were considered a success.

For almost a decade, politicians and journalists debated over what to do with the building. A special and substantial tax on cigarettes was levied to pay for the accumulating interest charges. The city sued the architect; the architect sued the city. Engineering studies found that the base of the tower was sinking and that the whole structure would eventually fall down. Finally, in 1983, it was decided to reinforce the base, complete the tower in stainless steel and install the roof. By 1987, the work was done, but the retractable roof, which is made of the same material as bulletproof vests, tends to rip; it seems that it will never function as designed.

The Biodome (2) was designed by Roger Tallibert to house the Olympic velodrome, or bicycle racetrack. Built of prestressed and poststressed prefabricated concrete, it is a huge, scalloped, skylighted and flattened dome with no interior supports. It covers an area of 16,200 square meters (174,000 square feet).

Today it houses an avant-garde museum of natural science. A mix of botanical garden, aquarium and zoo, it has been designed to bring a new understanding to the relationship between man and four ecosystems. The 10,000-square-foot "Tropical Forest" maintains its heat and 80 percent humidity even during power outages. Two huge ponds are home to the "Marine Life" (including beluga whales) of the St. Lawrence River. "Arctic World" and "Northern Forest" are cooled at night so that the plants go into dormancy for the winter. Open: every day 9 A.M. to 5 P.M.

Botanical Gardens

A minitrain runs from the Olympic Tower and Biodome to the Botanical Gardens, but if you feel like having an alienating, modern experience, walk up to and across the concrete plaza over the entrance to the stadium and underground garage. This plaza, which until the money dried up used to have water cascades, might be interpreted as a monstrous attempt at a Zen garden; in any case, it makes the stadium (the building that seemed so elegant from afar) look like a huge, dead clam stranded on a beach.

THE LEGACY OF BROTHER MARIE-VICTORIN

The Montreal Botanical Gardens were founded in 1931 by Brother Marie-Victorin on 180 acres of parkland that had been protected from development since 1910. Like the building of *vespasiennes,* which we have seen in many of the small parks, and the Jacques-Cartier Bridge, the construction of the greenhouses and the creation of the gardens was a make-work project of the Great Depression. At first arranged according to the intellectually disciplined concepts of botany, in recent years the planners have begun to develop gardens in which esthetics and artistry are the guiding forces of design. The Japanese and Chinese gardens are among the best of their kind. In less than sixty years, with 26,000 plants, the gardens have become the third most significant ones (after London and Berlin) in the world.

———————————————— ■ ————————————————

The **entrance gardens** (3) are in the formal tradition of Versailles. The blends of colors, the width of the beds and the central fountain give a feeling of form. The central buildings were built in 1939 to house L'Institut Botanique de l'Université de Montréal. The statue of Brother Marie-Victorin, the founder of both the gardens and the institute, is by Sylvie Daoust and was erected in 1954.

In nine large **greenhouses** (4), ferns, orchids, tropical economic plants, cacti, begonias, haciendas, "a garden of weedlessness" and a tropical rain forest grow.

The **Perennial Gardens** (5) are a favorite place for wedding parties to be photographed. The variety of bridal gowns competes with the flower beds and the trellis-work walkways with their romantic benches.

———————————————— ■ ————————————————

THE LOVERS' BENCH

For many years, The Lovers' Bench was exhibited outside a private art gallery on rue Sherbrooke, where it charmed and amused the public. When the 1979 sculpture, by Lea Vivot, was sold to Toronto, Montrealers were saddened. In Toronto, however, the depiction of a larger-than-life, nude, necking couple and separate, screaming nude woman caused shock rather than bemusement. With the breath of scandal hanging over it, The Lovers' Bench was sold to a hotel in New York, where it was exhibited in the lobby until American conventioneers objected. Afraid of losing customers, the hotel gave it back to the artist, who, in turn, gave it to Montreal. Compared to its place on rue Sherbrooke, the bucolic setting of the gardens mutes the "shock value" of the piece; but it's good to have the ménage à trois back home.

———————————————— ■ ————————————————

   The Economic (6), Annuals (7), Monastery (8) and Shrub
gardens (9), with clearly labeled varieties of food, cloth, dye, medici-
nal and even poison plants, not only show ordinary gardeners how
their plots should be growing, but also exhibit those plants that are
most economically important to the world. The monastery garden
grows plants that monks used as herbs and medicines.

   The Alpine Garden (10) displays plants from the Alps, Pyrenees,
Rockies and other mountain ranges. There is also a small mineralogi-
cal garden that displays different rocks and minerals from all over
Canada.

   The Flowery Brook (11) is in the English tradition of gardens. Its
collections of irises, peonies, daylilies, grasses and asters spread over
an expansive area. To the south of the lake, it is bordered, to the east,
by fragrant lilac trees. They are at their best in late May and early
June. The adjacent Natural Habitats Garden reproduces the floral
zones of southern Quebec.

   The majority of the trees in the Arboretum (12) have not reached
full size. Comprising the northern half of the land, the Arboretum
has over 3,000 species of trees, which are grouped according to
botanical family. In spring, the flowering trees are very pretty, and in
June, the magnificent collection of rhododendron and azalea are in
bloom in the Leslie Hancock Garden, which is on the western side of
the Arboretum. In late summer, the berry-bearing trees begin to
display fruit; in autumn, the leaves change; and in winter, the stark
silhouettes of trunks and branches stand in contrast to the snow. This
is a popular place for cross-country skiing.

   The Shade Garden (13) is tranquil, earthy and cool. Pathways
meander beside beds of delicate flowers that prefer to grow beneath a
canopy of maple, ash and lime trees.

   The Japanese Garden (14) was designed by Ken Nakajima. You
enter through a pavilion, where there is a small museum, an exhibition of traditional Japanese arts, a library and a Zen garden, which
although created entirely out of stones, gives one the feeling of
looking down on the peaks of mountains from above the clouds. The
full impact of this garden does not fully hit you until some hours
later. In a courtyard to the side is the largest and most comprehensive
bonsai collection outside Japan. Wu Yee-Sun, a Hong Kong indus-
trialist, had intended to donate the $1 million collection to the United
States, but the Americans would not allow it into the country. There
is a tiny beech forest of fifteen trees growing in a dish. One less-than-

one-meter-tall juniper is 350 years old—as old as Montreal. At the back of the pavilion is a fenced-in tea garden where formal tea ceremonies are demonstrated. The main garden is beyond the fence.

The Japanese garden is an allegorical representation of human life and death. At first, the shrubs, plants and rocks are small and arranged in threes (representing life), but they become larger until you reach the top of a hill that looks down onto a bridge (death) that crosses the narrows of a small lake that is home for hundreds of goldfish. The bridge is crooked because it is thought that evil spirits, which try to follow a person into the afterlife, can move only in a straight line. Across the bridge, the flowers are white and arranged in fours—the color and number of death. A small pine forest completes the garden.

The Chinese Garden (15) was created by Lei Wei-Zhong of Shanghai, China. Opened to universal praise in 1991, its official name is Meng Hu Yuan, which means "The Garden of the Lake of Dreams." With its keyhole doors, undulating dragon walls, pagoda, pavilions and pools, it is in the Yangtze River style, which dates from the fifteenth-century Ming dynasty, and is only the fourth garden of its kind outside China. The cost of construction was shared by Shanghai and Montreal.

A Chinese garden should feel as if nature had created it. At the same time, everything in it—the traditional yellow mountain, forests and structures—is miniaturized in an attempt to crowd into a narrow space as many vistas as possible.

The Marsh and Bog Garden (16) is formed by a hundred small and geometrically arranged pools. Here you can see a variety of water lilies, including the lotus, and an extensive array of indigenous and ornamental plants from humid or aquatic environments.

The Montreal Insectarium (17) houses a selection from the 250,000 specimens in the collections of Father Frimin Laliberté and Georges Brossard, two of Montreal's most enthusiastic entomologists. From the tower of the Olympic Stadium, it is easy to make out the insect-shaped design of this new (1990) museum. You can see the multifaceted eyes, the white wings and the buff-colored body. Inside is one of the world's great public exhibits of insects from all over the world. At first you are drawn to the splendor and colors of the wings of butterflies and moths, but the longer you stay, the more astounding the world of insects, "nature's winners," becomes. As well as the mounted specimens, there is a vivarium of fluttering butterflies and displays of live scorpions, stick insects, silkworms, millipedes, giant cockroaches, a bird-eating tarantula and more. Much thought has been given to providing young children, who tend to be less squeamish than adults, with display cases at their eye level. The insectarium (the only one in North America) has proved to be a hit with the public!

In **the Rose Garden** (18) eight thousand bushes bloom and perfume the air.

The **exterior gardens** are open every day, all year, dawn to dusk. Admission is free. The **greenhouses** are open every day, all year, 9 A.M. to 6 P.M. The **insectarium** is open every day, all year, 9 A.M. to 6 P.M.

The Château Dufresne and Musée des Arts Decoratifs (19) are at the corner of Pie IX and Sherbrooke. This forty-four-room mansion was built between 1916 and 1918 for two brothers, Oscar and Marius Dufresne, whose families occupied the two identical, semidetached wings. Reflecting the monumental taste of the brothers, it was designed by Lebon, who was inspired by Versailles's Petit Trianon. It was, however, the eclectic mix of sumptuous styles in the interior of the mansion that was most fascinating. The bedrooms evoked the courts of Louis XV and XVI, while the studies were Tudor and Gothic, the dining rooms Classical and Renaissance and the salons inspired by Second Empire styles. The ceiling frescoes were designed by the Italian painter Guido Nincheri, yet many of the moldings, ceiling decorations, fireplaces, and floor paneling were prefabricated and chosen from American catalogs.

Neither of the brothers had children, and the mansion became part of a college in 1948, but Madame Marius Dufresne saved much of the furniture. When the building was classified a historic monument in 1976, the Macdonald-Stewart Foundation subsidized the restoration of five rooms, including the Turkish smoking room. The building now houses the Lilian and David M. Stewart collection of international design, which dates from 1940, and the Musée des Arts Decoratifs, which regularly mounts displays from its collection of furniture, glassware, textiles and ceramics. Open: Wednesday through Sunday 11 A.M. to 5 P.M.

❧ 6 ❧

Life in Montreal

ACCOMMODATIONS

Hotels

The Montreal area has about 30,000 rooms to rent on a nightly basis. Half of the rooms are in large (more than 150 rooms), modern hotels with prices that reflect the market. The number of medium-size hotels (35 to 150 rooms) is limited, but they are all modern. Montreal has but a few good, small establishments in converted old houses, but there are excellent networks of bed-and-breakfast establishments, which I highly recommend. I have limited the hotels that I list to those that are centrally located and offer something special. I have inspected all of them, but the stars have been awarded by Quebec's Ministry of Tourism, with six stars being the best possible rating.

Abbreviations

PB = private bathroom
AC = air-conditioning
K = kitchenette
P = parking
P$ = parking fee
W = whirlpool bath
F = fireplace
Tel = telephone
TV = television
AmEx = American Express
DC = Diners Club
MC = MasterCard

The numbers in parentheses do not refer to exact positions, but only to those *closest* on the map of downtown (see page 88).

The Most Expensive

The Ritz-Carlton (37): *1228 rue Sherbrooke, H3G 1H6. Tel.: 842-4212, 1-800-363-0366.* 230 rooms with PB, AC, Tel and TV. 20 with F; 2 with W. P$. This Edwardian hotel has been considered the best in the city since 1912. *International Investor* ranks it first in Canada, fourth in North America and twenty-second in the world. Personal attention by the staff gives this grand hotel its reputation. The lobby alone is worth a visit. Elizabeth Taylor and Richard Burton were first married here.   AmEx, MC, Visa.   ★ ★ ★ ★ ★ ★

Le Quatre Saisons (7): *1050 rue Sherbrooke O., H3A 2R6. Tel.: 284-1110, 1-800-268-6282.* 300 rooms with PB, AC, Tel and TV. P$. This modern hotel is favored by celebrities. John Lennon and Yoko Ono staged their "love-in" here. Madonna ran up and down the emergency stairs to stay fit. Michael Jackson sallied out with his bodyguards to visit the Museum of Fine Arts. Queen Elizabeth The Queen Mother ordered her gin and tonic in a tumbler. The hotel has a year-round heated pool on the roof and its restaurants are noted for "power" meals. The Japanese breakfast is unique in the city. AmEx, MC, Visa.   ★ ★ ★ ★ ★ ★

The Very Expensive

Bonaventure Hilton International (1): *1 Place Bonaventure, H5A 1A4. Tel.: 878-2332, 1-800-268-9275.* 394 rooms with PB, AC, Tel and TV. P$. Above Montreal's exhibition center, this Hilton has a heated, rooftop, exterior pool that is open year-round and is accessible by an igloolike tunnel. Some of the outer rooms give fine views of the city, and the inner rooms look down on a garden with trees, a pond and a cascade.   AmEx, DC, MC, Visa.   ★ ★ ★ ★ ★ ★

Le Château Champlain (1): *1 Place du Canada, H3B 4C9. Tel.: 878-9000, 1-800-268-9420.* 616 rooms with PB, AC, Tel and TV. 2 with W. P$. Because of its distinctive half-moon-shaped windows, Canadian Pacific's tall, modern hotel is affectionately known as the great cheese-grater. Although it has an indoor pool, sauna and fitness center, it is also famous for its high-kicking dancers in the cabaret. It is situated at the south end of Dorchester Square, and many of the rooms on the north side offer a great view of the city and the illuminated cross on the mountain.   AmEx, DC, MC, Visa.   ★ ★ ★ ★ ★

Hôtel Inter-Continental Montréal: (43, Old Montreal): *360 rue Saint-Antoine O., H2Y 3X4. Tel.: 987-9900, 1-800-327-0200.* 359 rooms with PB, AC, Tel and TV. P$. The only hotel located in Old Montreal, this new building is exceptionally well-appointed. Above the seventeenth floor, the corner suites provide beautiful panoramas from the port to the mountain. Part of the World Trade Center, it is connected to the underground city.   AmEx, MC, Visa.   ★ ★ ★ ★ ★ ★

Le Meridien (18): *4 Complexe Desjardins, H5B 1E5. Tel.: 285-1450, 1-800-361-8234.* 601 rooms with PB, AC, Tel and TV. P$. Owned and operated by Air France, this first-class hotel is located on the stretch of rue Ste-Catherine that hosts the jazz, film and comedy festivals. Sauna, outdoor and indoor swimming pools.   ★ ★ ★ ★ ★ ★

The Expensive

La Citadelle (9): *410 rue Sherbrooke O., H3A 1B3. Tel.: 844-8851, 1-800-283-2967.* 181 rooms, 180 with PB, 18 with K, 4 with W. AC, Tel and TV. P$. This new high-rise hotel has a fitness center and pool.   AmEx, DC, MC, Visa.   ★ ★ ★ ★ ★

Hôtel de la Montagne (52): *1430 rue de la Montagne, H3G 2M4. Tel.: 288-5656, 1-800-361-8155.* 138 rooms with PB, AC, Tel and TV. 15 with W. P$. In the summer, the rooftop bar and swimming pool, which is open to the public, is a place for the young English in-crowd to be beautiful. The decor of the restaurant (one of the best in the city) is a strange mix of Baroque, Victorian and yuppie fantasy, but the rooms, decorated in several styles, are simple and comfortable. A fun, young place to stay in the center of the downtown night-life.   AmEx, MC, Visa.   ★ ★ ★ ★ ★

Le Château Versailles (40): *1659 rue Sherbrooke O., H3H 1E3. Tel.: 933-3611, 1-800-361-7199.* 70 rooms with PB, AC, Tel and TV. P. Long a popular hotel with loyal customers; most rooms have old plaster moldings on the ceiling and are furnished with French antiques. It has a reputation for meticulous service.   AmEx, DC, MC, Visa.   ★ ★ ★ ★

The Medium Priced

Hôtel de l'Institut (27): *3535 rue St-Denis, H2X 3P1. Tel.: 282-5120, 1-800-361-5111.* 42 rooms with PB, AC, Tel and TV. P$. Because this hotel is a training ground for the students of L'Institut du Tourisme et d'Hôtellerie du Québec, it could very well be one of the most interesting in the city. During term (September to May) the student chefs and waiters cook and serve. AmEx, MC, Visa. Not rated.

Le Roussillon Royal (32): *1600 rue St-Hubert, H2L 3Z3. Tel.: 849-3214, 1-800-363-6223.* 147 rooms with AC, Tel and TV. 95 with PB. P. Located close to the Voyageur bus station, this hotel is one of Montreal's better bargains. AmEx, MC, Visa. ★ ★ ★ ★

The Inexpensive

Auberge le Jardin d'Antoine (30): *2024 rue St-Denis, H2X 3K7. Tel.: 843-4506.* 34 rooms, 30 with PB, AC and TV. For twenty years, it was Pierre-Antoine Giardina's ambition to open a small hotel. In 1989 he managed to buy this three-floor building. The pride and happiness of the whole Giardina family are evident. AmEx, MC, Visa.

Le Château de l'Argoat (28): *524 rue Sherbrooke E., H2L 1K1. Tel.: 842-2046.* 29 rooms with PB, AC, Tel and TV. P$. The staff is friendly, the rooms comfortable and the prices very fair. Book in advance. MC, Visa. ★ ★ ★

Hôtel de Paris (28): *901 rue Sherbrooke E., H2L 1L3. Tel.: 522-6861.* 26 rooms with PB, AC, Tel and TV. 4 with efficiency units. This converted house has several elegant rooms with balconies. The cheaper rooms in the back are more modern. The management is very friendly and helpful. AmEx, MC, Visa. ★ ★

Hôtel St-Denis (32): *1254 rue St-Denis, H2X 3J6. Tel.: 849-4526.* 60 rooms with Tel and TV. 44 with PB; 20 with AC. P$. I mention this hotel because it is the least expensive with access for wheelchairs. AmEx, MC, Visa. ★ ★

The Least Expensive

Hôtel Armor (28): *151 rue Sherbrooke E., H2X 167. Tel.: 285-0894.*

14 rooms with AC and TV. 7 with PB. In a converted, old house, this low-priced hotel has a lower rating than I would give it.   MC.   ★

Hôtel Casa Bella (22): *258 rue Sherbrooke O. H2X 1X9. Tel.: 849-2777.* 20 rooms with AC, Tel and TV. 8 with PB. P. One of the better and friendliest of the least-expensive hotels.   AmEx, MC, Visa.   ★ ★

Hôtel des Touristes a l'Américain (32): *1042 rue St-Denis, H2X 3J2. Tel.: 849-0616.* 53 rooms with AC, Tel and TV. 25 with PB. P. This very funky hotel is a converted brothel that still has the old alarm system to warn the clientele of police raids. If you want to imagine that you're a private eye of the 1940s, this is the place for you.   AmEx, MC, Visa.   ★

Gay and Lesbian Hotels

Auberge du Centre-Ville (48): *1070 rue MacKay, H3G 2H1. Tel.: 878-9393.* 49 rooms, 29 with PB. AC, Tel and TV. P$. Men only.   AmEx, MC, Visa.   ★ ★

La Concierge (33): *1019 rue St-Hubert, H2L 3Y3. Tel.: 289-9297.* 17 rooms, 9 with PB. Montreal's most popular gay and lesbian hotel is in two converted Victorian houses near the Gay Village.   AmEx, MC, Visa.

Bed-and-Breakfasts

For those who want an intimate visit or those with limited budgets, staying in B&Bs in private houses is probably the best way to visit Montreal. Generally, they do not have signs outside their doors, but are organized into networks. For the best rooms, it is advisable to reserve two weeks in advance. Parking on the street is safe and generally easy. Ask about proximity to the metro (subway).

A Bed and Breakfast—A Downtown Network: *3458 avenue Laval, H2X 3C8. Tel.: 289-9794.* Running the largest of the networks, Bob Finkelstein has over 90 rooms not far from McGill University and close to the Peel and McGill metro stations.   AmEx, MC, Visa.

A Bed and Breakfast in Montreal: *P.O. Box 575, Snowdon Station, H3X 3T8. Tel.: 738-9410.* Marion Khan started Montreal's first network in 1980. The majority of her homes are located on the quiet, tree-lined, residential streets to the west of downtown.   AmEx, MC, Visa.

A Montreal Oasis in Downtown: *3000 rue Breslay, H3Y 2G7. Tel.: 935-2312.* This downtown network is slightly more expensive because it specializes in giving gourmet breakfasts.   AmEx, MC, Visa.

Bed & Breakfast de Chez Nous: *3717 rue Ste-Famille, H2X 2L7. Tel.: 845-7711.* Jacqueline Boulanger's 30 homes are in different parts of the city, but the majority are in the residential area to the west of downtown. She also has some furnished apartments for families.   MC, Visa.

Bed & Breakfast Mount Royal: *4514 avenue Royale, H4A 2M9. Tel.: 484-7802.* Ginette Houle's network is mostly downtown around McGill University. She also has furnished apartments.

Bed & Breakfast Network Hospitality Montreal Relay: *3972 avenue Laval, H2W 2H9. Tel.: 287-9635.* Madame Pearson's 30 homes are concentrated in the more French residential neighborhoods close to the Sherbrooke and Mont-Royal metro stations.   MC, Visa.

Welcome Bed & Breakfast Bienvenue: *3950 Laval, H2W 2J2. Tel.: 844-5897.* Carole Sirois has 50 rooms, some downtown and some in the French residential area to the east of Mont-Royal.

Residences and Youth Hostels

The youth hostel is the least expensive and the YMCA and YWCA are the most expensive.

Auberge de Jeunesse Internationale de Montréal (Youth Hostel) (7): *3541 rue Aylmer, H2X 2B9. Tel.: 843-3317.* 104 beds in 19 rooms. Open all year, centrally located and close to McGill University.

McGill University Residences (7): *3935 rue Université, H3A 2B4. Tel.: 398-6367.* 1,000 beds in 1,000 rooms. Located on the downtown slope of Mont-Royal, these are the best residence rooms in the city if you don't mind a bit of a walk up the hill. Check in advance for availability.

Residence des Étudiantes Université de Montréal: *2350 rue Edouard-Montpetit, H3C 1J4. Tel.: 343-6531.* 1,170 beds in 1,130 rooms. These residences are located on the north slope of Mont-Royal away from downtown. Check for availability. Metro Université-de-Montréal.

YMCA (34): *1450 rue Stanley, H3A 2W6. Tel.: 849-8393.* 429 beds in 330 rooms. Located in the center of the downtown core.

YWCA (48): *1355 boulevard René-Lévesque, H3G 1T3. Tel.: 866-9941.* 128 beds in 107 rooms. Located downtown.

Efficiency Units

Hôtel l'Appartement a Montréal (9): *455 rue Sherbrooke O., H3A 1B7. Tel.: 284-3634.* 125 units with PB, AC, Tel and TV. Swimming pool and sauna.   AmEx, MC, Visa.   ★ ★ ★ ★

Le Richbourg de Montréal (46): *2170 avenue Lincoln, H3T 7N5. Tel.: 935-9224.* In a pleasant, downtown residential area, this hotel, which looks like an apartment block, offers a pool, fitness center and sauna. 221 efficiency units with PB, AC, Tel and TV. P$.   AmEx, MC, Visa.   ★ ★ ★ ★

Manoir Lemoyne (46): *2100 boulevard de Maisonneuve O., H3H 1K6. Tel.: 931-8861, 1-800-361-7191.* Located in a downtown residential area, this converted apartment block has a sauna and fitness center. 286 efficiency units with PB, AC, Tel and TV. P$.   ★ ★ ★ ★

Short-term Apartments

Rented for eight days or more, the listed apartments are in modern high-rise buildings, the upper floors of which afford fine views of the city.

Le Château Royal Hôtel Appartements (52): *1420 rue Crescent, H3G 2B7. Tel.: 848-0999.* 135 units with AC, Tel and TV. P$.   AmEx, DC, MC, Visa.

Le Montfort (46): *1975 boulevard de Maisonneuve O., H3H 1K4. Tel.: 934-0916.* 220 units with AC, Tel and TV. P$.   AmEx, MC, Visa.

La Tour Belvedere (46): *2175 boulevard de Maisonneuve O., H3H 1L5. Tel.: 935-9052.* 135 units with AC, Tel and TV.   AmEx, MC, Visa.

RESTAURANTS: THREE LISTS

Montreal has long been considered a gastronomic capital of North America. The citizens dine out often, expect to be able to eat in a leisurely fashion and are quick to recognize good food. There are more than five thousand restaurants in the city. They offer a huge variety of cuisines, prices and atmospheres. For instance, at the corner of boulevard St-Laurent and rue Laurier you are a two-minute walk from a Russian, a Thai, a Chinese, a vegetarian, two Italian, an Indian and two French restaurants—not to mention a café and a bistro. Although some establishments have been serving consistently excellent meals for more than forty years, competition is stiff and it does not take long for a poorly managed place to go bankrupt.

The numbers in parentheses do not refer to exact positions, but only to those *closest* on the maps (for restaurants in Old Montreal, refer to page 40; for those downtown, refer to page 88).

Old Montreal

Hamburgers, Pizzas, Salads and Sandwiches

Il Était une Fois (11): *600 d'Youville. Tel.: 842-6783.* Located in a converted station and decorated with memorabilia, this family restaurant is noted for its hamburgers.

I am afraid that I can recommend no other Old Montreal establishment in this category. On **Place Jacques-Cartier** there are a number of places that sell fast food. There, if you want to try a dish that is much loved in Montreal, the **Nelson Crêperie** offers light, extra-thin, Breton pancakes made from a variety of flours and which form an envelope for meat, fruit and vegetable sauces. They are not the best *crêpes* in town, but they are a satisfying alternative to fast food. Just to the west, **Chez Better,** *160 Notre-Dame E.,* offers good sausages and beers at reasonable prices.

Inexpensive Restaurants

Fiesta Tapas (40): *479 St-Alexis. Tel.: 287-7482.* Spanish. This attractive restaurant offers superb tapas, a tasty snack that can become a meal. The paella is recommended.

Stash Café Bazaar (5): *461 St-Sulpice. Tel.: 861-2915.* Polish. The soups, goulash, pierogis and cakes are good. Rib-sticking food at low prices.

Alexandre (31): *438 Place Jacques-Cartier. Tel.: 866-9439.* This

Parisian-style brasserie is fun, lively and fast. It's noted for mussels, french fries, sausages and imported beers.

Moderately Priced Restaurants

Casa de Mateo II (5): *440 St-François-Xavier. Tel.: 844-7448.* Mexican. The *fragita* (marinated sliced steak) and *pescado Veracruzana* are excellent. Portions are generous.

Menara (22): *256 St-Paul E. Tel.: 861-1989.* Moroccan. Belly dancers perform as you eat.

Les Filles du Roy (22): *414 rue Bonsecours. Tel.: 849-3535.* Quebec. This restaurant is noted for its wild game (when in season) and costumed waitresses. The *cipaille de Lac St-Jean* is a pie made of six different meats, including game, and vegetables. Maple syrup haven.

Troquet à Lina (40): *465 rue St-Jean. Tel.: 842-6403.* French. Lina's has created a relaxing atmosphere and built up a regular clientele. Her French cuisine is the best priced in Old Montreal.

Expensive Restaurants

Chez Delmo (2): *211 rue Notre-Dame O. Tel.: 849-4061.* Seafood. Chez Delmo has been rated highly for forty years. The bar, where business executives eat lunch, is one of the most beautiful in the city.

Gibby's (9): *298 Place d'Youville. Tel.: 282-1837.* Steaks. This elegant restaurant is considered to be one of the best in the city. Portions are huge.

Very Expensive Restaurants

Claude Postel (31): *443 St-Vincent. Tel.: 875-5067.* French. Claude Postel, one of Montreal's best chefs, is also the owner of this restaurant. A charming man, he may wax eloquently to guests about his creation of the day. Believe him. His pastries are also superb.

La Marée (31): *404 Place Jacques-Cartier. Tel.: 861-9794.* Seafood. The French haute cuisine is considered triumphant. Go for the lobster dishes and expect to be pampered.

Le Fadeau (20): *423 rue St-Claude. Tel.: 878-3959.* French nouvelle cuisine. The *menu de dégustation* is an adventure for the palate. Relax and enjoy the taste treats.

Le St. Amable (31): *188 rue St-Amable. Tel.: 866-3471*. French. This beautiful restaurant has been recognized for over twenty years. Ask for the specialties of the house.

Downtown: The English Quarter

This area offers the greatest concentration of Montreal's best restaurants. Prices tend to be higher and the atmosphere less relaxed than you will find in the St-Denis and St-Laurent area.

Hamburgers, Pizzas, Salads and Sandwiches

American Rock Cafe (10): *2080 rue Aylmer. Tel.: 288-9272*. McGill University students create the lively, loud atmosphere for this hamburger and sandwich restaurant.

Beezers (49): *1242 rue MacKay. Tel.: 874-5442*. A family restaurant specializing in hamburgers and foot-long hot dogs.

Ben's (34): *1475 rue Metcalfe. Tel.: 844-1000*. Ben's, a delicatessen that has been run by the Kravitz family for fifty years, is an unchanging Montreal institution. The unique taste of the famed smoked meat sandwich was discovered by accident in the 1930s.

La Pizzaiolle (50): *1446-A rue Crescent. Tel.: 845-4158*. Some say that these are the best pizzas in town.

La Tulipe Noir (36): *2100 rue Stanley. Tel.: 285-1225*. You may have to queue to buy the excellent sandwiches and desserts that are served in this *haute café* located in the new and architecturally interesting Alcan Building.

Le Faubourg (48): *1616 Ste-Catherine O. Tel.: 939-3663*. This food emporium offers a number of good lunch restaurants.

Les Palmes (6): *1500 McGill College. Tel.: 499-9903*. This California-style bistro is noted for its salads. Light and airy, it is located in Place Montreal Trust.

Best Tearooms

Les Jardins du Ritz (37): *1228 rue Sherbrooke O. Tel.: 387-5959*. In summer, watch ducklings paddle in the pond as you enjoy afternoon tea in this elegant restaurant that has been an institution for eighty years. Expensive.

Toman Pastry Shop (49): *1421 rue Mackay. Tel.: 844-1605*. This

Czech tearoom is considered to be the best in the city. The pastries are worth a special trip.

Inexpensive Restaurants

Bar-B Barn (47): *1201 rue Guy. Tel.: 933-3811.* Ribs and chicken. Noisy and crowded, this caters to families.

Carlos and Pepé's (35): *1423 rue Stanley. Tel.: 288-3090.* Mexican. This is a very popular student hangout.

Cracovie (3): *1246 rue Stanley. Tel.: 866-2195.* Polish. Noted for goulash and pierogis, this warm European restaurant offers the best downtown bargain.

Le Commensal (10): *680 Ste-Catherine O. Tel.: 845-2627.* Vegetarian. From a large selection of dishes, you serve yourself and pay by weight. A tasty bargain.

Le 9e (10): *677 rue Ste-Catherine O. Tel.: 284-8421.* On the ninth floor of the Eaton department store, this Art Deco restaurant is a reproduction of the dining room in Mrs. Eaton's favorite pre–World War II passenger liner, *Île de France.* The food is no better than might be expected in a department store, but the decor is magnificent.

New Woodlands (47): *1241 rue Guy. Tel.: 933-1553.* Indian. Service is slow, but the vegetarian cuisine of southern India is exceptional.

Moderately Priced Restaurants

Café Mozart (50): *2090 rue de la Montagne. Tel.: 849-1482.* Hungarian. The Old European atmosphere is here. A window seat upstairs gives a good view of the street.

L'Actuel (3): *1194 rue Peel. Tel.: 866-1537.* This Belgian restaurant is noted for its excellent mussels and is considered one of the best seafood restaurants in the city.

Le Paris (48): *1812 rue Ste-Catherine O. Tel.: 937-4898.* French. The decor of this thirty-year-old restaurant gives you no hint of the excellent, simple cuisine. For value, this is perhaps the best French restaurant in town.

Matty's (37): *2075 rue de la Montagne. Tel.: 843-3591.* Greek and Armenian. This comfortable restaurant offers good value and a relaxing atmosphere. Ask Matty for his specialties.

Piment Rouge (3): *1170 rue Peel. Tel.: 866-7816.* Szechuan. This restaurant is in a magnificent Edwardian room. The fish and the tofu dishes are excellent.

Sushi Maki (50): *1240 rue Crescent. Tel.: 861-2050.* Japanese. A gentle, intimate sushi bar that has a growing number of fans.

Expensive Restaurants

Costas (49): *1236 rue MacKay. Tel.: 933-4565.* Greek seafood. Go for the catch of the day.

Henri II (49): *1175-A rue Crescent. Tel.: 395-8730.* This small, attentive restaurant is said to offer the best French nouvelle cuisine in town. Ask for the daily special.

Katsura (50): *2170 rue de la Montagne. Tel.: 849-1172.* Japanese. This large restaurant offers the best sushi and sashimi in town. You can reserve a private tatami room or get a bento box lunch at noon.

La Vigna (50): *2045 rue Crescent. Tel.: 288-2532.* Natale Defazo's pasta is fantastic. Try milk-fed *scallopine della Vigna.*

Le Chrysanthème (49): *1208 rue Crescent. Tel.: 397-1408.* Szechuan and Peking. The Hunan dumplings, the Mongolian beef and the sizzling duck are great. Some people find the atmosphere cold.

Le Mas des Oliviers (49): *1216 rue Bishop. Tel.: 861-6733.* Provençal Chef Jacques Muller is noted for his bouillabaisse, lamb and "farmer's stew."

Very Expensive Restaurants

Café de Paris (37): *1228 rue Sherbrooke O. Tel.: 842-4212.* French. In the Ritz-Carlton Hotel, this restaurant is a trip into the rarified world of old money.

Chez la Mère Michel (47): *1209 rue Guy. Tel.: 934-0473.* French. Owner Micheline Delbuguet serves beautifully prepared regional cuisine in a beautifully converted house.

Le Lutetia (50): *1430 de la Montagne. Tel.: 288-5656.* French. The decor of this hotel's restaurant is an opulent mix of Baroque and High Victorian. The kitchen is behind plate glass and the cuisine is touted.

Les Chenets (49): *2075 rue Bishop. Tel.: 844-1842.* French. With one of the best wine lists in town, this cozy restaurant is noted for its soups, fresh salmon and pheasant.

Les Halles (49): *1450 rue Crescent. Tel.: 844-2328.* French. This restaurant is reputed to be the best in town. The decor downstairs is inspired by the famous Parisian market. Ask the waiter to describe the daily special. The desserts are astounding.

Troika (50): *2171 rue Crescent. Tel.: 849-9333.* For atmosphere, cuisine and music, this romantic Russian restaurant has long been a well-loved fixture in Montreal. The caviars are imported fresh weekly.

Downtown: Rue St-Denis and Boulevard St-Laurent

This area is probably the most favored of Montreal's dining districts. On rue Prince-Arthur (27), the restaurants spill onto the pedestrian street, where buskers, artists and vendors create a festival atmosphere; and a few blocks north, on parallel rue Duluth, there is another concentration of eateries. When there is no number following the name, the restaurant is off the map, but no farther than a ten-minute walk from rue Sherbrooke.

Hamburgers, Pizzas, Salads and Sandwiches

Da Pizzattaro (14): *1121 Anderson. Tel.: 861-7076.* "Nouveau pizzas" are baked in wood-fire ovens.

Pizza Mella (26): *107 Prince-Arthur E. Tel.: 849-4680.* This parlor offers a large variety of "yuppie" pizzas.

La Paryse (30): *302 Ontario E. Tel.: 842-2040.* The best hamburgers in town.

Inexpensive Restaurants

Au Coin Berbère: *73 rue Duluth E. Tel.: 844-7405.* North African. The decor is rundown, but the couscous is the best in town.

Crêperie Québecoise (33): *1775 rue St-Hubert. Tel.: 521-8362.* Crepes. The micro-thin pancakes stuffed with meat, vegetable and fruit sauces are among the best in the city.

Le Commensal (29): *2115 rue St-Denis. Tel.: 845-2627.* Vegetarian. You serve yourself and pay by the gram.

Mazurka (26): *64 Prince-Arthur E. Tel.: 844-3539.* Polish. This was the first restaurant on this now-fashionable street. Rib-sticking food at low, low prices.

Moderately Priced Restaurants

Café Cherrier (28): *3635 rue St-Denis. Tel.: 843-4308.* French. This trendy bar and restaurant is a favorite with artists and intellectuals.

Bon Blé Riz (16): *1437 boulevard St-Laurent. Tel.: 844-1447.* Chinese. The neighborhood is seedy, the decor not much better, but the food is good. The chef sometimes displays the art of making noodles completely by hand—it looks like magic.

Delta-Ba (26): *131 Prince-Arthur E. Tel.: 843-7147.* Vietnamese. One of Montreal's first Vietnamese restaurants, remains unpretentious and offers good value.

Schwartz: *3895 boulevard St-Laurent. Tel.: 842-4813.* Steak. The Montreal Hebrew Delicatessen is an institution. There are often lines of hungry customers salivating for steaks.

L'Exotic (27): *3788 rue Laval. Tel.: 843-4741.* Madagascan. Spicy and succulent cuisine from an exotic land.

L'Express: *3927 rue St-Denis. Tel.: 845-5333.* French. This Parisian bistro is lively and trendy.

Expensive Restaurants

Citronlime: *4669 rue St-Denis. Tel.: 284-3130.* French. This innovative restaurant incorporates South American and Asian influences into the French tradition. It's highly recommended.

Le Piémontais (16): *1145A rue de Bullion. Tel.: 861-8122.* One of Montreal's best Italian restaurants is in an out-of-the-way neighborhood, but the veal dishes are highly recommended. The owner, Remo Pompeo, welcomes all.

Moishe's: *3961 boulevard St-Laurent. Tel.: 845-3509.* An old-world, Jewish, steak restaurant with efficient service and an envied reputation.

Witloof (28): *3619 rue St-Denis. Tel.: 281-0100.* Belgian. This elegant but lively restaurant is famous for its mussels and Belgian stew. There are often lines.

Very Expensive Restaurants

La Sila (29): *2040 rue St-Denis. Tel.: 844-5083.* Italian. The pasta is exquisite. Ask the waiters for suggestions in one of Montreal's best Italian restaurants.

Les Mignardaises (29): *2037 rue St-Denis. Tel.: 842-1152.* French. According to many, J. P. Monet's table is considered formidable. Ask your waiter to describe the special of the day and be amazed by the inventiveness of the cuisine. Be prepared for a treat.

SHOPPING

You can buy just about anything you want in Montreal, but it is in clothes and fashion that the city truly excels. There are two reasons for this. First, Montrealers, both men and women, no matter what their income, have a flair for style and a confidence in their taste. They are creative and will mix styles and improvise to express their personality rather than accept "total looks." Second, North American designers and manufacturers have found that clothes move faster in Montreal shops than anywhere else. This means that, without going to Europe, they can determine fashion trends more quickly by first selling them here. Europeans can also determine the trends of North America. As a result, Montreal is always on the cutting edge of fashion.

A word of warning: Before you purchase anything, ask whether or not the Goods and Services Tax (GST) is included in the marked price. Also, save your receipts for a rebate of the tax when you return home. See the information on taxes in the "Basic Information" section at the beginning of this book.

The numbers in parentheses refer to the positions *closest* on the map of downtown (see page 88).

The Complete Downtown Shopping Tour

Les Cours Mont-Royal (34) is the most attractive shopping mall in the city. The stores are arranged around a magnificent chandeliered lobby that was once the entrance hall to the largest hotel in the British Empire. Curving staircases wind elegantly to the different levels; there is a fascinating fountain hidden away in the back, and you might be treated to a fashion show or a pianist playing on the central level. More than half of the ninety boutiques sell clothes, many carrying designer labels. Alfred Sung, Aquascutum, Le Château, Club Monaco, Giorgio, Lancia Uomo, Parachute and others.

Place Montreal-Trust (6) is a modern complex with 120 boutiques and restaurants that offer a range of prices and styles in clothes and home furnishings. The large central foyer boasts palm trees and a fountain that squirts water six levels high. Abercrombie and Fitch, Alfred Sung, Bally, Gigi, Jacob, Marks and Spencer, Rodier and others.

An underground tunnel takes you to Le Centre Eaton, 2020 University, 2001 University, Les Promenades de la Cathédrale and La Baie, all of which open directly to the expansive McGill metro station, where pedestrian streets look directly over the rubberwheeled blue trains. Above the eastbound platform there is a stained-glass mural (Nicolas Sollogoub, 1966) that honors Montreal's first two mayors, Benjamin Viger and Peter McGill.

Torontonians should not compare **Le Centre Eaton** to their spacious, airy Eaton Centre. Montreal's is a disappointment and by no means the city's most attractive shopping mall. It opens into the Eaton department store, part of the chain of retail outlets that has the greatest sales volume in Canada. Founded in Toronto by Timothy Eaton, it is still a family business with a loyal staff and clientele. The restaurant on the ninth floor is a replica of the Art Deco dining hall on the *Île de France,* Lady Eaton's favorite Atlantic passenger liner. Here, there are thirty-five-foot columns of pink and gray marble, Italian alabaster vases, Monet grills and banisters, mural paintings by Natatcha Carlu and bas-reliefs by Denis Gelin. Strangely, the restaurant is still a department store's cafeteria, and amid all this romantic opulence, the most ordinary people sit surrounded by their shopping bags.

Les Promenades de la Cathédrale (10), with its ninety businesses on three levels around an attractive open space, gets its name from the fact that it is built under Christ Church Cathedral. It offers a wide range of boutiques and opens into La Baie department store.

La Baie (11) sells what you might expect in a large department store, but is famous for its traditional red-green-and-white Hudson's Bay blankets. Lately it has gained a reputation for selling stylish clothing at a moderate price.

Henry Birks et Fils (11) is Montreal's Tiffany's. On Phillips Square, this upper-class shop is not connected to the metro. The store, which still employs its own designers, is noted for its gems, jewelry, silver, crystal and fine china.

Hemsleys, 650 Ste-Catherine O., is another china and jewelry store. It was founded in 1885, when Mr. Hemsley arrived from England with an impressive and valuable collection of clocks, watches and objets d'art. Hardly was he installed in his new premises than the great flood of 1886 inundated his shop, upending his display cases and ruining much of his inventory. When the flood subsided, he nailed his counters to the floor and began again.

Place-Ville-Marie (5) is a short detour down rue McGill College from St-Catherine, which brings you to the "grandmammy" of the world's downtown malls. With almost ninety retail outlets, it offers a mix of prices on clothes, household items and handicrafts. Brown's, Cactus, Cemi, Dalmy's, Francois Villon, Gazebo, Holt Renfrew, Jacnel, Lalla Fucci, Marie-Claire, Mayfair, Reitman's, Le Rout Metiers d'Art and others.

Farther south and connected to PVM by underground passages is **Place Bonaventure,** which is built over a metro station. The one hundred stores of this complex offer a wide range of products at various prices. It is especially good for shoes and has one of Montreal's best bridal salons, Alain Giroux, Au Coton, Bally, Bikini Village, Dack, Pegabo, Pronuptia and others.

Along rue Ste-Catherine from McGill College to de la Montagne and beyond, you will find a wide range of shoe, clothing, sporting goods and specialty shops. **Marshalls,** 1145 Ste-Catherine, is Montreal's preeminent fabric store and has a vast collection of clothing patterns. **Ogilvys,** 1307 Ste-Catherine, is a refurbished department store that now also houses some of Montreal's most elegant clothing boutiques. The open building, with its pink-glass chandeliers, has a dignity that the other malls tend to lack—at noon, in keeping with a tradition that dates back to 1865, a Highland piper walks around the store, serenading the customers. As one of the saleswomen told me, "It's an experience that you never forget, and it never ceases to surprise you!" Aquascutum, Crabtree and Evelyn, Don Sayres, Jean Muir, Joan and David, Jaeger, Karl Lagerfeld, Valentino and others.

Holt Renfrew, at 1300 Sherbrooke (37), is just up rue de la Montagne. This clothing and tailoring shop has been catering to the men and women of the Canadian establishment since 1837. They will not only design clothes for you, but stock one-of-a-kind designer dresses and the most exclusive of designer labels. Prices, as might be expected, are high.

From de la Montagne (37) **to Guy** (40) are a number of exclusive boutiques for men's and women's clothing. Ralph Lauren is at 1316; Yves St. Laurent is at 1330; Ungaro is at 1430. Les Gamineries, for children, is at 1458; Brisson & Brisson, for men, is at 1472. Lily Simon, at 1480, sells Armani and Valentino; Bruestle, for the tailored woman, is at 1490. At the corner of rue Simpson, the internationally known jeweler, Cartier, has a green-marble-faced shop where diamonds sparkle in the window. This short length of Sherbrooke is also occupied by Montreal's finest art galleries and some of its better antiques shops. Among others, Galerie d'Art Eskimau, at 1434, specializes in Eskimo sculpture, as does Elca London Gallery, at 1616; Dominion Gallery, at 1438, and Waddington & Gorce, at 1504, sell the works of internationally known sculptors and painters. Across the street, Robert Buckland sells oriental carpets.

On **rue Crescent** (50), Celine sells crisp Parisian styles at 2142, and Laura Ashley sells romantic English clothes, linens and fabrics at 2110. Ferroni, at 2145, and Andre Antiques, at 2125, deal in antiques and furniture, and Davidoff will sell you the best cigars in the world.

Les Faubourg (48) is Montreal's best food emporium. It is spacious, relaxed and has islands of café tables and chairs. It also has one of the better wine stores in the city, some clothing and craft boutiques and a cinema.

If you haven't spent your money by this time, you may wish to take the metro west to Atwater, which opens into Alexis Nihon Plaza and has a tunnel that leads to exclusive Westmount Square and British-like **Greene Avenue,** where there are a number of good antiques shops. The Double Hook Book Shop, at 1235A, sells Canadian books that are not readily available in other shops.

If you are truly born to shop (especially for the more avant-garde fashions), you should not miss the blocks that run **north from rue Sherbrooke on either boulevard St-Laurent** (25) **or rue St-Denis** (28). Then, if you really must, take a taxi to **rue Laurier at avenue du Parc** (take the 80 bus from Place-des-Arts metro), where elegant boutiques cater to the well-heeled of Outremont.

A LEGEND FOR SHOPPERS

In 1793, a young man from Repentigny, Hervieux de Lanoraie, decided to go shopping in Montreal on New Year's Day. His little adventure would become a legend.

Hervieux, knowing that it would take a day to get to town, hitched his horse to a sleigh and set out early New Year's Eve. He had not gone far when snow began to fall and he decided to take a shortcut across some fields. It was a mistake, for it was not long before he was in a real blizzard and his horse could no longer move forward. Unable to see more than a dozen yards in front of him, Hervieux covered the animal with a blanket and, conscious that he should not fall asleep in the cold, wrapped himself as best he could. To stay awake he had to pinch himself and think of the trees in summer as the white blanket fell all around him.

As night fell, Hervieux noticed a glimmer of light coming from a small house that he had not noticed in the muffled, white light of day. He climbed out of the sleigh, put on his snowshoes and walked easily to the cabin. He knocked at the door and waited, but no one came. He looked through the window and saw a huge fire burning in the fireplace, but the house seemed empty. He pushed open the door and called out to the inhabitants. After a while, when no one replied, he took off his coat and sat warming himself at the hearth. He kept looking around, expecting someone to appear.

He had been staring into the fire for some time when he suddenly heard a creaking sound behind him. He turned and saw an old, white-bearded man sitting on a chair in the corner. Hervieux got up immediately and apologized for having entered the house without permission. The old man waved his hand and said, "I have been condemned to sit here every New Year's Eve until I save the life of an unfortunate traveler. God gave me this punishment because, when I was alive, I refused a stranger lodging in just such a blizzard on a New Year's Eve many years ago. The next day, I found him curled up and frozen in front of my door."

Young Hervieux fell asleep by the fire. The next morning, he awoke in his sleigh. The snow had stopped falling, his horse was able to get back onto the road, and the young man from Repentigny was able to go shopping in Montreal.

––––––––––––––––– ■ –––––––––––––––––

MONTREAL AT NIGHT

The *Montreal Mirror,* a weekly publication, provides a complete list of films, theater, music, dance and art in the city. This free publication is readily available in many bars, restaurants, cafés and shops. I shall therefore limit my entries to information and attractions that are not made evident by the *Mirror*'s listings. The numbers in parenthesis refer to the positions *closest* on the maps of downtown (see page 88).

Theaters and Movie Houses

Cinemas: *The Egyptien,* in Les Cours Mont-Royal (34), has an interesting, postmodern decor, while the *Imperial,* 1430 rue Bleury (18), is a renovated movie palace of the 1930s. The *Cinemathèque Québecoise,* 335 de Maisonneuve E. (31), and *Le Conservatoire,* 1455 de Maisonneuve O. (50), usually present minifestivals of films from the past or from foreign countries. *Cinema Parallele,* 3682 St-Laurent (25), is a tiny house that presents the most avant-garde of new films.

Cabaret: The most lavish of Montreal's dinner shows is in the CAF' CONC', 878-9000, in the *Chateau Champlain Hotel* (1), where a costumed, high-kicking, Moulin Rouge–type review is staged. It has to be seen to be believed! Monday through Saturday 9 P.M.; Friday and Saturday 11 P.M. Cover charge.

Classical Music: *The Montreal Symphony Orchestra* is considered to be one of the better orchestras in North America. *Pollack Hall,* 555 rue Sherbrooke O. (9), Tel.: 485-3736, is a much-used facility where McGill's Faculty of Music and the Canadian Broadcasting Corporation often present free concerts.

Comedy Clubs: *The Comedy Nest,* 1459 rue Crescent (50), Tel.: 849-NEST; and *Comedy Works,* 1234 rue Bishop (49), Tel.: 398-9661, both offer live stand-up comics. Tuesday to Sunday at 8:30 P.M. and Friday and Saturday at 11 P.M. Telephone for reservations.

Contemporary Music: *Spectrum,* 318 Ste-Catherine O. (18), Tel.: 861-5851, is the main venue for Quebec artists but also presents international stars. It is more like a club than a theater—drinks are served in the hall and there are no seating reservations.

Dance: Montreal is home to some of Canada's most exciting chore-ographers. For information on dance performances in the city, con-tact *Maison de la Dance,* Tel.: 849-8681.

Theaters: With some forty theater companies in Montreal, the city usually has a diverse bill of fare to offer. However, *Centaur Theatre,* 453 St-François-Xavier (36 on the map of Old Montreal), is the only stage that regularly presents English-language productions. *Théâtre du Nouveau Monde,* 84 Ste-Catherine O. (18), is the flagship of the French theater. *Théâtre de Quat'sous,* 100 avenue des Pins E. (25), Tel.: 845-7277; and *Théâtre d'Aujourd'hui,* 1297 Papineau (metro Pa-pineau), Tel.: 523-1211, favor original Quebec works. *Éspace Libre,* 1945 Fullum (metro Frontenac and bus 125), Tel.: 521-4191; *Théâtre de l'Eskabel,* 1235 Sanguinet (33), Tel.: 849-7164; and *Théâtre de la Veillée,* 1371 Ontario E. (metro Beaudry) are considered experimen-tal. The best-known café-theater is *La Licorne,* 2075 St-Laurent (23), Tel.: 849-7164; and the *Ligue Nationale d'Improvisation,* Tel.: 849-9726, present (in a miniature hockey ring) competing teams of actors that win "games" after being judged by the audience.

Live Music

In Montreal, clubs serve drinks until 3 A.M.

Alternative Music: *Les Foufounes Electriques* (Electric Buttocks), 87 Ste-Catherine E. (33), Tel.: 845-5484, is the mecca for punk and new wave fans. The outside of the building has been fantastically painted and there is a sculpture garden in front of the entrance.

Boîtes à Chansons: For a visitor who wants to be part of a lively, young, 500-strong, Québecois crowd having fun, drinking and occa-sionally making fools of individuals who are invited on stage, *Aux Deux Pierrots,* 114 rue St-Paul E. (18), is the place to go. The musician-animators encourage clapping, singing and general participation in a continuous partylike atmosphere from 8:15 P.M. to 2:30 A.M., Thurs-day through Sunday. There can be long lines here, but it's not to be missed! The neighboring *Aux Pierrots*, 104 rue St-Paul, is a smaller *boîte* where the entertainment is more local, more "folky" and more French. The musicians are often more like stand-up comics than animators. Both are under the same management. Around the corner, on rue St-Vincent, is *Le St-Vincent*. With its two floors and balcony in an almost-200-year-old building, it has been open 20 years and is the granddaddy of all Quebec's *boîtes*. The small cover charge goes to the musicians, who usually play songs dear to the Québecois.

Country Music: *The Blue Angel*, 1230 rue Drummond (35), Tel.: 866-7146, is the last of Montreal's downtown country clubs. It's seen better days—it's been in business since before World War II, when you were refused entrance if you were wearing jeans.

Heavy Metal and Hard Rock: *Back Street*, 382 rue Mayor (18) (just off Bleury north of Ste-Catherine), Tel.: 987-7671.

Irish Music: *Le Vieux Dublin*, 1219A rue Université (10), Tel.: 861-4448.

Jazz and Blues: In the 1930s, Montreal was a favorite destination and a major center for American jazz musicians. Oscar Peterson is undoubtedly the city's most famous Montrealer to come out of this great period. Since then, jazz has fallen on harder times, but the internationally renowned yearly festival has renewed interest in the art form. In the downtown area there are *Bar G Sharp* at 4062A boulevard St-Laurent (26), Tel.: 845-6932; *Beaux Esprits* at 2073 rue St-Denis (30), Tel.: 844-0882; and *Biddle's* at 2060 Aylmer (9), Tel.: 842-8656. In Old Montreal there are *l'Air du Temps*, at 191 St-Paul O. (6), Tel.: 842-2003; and *Claudio's* at 124 rue St-Paul E. (31), Tel.: 866-0845.

Karaoke: *Shad-O*, 3732 rue St-Dominique (25), and *Beepers*, 1474 rue Crescent (50), are karaoke bars where customers are invited to choose from hundreds of songs that have been recorded without the lead singer, are given a microphone and, while the lyrics are flashed on a monitor, become stars.

Rock: In Old Montreal, *Nuit Magique*, 22 rue St-Paul E. (18), Tel.: 861-8143, offers a house band that nightly plays Top 40 and classic rock. In the rear is a quieter room with a fireplace and sofas for regulars. Downtown, *Déja-vu*, 1224 rue Bishop (49), and *Charlies*, almost next door, are in friendly competition—the bands have been known to trade stages in mid-evening.

Strip Clubs: Montreal has a great number of strip clubs, especially along rue Ste-Catherine. *Danceurs nus* means the strippers are male; *danceuses nues* means they're female. Because of their proximity to each other, I mention the *Bar Appollon*, 1250 rue Staley (2), where men strip for women, and *Chez Parée*, next door at 1258, where women strip for men.

Varied Artists: *Club Soda*, 5420 avenue du Parc (take the 80 bus from Place-des-Arts metro), Tel.: 270-7848, may present big bands, motown or stand-up comedy. It's a lively place.

World Beat Music: *Club Balattou*, 4372 boulevard St-Laurent (take the 55 bus from St-Laurent metro), presents many African and Caribbean artists.

Bars and Dance Clubs

It is well known that the French language has an elegance that English never approaches. Nowhere is this more apparent than in the expression *La tournée des grands ducs* ("the Grand Dukes' tour"), which means a pub crawl or bar hop. Whether one tours, hops, or crawls from watering hole to watering hole, it is a favorite pastime in Montreal. In French, "I'll pay for the next round" is "Je payerai la prochaine tournée."

With hundreds of bars to choose from, I can only mention a few. In the English Quarter, where there are over forty bars, *Sir Winston Churchill Pub* and *Thursday's* at 1459 and 1449 rue Crescent (50), have long been popular. For a quieter time, head for *Escapade*, which has a fine view from the top of the Château Champlain Hotel (1), or the *Grand Prix Bar*, the most dignified in the city, in the Ritz-Carlton Hotel (36). In Old Montreal (refer to map on page 40), *Le Keg*, 22 rue St-Paul E. (18), is the most lively. In the Latin Quarter, where there are eighteen bars and clubs in a two-block stretch, the *Saint-Sulpice*, 1680 rue St-Denis (30), has a large terrace in the rear and offers inexpensive beer by the pitcher. *City-Pub*, 3820 St-Laurent (25), has Heineken, Bass, and Newcastle, as well as the local brews Belle Guelle and St. Ambroise, on tap. Bottled beers come from twelve different countries, including China, Czechoslovakia and Libya.

If you are under thirty-five and want to dance, I suggest that you go to boulevard St-Laurent, just north of rue Sherbrooke (25), where there are eight dance bars within a few blocks. *Business*, at 3500 St-Laurent, is very popular with the young and the beautiful and has a doorman who may screen you. The decor is minimal and may be described as urban-harsh; the music is alternative. *Di Salvio,* at 3519, is Montreal's most exclusive dance bar. An intimate size, with a fireplace and comfortable chairs, it is where visiting movie stars and even the prime minister of Canada have been seen dancing. It is technically a private club, but if you arrive early in the evening or have an air of "intelligence or power" you may be invited to enter. Bring your limo, for even the owner-manager, Bob Di Salvio, says that he's not sure that the doorman would let him in. The music varies according to the mood and size of the crowd—and the crowd can be wild or subdued. *Blue Dog,* at 3550 St-Laurent, takes the overflow from Business. *Zoo Bar,* at 3556, is the largest dance bar in the area. The crowd is young and well-heeled and the atmosphere is welcoming. The Art Deco decor of *Chez Swann* at 57 Prince-Arthur E. (26), makes it the best-looking dance bar. A little farther up St-Laurent is the *Garage St-Laurent,* at 3699, which has a rock-and-roll bar (sometimes with live music) upstairs and a dance music bar downstairs. The *Bar St-Laurent,* at 3868, has a small dance floor, two pool tables and tables for conversation. The low prices attract students and young immigrants from all over the world.

There are dance bars in other neighborhoods that should be mentioned. *Club Balattou,* at 4372 St-Laurent (take the 55 bus from St-Laurent metro), is Montreal's best World Beat dance bar. There is a cover charge when live music is played. Telephone 845-5447. Also popular with black people is *Isaza,* 5149A avenue du Parc, just north of rue Laurier (take the 80 bus from Place-des-Arts metro). *Passeport,* 4156 St-Denis (Mont-Royal metro), is a popular dance bar. Across the street, at 4177, is *Le Lézard,* where on Mondays the customers are invited to body paint each other and on Thursdays are asked to come in drag. *Metropolis,* at 59 Ste-Catherine E. (16), Canada's largest discotheque, occupies a converted and largely preserved movie palace. It is immense and there is a cover charge. *Foufounes Électriques,* 16 Ste-Catherine E., is the most *branché* (or alternative) of Montreal's dance clubs and also presents concerts performed by internationally known alternative musicians. Telephone 845-5484.

There are also a number of dance bars in the English Quarter. *Studebaker's,* 1255 rue Crescent (50), plays music from the 1960s and 1970s while bartenders dance on the bar. For Lambada fans there is *Alexandre,* 1454 rue Peel (34), which has a Club Med kind of atmosphere, and *Salsathèque,* 1220 rue Peel (2), which has a house orchestra that plays Latin American and tropical rhythms. The clientele of the *Pacha Club*, 1212 de Maisonneuve O. (35), which plays dance music, and Club 6/49, 2139 de la Montagne (35), which has a house band that plays Latin music, tends to be more mature than patrons of most dance bars. For dinner and dancing on Saturday night, try *L'île de France*, 801 de Maisonneuve O. (6), Tel.: 849-6331. *Flamingo Joe*, 2080 Aylmer (10), Tel.: 288-9272, offers dinner, a Brazilian dance troupe and dancing. And not to be forgotten is the *Vieux Munich*, 1170 St-Denis (33), a large and popular German beer garden and restaurant where you can polka until you drop.

Gay and Lesbian Bars

Montreal's gay nightlife is so extensive that the area between the Beaudry and Papineau metro stations is known as the Gay Village. *Max*, at the corner of rue Ste-Catherine and rue Montcalm, and *Bronx*, at 1279 St-Hubert, are discotheques. Station "C," at 1450 Ste-Catherine E., is a complex of four bars. *Track*, 1584 Ste-Catherine E., is a cruising bar that attracts a varied crowd. *Terrasse du Village*, 1366 Ste-Catherine E., which closes at midnight, has the best outdoor facilities. *Campus*, 1111 Ste-Catherine E., is the largest gay strip club, and you can pay to have a dancer perform at your table. *Entre-Peau*, 1115 rue Ste-Catherine, presents Montreal's favorite drag artists. The best bar for a quiet talk is *California*, 1412 rue Ste-Elizabeth (two blocks west of St-Denis) (33), which has a large outdoor patio in summer.

Bilitis St-Denis, 1250 rue St-Denis (33), is exclusively for women. Farther up St-Denis, *Lilith*, at 3882 (29), is a private club for women. *Loubar* is at 1364 Ste-Catherine E.

✤ 7 ✤

Vacation and Ski Resorts Outside Montreal

ESTRIE, OR THE EASTERN TOWNSHIPS

How to Get There

Leave the island of Montreal by the Champlain Bridge and take Autoroute des Cantons-de-l'Est (Highway 10) to Chambly, which is situated on the Richelieu River, twenty minutes from downtown Montreal.

History

The Abenakis, a hunter-gatherer tribe, continued to be the primary inhabitants of most of the area to the south and southwest of Montreal until the nineteenth century. The Richelieu River Valley had been granted as *seigneuries* during the French regime, and many of the farmers joined Ethan Allen's aborted invasion of Montreal during the American Revolution. However, the valley was the only part of Quebec that joined the Thirteen Colonies. After American independence, the British, with the goal of securing the border, set aside the undeveloped areas for the United Empire Loyalists who had fled north.

The land was to be given freely, held freehold and divided into English-type townships. But, with more land available than was needed, corruption became the order of the day. John Manners, the Marquis of Granby, a friend of George III, became a major landholder; on this precedent, huge estates were given away. Nicholas Austin received over 60,000 acres; one British governor, Sir Robert Shore Milnes, "accepted" 48,000 acres. This liberal distribution was shared by Montreal's small merchant class, who would bribe the government officials in Quebec City. By 1805, almost 1½ million acres had been given to just seventy men.

The government, still afraid of American invasion but also aiming to anglicize Quebec, responded to the charges of corruption by selling (at bargain prices) over 1 million acres to the British-American Land Company, on the condition that it encourage British and Irish immigrants. The citizens of the towns along the Richelieu Valley were especially vexed by this, for it meant that they could not expand south and east. A call for arms by Wolfred Nelson, an anglophone from St-Denis-sur-Richelieu, sparked the Rebellions of 1837–38.

After the short-lived uprising, the company was forced to give back some of the land, but retained enough to make a good profit (from sales to British immigrants) for men such as Sir A. T. Galt. In the 1850s, when it was decided that Montreal should be connected by rail to an Atlantic port—either Portland, Maine, or Boston, Massachusetts—he was a substantial backer of the Portland route, which would run through the land that he controlled. The competition for the two routes was so intense that it was finally decided by a race between two runners, who set out from Montreal at the same time. Portland won; and so, the railway passed through Sherbrooke. This opened the Eastern Townships to the lumber trade. A textile industry (founded by Galt) began to grow in the towns of Sherbrooke and Magog.

The first French-Canadians arrived not as settlers but as lumberjacks and factory workers. In 1858, the area was so overwhelmingly English that it did not even have a French name—when A. Guérin-Lavoie, a novelist, wrote *Jean Rivard, le défricheur,* about a settler clearing land in the area, he purposefully invented the name *Cantons-de-l'est,* a translation of "Eastern Townships." Over the next hundred years, the francophone workers began to buy land and build houses. Today there is still a sizeable English community, but it no longer forms the majority. The official name for the area, Estrie, comes from a regional anthem, *L'Esterie* ("The Eastern Kingdom"), written in 1946 by Monsignor Maurice O'Bready.

The Tour

Fort Chambly (1), first built in 1711 and restored in 1982, is an example of French medieval-type architecture with fronton, bastions and machicolation. The drawbridge, however, has been replaced by a footbridge. Inside, the guardhouse, which dates from

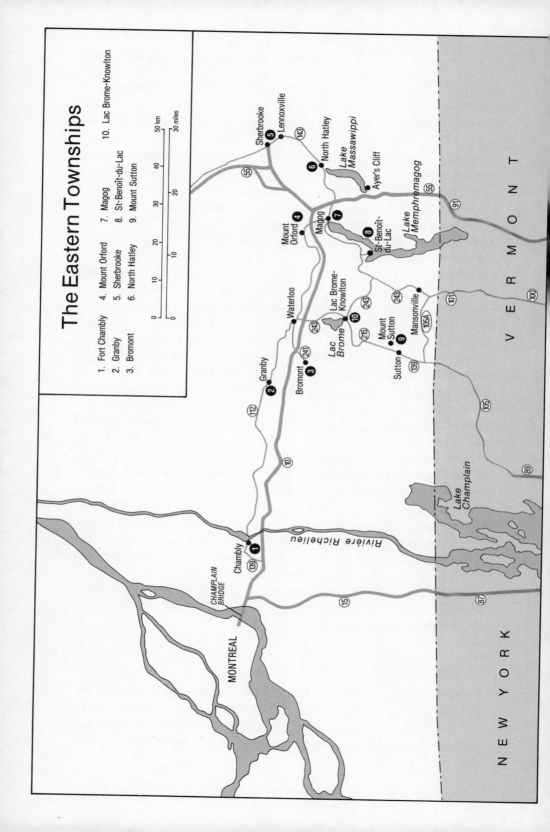

The Eastern Townships

1. Fort Chambly
2. Granby
3. Bromont
4. Mount Orford
5. Sherbrooke
6. North Hatley
7. Magog
8. St-Benoît-du-Lac
9. Mount Sutton
10. Lac Brome-Knowlton

1815, houses an exhibition that shows the history of the fort, a scale model of the valley and the daily life of an eighteenth-century soldier. Open: May to October: Tuesday through Sunday 10 A.M. to 6 P.M.; Monday 1 P.M. to 6 P.M.

Because the Richelieu River has its source in Lake Champlain, which leads to the Hudson, this river system was long an Iroquois canoe route. In fact, in the early 1600s, Henry Hudson, coming up from New York, and Samuel de Champlain, descending from Quebec, came very close to meeting. During the French-English wars, the route was the preferred invasion route of the English armies, and Fort Chambly was first built in 1711. In 1775, Ethan Allen led his Green Mountain Boys up the Richelieu to invade Montreal, but he did not take Fort Chambly.

Granby (2) offers a fascinating marsh teaming with life at the *Lac Boivin Nature Center* on Route 139. Four well-marked trails and an observation tower make it a good place to study wetlands. *Granby Zoo* is on Route 112, east of Chambly. The Montreal area's only zoo is home to 1,200 animals from five continents. Open: May to October: 10 A.M. to 5 P.M.

Bromont (3) was founded in 1964 and is already a major tourist center with water and alpine slides, an obstacle course, mountain coasters and hiking trails. The *SpaConcept International* (P.O. Box 300, 90 Stanstead Street, J0E 1L0, Tel.: 514-534-2717) is a health center that specializes in massage therapy and hydrotherapy. In June, the *Bromont International* is held in the Olympic Equestrian Center.

Hotels: In Bromont, there are six hotels with a total of 365 rooms. The most luxurious and expensive is the 154-room *Hôtel Le Château Bromont*, at 90 rue Stanstead, Tel.: 514-534-3643, 1-800-363-8920. The 54-room *Auberge Bromont*, 95 rue Montmorency, Tel.: 514-534-2200, 1-800-363-8920, is as highly rated, but is less expensive. It has a much better restaurant, but lacks the indoor pool and sauna.

Skiing: Equipment rental, dining, weekend nursery, ski boutique and school. *Downhill:* Tel.: 514-534-2200, 1-800-363-8920. 26 slopes—easy to very difficult. Night skiing on 20. Vertical drop: 405 meters. Longest slope: 2,110 meters. 3 chair lifts, 1 rapid, 2 T-bars, 1 beginner's lift. *Cross-country:* Tel.: 514-534-2277 and 514-534-2200. 9 trails—easy to difficult. 2 heated relay stations.

Mount Orford (4) *Recreational Park* (Tel.: 819-843-6233) was created fifty years ago. In summer, there are facilities for camping, canoeing, windsurfing, swimming, hiking and golf. Parking and entrance fees. In summer, *Festival Orford* is an annual music festival that combines international-caliber courses with popular and classical concerts and art exhibitions. It runs at the *Centre d'Arts* on chemin du Parc (Route 141) from late June to early August. Tel.: 819-843-3981, 1-800-567-6155.

Skiing: Equipment rental, dining, nursery, ski boutique and school. *Downhill:* Tel.: 819-843-6548. 33 slopes—easy to difficult. Vertical drop: 540 meters. Longest slope: 4,000 meters. 6 chair lifts, 1 T-bar, 1 beginner's lift. *Cross-country:* 11 trails—easy to difficult. 42 kilometers of trails. 1 heated relay station. Tel.: 819-843-9855.

Sherbrooke (5), with a population of 75,000, is the regional center of the Eastern Townships. In the North Ward there are some fine Victorian houses; downtown there is a small *art museum* (it's best for primitive art) on rue Palais, and there is a *natural history museum* at the seminary, 195 rue Marquette. Both museums are open only in the afternoons; both are closed Monday and Friday. The *Auberge Elite,* at 4206 rue King O., has one of the better restaurants, but for excellent dining and charming accommodations, I would try to make a reservation in one of the three country inns at North Hatley.

Just to the south (Route 143) of Sherbrooke is **Lennoxville** (population 4,000), the home of Bishop's University, and on rue du College there is a **research farm** that gives guided tours. Open: mid-May through August: 8:30 A.M. to 3:00 P.M.

North Hatley (6), a small (population 715) town at the northern end of Lake Massawippi, is home to two of the region's best country inns, both with excellent restaurants. The thirty-five-room *Hovey Manor,* Tel.: 819-842-2421, because it is a converted lakeside manor furnished with antiques, is the more romantic. But both the twenty-five-room *Hatley Inn,* Tel.: 819-842-2451, and the twenty-six-room *Ripplecove Inn,* Tel.: 819-838-4296, in Ayer's Cliff, at the other end of the lake, are fine country inns. North Hatley also offers sailing, golf, a hundred kilometers of trails for horseback riding, and is the home of an English summer theater, the Piggery.

Skiing: Equipment rental, dining and ski school. Tel.: 819-842-2447. *Downhill:* 17 slopes—mostly easy. Vertical drop: 230 meters. Longest slope: 1,100 meters. 1 chair lift, 1 T-bar. Night skiing until 10 P.M. *Cross-country:* 6 trails—easy to difficult. In winter, the three inns that I have mentioned are connected by a 35-kilometer ski trail around the lake, and the management of each inn will arrange to have your car and luggage transferred to the next.

SOUTHERNERS AVOID YANKEES

North Hatley has one of the more interesting histories in the region. After the American Civil War, Southern families who could still afford to have summer homes in the North adopted the twenty-mile-long lake. Such was their hatred of Yankees that they would take the train from Atlanta, pull down the window blinds as they crossed the Mason-Dixon Line, and not raise them until they arrived in Canada. The town has remained a favorite with Americans ever since.

Magog (7), with a population of 13,500, is just a short scenic drive from North Hatley. The town is at the head of forty-kilometer-long Lake Memphremagog, in which a monster, said to be related to the one in Loch Ness, is occasionally seen swimming across the U.S.-Canada border. Magog has facilities for waterskiing, sailing, sailboarding, rowing, scuba diving, motorboating and swimming. There are three eighteen-hole golf courses, stables, restaurants and night spots. A health spa, *Institut Andréanne,* 2283 chemin du Parc, J1X 3W3, Tel.: 819-843-4615, employs a beautician and specializes in hydrotherapy—particularly a seawater cure. *Auberge St-Bernard,* 3159 Route 112 Ouest, Tel.: 819-843-6657, 1-800-567-7378, is a twenty-six-room inn, where there is a good restaurant and almost every room has a fireplace.

The Benedictine monastery, **St-Benôit-du-Lac** (8) is south of Magog and on the western side of Lake Memphremagog. The abbey was designed by Dom Paul Bellot (1876–1944), who created a style of architecture that sought perfect harmony in accordance with nature's geometric laws. Inside, there are forty rooms that are reserved for men who wish to pass some days in contemplation and tranquility. In a nearby villa, there are fifteen rooms reserved for women. In accordance with St. Benedict's wishes, the Divine Office is a priority, and a Gregorian mass is celebrated daily at 11 A.M. Vespers are also chanted in Gregorian at 5 and 7 P.M. on Thursday. The cheese and cider that are produced by the monks is for sale, morning and afternoon, Monday through Saturday.

Skiing: *The Owl's Head Ski Resort* (P.O. Box 35, Mansonville, J0E 1X0, Tel.: 514-878-1453), which was opened by Fred Corman, a German who fell in love with the spectacular beauty of the country, is at Vale Perkins, just to the south. Apartment-hotel, inn, equipment rental, dining, nursery, ski boutique and school. 27 slopes—easy to expert. Vertical drop: 540 meters. Longest slope: 3,219 meters. 6 chair lifts, 1 rapid.

Mount Sutton (9) is a resort that opened in 1960. It and the village of Sutton offer the broadest range of lodging, the best hiking and the most diversified woodland skiing in the Eastern Townships. It is especially appreciated by those who wish to enjoy the autumn colors and those who are learning to ski. *Appartements-Hotel Val Sutton*, 575 chemin Real, Tel.: 514-538-4444, offers the most luxurious accommodations; but *Motel l'Estancia*, 264 rue Maple, Tel.: 514-538-3501, with its kitchens and fireplaces, offers the best value. Unfortunately, there is no restaurant that I can recommend.

Skiing: Equipment rental, dining, nursery, ski boutique and school. *Downhill:* Tel.: 514-538-2339. 53 slopes—easy to very difficult. Vertical drop: 460 meters. Longest slope: 4,023 meters. 8 chair lifts, 1 rapid. *Cross-country:* 6 trails—easy to difficult. 1 heated relay. Tel.: 514-538-2271.

Lac Brome—Knowlton (10) has preserved many of its nineteenth-century homes. It is a center for antiques and home of a *historical museum* with a Fokker D VII, a World War I–vintage airplane. The *Le Malard* restaurant, which overlooks the lake, is highly recommended for its duck.

Skiing: Equipment rental. *Cross-country:* Tel.: 514-243-6843. 11 trails—easy to very difficult. 53 kilometers of trails. 2 heated relay stations.

THE LAURENTIAN MOUNTAINS

How to Get There

Autoroute Laurentides (Highway 15) is a fast, modern road that starts at the Metropolitain Expressway (Highway 40) and, within forty-five minutes, takes you into the mountainous resort area north of Montreal. Parc Mont-Tremblant, the farthest area mentioned here, is slightly over one and a half hours away from Montreal.

History

The Laurentians, considered to be the oldest mountain range in the world, were formed 950 million years ago and were shaved to their present, modest height by the last ice age. The first known inhabitants were the Algonquins, who believed that their spirit-god, Manitou, lived on Mont-Tremblant (literally: Trembling Mountain).

The lowlands, close to Montreal, were colonized during the French regime, and the timber resources of the area began to be exploited during the Napoleonic Wars; but St. Jerome, "the gateway to the Laurentians," was not founded until 1834. It was not until the late nineteenth century that the mountain valleys farther north began to be settled on a permanent basis. In 1868, Antoine Labelle was appointed curé of St. Jerome, and for the following thirty years he actively promoted the colonization in a period during which tens of thousands of French-Canadians were being forced, by economic hardship, to emigrate to New England, where the textile mills gave them employment. This exodus so disturbed both church and government that they swung behind Curé Labelle, who, before he died, had founded some twenty towns.

In the twentieth century, Americans were the first to develop the recreational potential of the mountains, lakes, valleys and rivers.

St-Sauveur-des-Monts and Mont Habitant (1), with a population of 4,000, is the center of the resort area closest to Montreal. It has a number of excellent restaurants, craft shops and a variety of accommodations. The French-language theater produces comedies in the summer, and there are two large aqua parcs (one in neighboring Piedmont) with waterslides. The French restaurant at the *Auberge St-Denis*, 61 rue St-Denis, Tel.: 514-227-4466, a forty-seven-room country inn, has an international reputation. *Marie-Philip*, 352 rue Principale, Tel.: 514-227-2171, is an exciting little restaurant owned by an inventive chef, Philip Filipovic, and his wife, Marie.

Morin Heights, on Route 364, is noted for its cross-country skiing, and leads, via the scenic Route 329, to **St-Adolphe-d'Howard,** where there is swimming, hiking and horseback riding. Route 329 leads to Ste-Agathe-des-Monts.

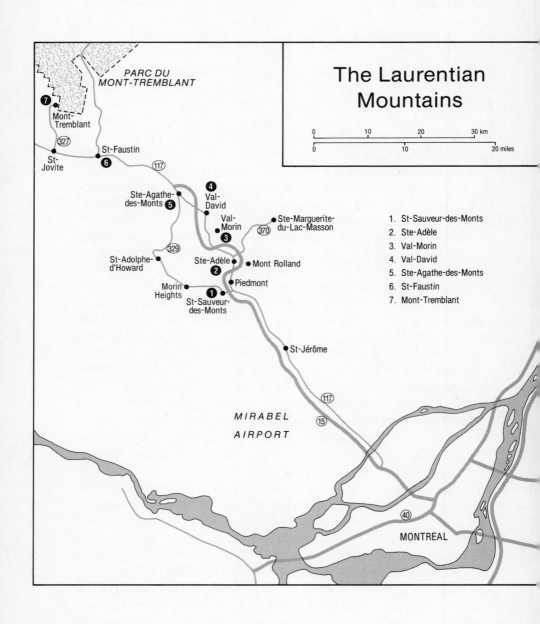

The Laurentian Mountains

0   10   20   30 km

0   10   20 miles

PARC DU MONT-TREMBLANT

Mont-Tremblant

St-Faustin

St-Jovite

Ste-Agathe-des-Monts

Val-David

Val-Morin

Ste-Marguerite-du-Lac-Masson

St-Adolphe-d'Howard

Ste-Adèle

Mont Rolland

Morin Heights

Piedmont

St-Sauveur-des-Monts

St-Jérôme

MIRABEL AIRPORT

MONTREAL

1. St-Sauveur-des-Monts
2. Ste-Adèle
3. Val-Morin
4. Val-David
5. Ste-Agathe-des-Monts
6. St-Faustin
7. Mont-Tremblant

Downhill skiing: *Mont-Christie (exit 60 from Route 15), Tel.: 514-226-2412.* 12 slopes—easy to difficult. Vertical drop: 170 meters. Longest slope: 1,212 meters. 3 T-bars. Equipment rental, dining, ski school. *Mont-Habitant (exit 60), Tel.: 514-393-1821.* 8 slopes—easy to difficult; night skiing on 8. Vertical drop: 167 meters. Longest run: 1,524 meters. 2 chair lifts, 1 poma. Equipment rental, dining, nursery, ski school. *Mont-St-Sauveur (exit 58 from Route 15), Tel.: 514-277-4671.* 26 slopes—easy to difficult; night skiing on 23. Vertical drop: 213 meters. Longest slope: 1,500 meters. 3 chair lifts, 4 rapid, 1 T-bar, 2 beginner's lifts. Equipment rental, dining, nursery, ski school.

Cross-country skiing: *Morin Heights—Centre ski de fond, 612 chemin du Village (exit 60, Route 364), Tel.: 514-226-2417.* 37 trails—easy to difficult. 150 kilometers of trails. Heated relay stations. Equipment rental.

Ste-Adèle (2), with a population of 7,000, is the second largest Laurentian town and has the most active nightlife. It offers downhill skiing, swimming and golf, and boasts the area's top-rated hotels. *The Hotel Chantecler, Tel.: 514-239-5555, 1-800-363-2420,* with 294 rooms, is a grand old favorite that offers its guests excellent sports facilities— including squash and tennis courts, 22 ski runs, an indoor pool and spa, a golf course and a beach. *Musée-village de Séraphin* is a faithful reconstruction of a village of the last century. *L'Eau à La Bouche, 3003 boulevard Ste-Adèle (Route 117), Tel.: 514-229-9991,* is a restaurant recommended for its *menu de dégustation. Loup Garou, 574 rue Patry, Tel.: 514-229-2080,* is a very attractive restaurant where Louise Duhamel practices her highly touted culinary skills.

A few miles along Route 370 are the *Alpine Inn, Tel.: 514-229-3516, 1-800-363-2577,* which offers five-night organized vacations for families; and *L'Esterel, Tel.: 514-228-2571, 1-800-363-3623,* a highly rated and popular 135-room hotel with 7 tennis courts, a marina, a beach, an indoor pool, cross-country skiing and an 18-hole golf course. The best horseback riding (with overnight excursions) in the Laurentians is at the *Centre d'equitation Ste-Marguerite, on Route 75, Montée Gagnon, Ste-Marguerite-du-Lac-Masson, Tel.: 514-288-4141.*

Downhill skiing: *Le Chantecler (exit 67 from Route 15), Tel.: 514-229-3555, 1-800-363-2420.* 22 slopes—easy to difficult; night skiing on 13. Vertical drop: 195 meters. Longest slope: 1,700 meters. 6 chair lifts, 2 poma. Equipment rental, dining, nursery, ski school.

Cross-country skiing: *Alpine Inn (Route 370), Tel.: 514-229-3516.*

5 trails—easy to difficult. 18 kilometers of trails. Heated relay stations. Equipment rental, dining.

Val-Morin (3) *(exit 76, Route 117)*, is an all-year resort town. Home of *Val-Va Sports ltée, 5275 boulevard Labelle, Tel.: 514-229-7842*, it offers go-carts and high-speed boats in summer, and bobsleds and luges in winter. *Hotel Far Hills, rue Far Hills, Tel.: 514-866-2219, 1-800-567-6636*, is a highly rated hotel with a good restaurant.

Downhill skiing: *Mont-Sauvage (exit 72 from Route 15), Tel.: 819-322-2337.* 9 slopes—easy to difficult. Vertical drop: 175 meters. Longest run: 1,600 meters. 3 T-bars. Equipment rental, dining, boutique and school. One of the least expensive slopes. *Belle-Neige (exit 76 from Route 15), Tel.: 514-430-8092.* 14 slopes—easy to difficult. Vertical drop: 154 meters. Longest slope: 1,272 meters. 2 chair lifts, 1 T-bar. Equipment rental, dining, weekend nursery, ski boutique and school.

Cross-country skiing: *Centre de ski de fond Far Hills, Tel.: 819-322-2014.* 13 trails—easy to difficult. Heated relay stations. Equipment rental, dining.

Val-David (4) (farther along Route 117) has three campsites, horseback riding and is also the summer home of Santa Claus, who can be visited (believe it or not) from late May to early October. The 69-room *Hôtel La Sapinière, Tel.: 819-322-2020, 1-800-567-6635*, is a fine country hotel that is recognized in France and is famous for its restaurant (reserve a week in advance).

Downhill Skiing: *Mont-Alta (exit 76 from Route 15), Tel.: 819-322-3206.* 22 slopes—easy to very difficult. Vertical drop: 180 meters. Longest slope: 1,600 meters. 2 chair lifts. Equipment rental, dining, weekend nursery, ski boutique and school. *Vallée-Bleue (exit 76), Tel.: 819-322-2337.* 15 runs—easy to difficult. Vertical drop: 115 meters. Longest run: 1,609 meters. 2 chair lifts, 1 poma. Equipment rental, dining, ski school.

Ste-Agathe-des-Monts (5), the largest of the Laurentian towns, is at the end of the autoroute. It has a popular municipal beach on Lac des Sables, good camping facilities and two 18-hole golf courses. *Auberge Watel, 250 rue St-Venant, Tel.: 819-326-7016, 1-800-363-6478*, a 20-room hotel, is considered the town's best.

St-Faustin (6) is the home of the *Centre educatif forestier des Laurentides* (chemin du Lac-du-Gordon), which offers an interpretation center and hiking trails that allow the visitor to discover the flora and fauna of the Laurentians. In winter, the quality of skiing on Mont

Blanc is so high that, in the 1960s, the Canadian Ski Instructors' Alliance considered buying the mountain to train its own instructors. Since then, the *Mont Blanc Ski Resort, Tel.: 819-688-2444*, has built luxury condos and rooms. There is a dining room, bar, indoor pool, sauna and steam bath as well as exercise areas and conference rooms.

Downhill skiing: 25 slopes—easy to very difficult. Vertical drop: 300 meters. Longest slope: 1,600 meters. 3 chair lifts, 4 T-bars. Equipment rental, dining, ski boutique and school.

St-Jovite and **Mont-Tremblant** (7) are in the most spectacular of developed Laurentian resort areas. The 175-room *Gray Rocks Inn, Tel.: 819-425-2771, 1-800-567-6767*, is on the shore of Lac Ouimet, on Route 327, outside the town of St. Jovite. Founded in 1906 by the Wheeler family, Gray Rocks is the oldest and one of the most luxurious resorts in the Laurentians. It has long been popular with American visitors. A few miles beyond is the picturesque town of Mont-Tremblant, which offers a variety of accommodations, and Parc du Mont-Tremblant, a 1,248-square-kilometer area with hundreds of lakes and seven rivers. Founded in 1894, the park protects the mountain, sacred to the Algonquins, from development and offers camping, canoeing, bicycling, fishing, hiking, hunting in season, skiing and swimming in spectacular scenery.

Downhill skiing: *Gray Rocks, Tel.: 819-425-2271.* 18 runs—easy to difficult. Vertical drop: 189 meters. Longest run: 1,600 meters. 4 chair lifts. Equipment rental, dining, nursery, ski boutique and school. *Mont-Tremblant Station, Tel.: 819-425-8711.* 34 runs—easy to very difficult. Vertical drop: 630 meters. Longest slope: 5,600 meters. 7 chair lifts, 1 rapid, 3 T-bars. Equipment rental, dining, day care, ski boutique and school.

Cross-country skiing: *Centre ski de fond Mont-Tremblant/St-Jovite, 305 chemin Brébeuf, Tel.: 819-425-2434.* 35 trails—easy to difficult. 100 kilometers of trails. There are few heated shacks, but the scenery is spectacular and wild.

Part Two

QUEBEC CITY

❧ 8 ❧

An Introduction to Quebec City

GEOGRAPHY AND CHARACTER

Quebec City is unique in North America and the world. It is the oldest American city north of Mexico, has been declared a World Heritage Site by the United Nations and, in times past, controlled the entrance to a continent. Repeatedly under siege, it is one of the last walled cities ever built. It is a capital city that feels like a town, a bureaucratic city filled with romance. It is a French city that, in its politeness and quiet dignity, feels strangely British; yet it has a joie de vivre that can only be French. At the same time, it makes Montreal feel American. Whatever Quebec City is, it owes much to its magnificent position, high on cliffs that overlook one of the great rivers of the world.

ARRIVAL IN QUEBEC

By public transportation: Quebec has a regional airport. If you are traveling from Montreal by public transportation, take the train. Quebec's rail station is a magnificent old Château-style building in the Lower Town. When you exit from it, you are immediately presented with an expansive view of the walled city above you. The bus station, on the other hand, is unattractive and in a run-down neighborhood that gives you no inkling that you are about to visit one of the most beautiful cities in the world.

By car from Montreal: From Montreal, Highway 20, on the south shore of the river, is as dull and truck-filled an expressway as you will find. I much prefer taking Route 40 (the Metropolitain) from the north end of Montreal. If you are west of Montreal, you take the Decarie Expressway north to get to it; if you are downtown, take rue

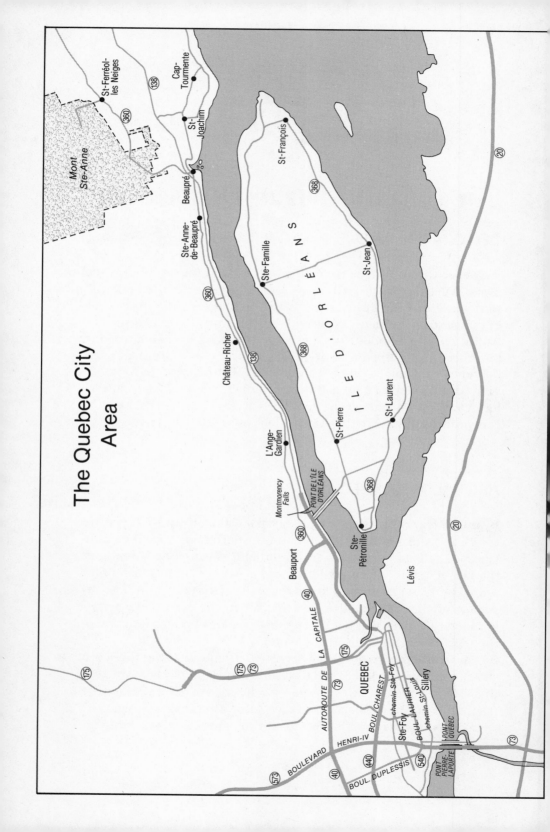

The Quebec City Area

St-Ferréol-les Neiges
Cap-Tourmente
(138)
(360)
St-Joachim
Mont Ste-Anne
Beaupré
St-François
Ste-Anne-de-Beaupré
(360)
Ste-Famille
St-Jean
Château-Richer
(138)
Î L E   D ' O R L É A N S
(368)
(368)
L'Ange-Gardien
St-Pierre
St-Laurent
Montmorency Falls
PONT DE L'ÎLE D'ORLÉANS
(368)
(360)
Beauport
Ste-Pétronille
Lévis
(40)
(20)
(20)
AUTOROUTE DE LA CAPITALE
(175)
(175)
(73)
(175)
QUEBEC
(73)
BOUL. CHAREST
Ste-Foy
chemin Ste-Foy
Sillery
chemin St-Louis
BOUL. LAURIER
PONT QUEBEC
HENRI-IV
BOULEVARD
(573)
(40)
(440)
(540)
PONT PIERRE-LAPORTE
BOUL. DUPLESSIS
(73)

Sherbrooke to Pie IX, where you turn left at the Olympic Stadium and then head north.

It is a fast, easy drive (once you get out of Montreal) to Trois-Rivières. Here, Route 40 breaks. Take 55 south to 755 east (before you get to the suspension bridge over the river), which becomes the continuation of 40 on the other side of the small city. It sounds more difficult than it is, but if you do make an error, the boardwalk along the banks of the St. Lawrence River and in front of the old (built in 1794) Ursuline Convent in Trois-Rivières is a pleasant place to spend an hour. And it is said, in legend at least, that it is close to the place where the Devil likes to trim his beard.

It is a fast drive from Trois-Rivières to Quebec City. Once you are in the suburbs, Route 40 becomes boulevard Charest, which leads directly and easily to Vieux-Québec (Old Quebec), the old walled city that you have come to visit.

THE DEVIL TRIMS HIS BEARD

It is said that one winter night, after the men of Trois-Rivières were coming back from Vespers, they noticed that the moon was so bright that the snow took on an eerie, yellow color and all the houses through the forest were strangely visible. When they arrived at the mouth of the St. Maurice River, they found that they could see the color of water under the ice. And there, on the bank in front of them, was a stranger, dressed in black, who hopped from one foot to another as if he were keeping himself warm.

As they approached, the better to talk with him, he stopped jumping, arranged something that was hanging from the back of his crimson-lined coat, and hung a mirror on the stub of an old branch of a tree. He then took out a razor and began trimming his beard.

The men froze in their tracks. They realized that the thing hanging from the stranger's coat was a tail and that he had cloven hooves for feet. They hightailed it into the woods, and for this reason, even into the twentieth century, the men of Trois-Rivières avoided passing by the place that the Devil had chosen to trim his beard.

By car from points south: Routes 20 and 73 lead to the Pierre-Laporte Bridge (the adjacent Quebec Bridge is the longest single-span cantilever bridge in the world—during construction it collapsed twice). After you have crossed the bridge, take boulevard Laurier, which leads directly to Old Quebec.

TRAVEL IN THE CITY

Because Quebec City is amazingly compact, and because the streets are narrow and occasionally confusingly crooked, there is only one way to see it—on foot. If your hotel does not have private parking, it will invariably arrange for discount rates at the extensive municipal garages.

9

The Story of Quebec City

QUEBEC'S HARD AND SLOW BEGINNINGS

Before the first Europeans sailed up the St. Lawrence River, the area called Canada—an old Amerindian term that meant "small community"—extended from Quebec, which means "where the river narrows," to about sixty miles downriver.

As I have said in the essay on the founding of Montreal, Jacques Cartier and his crew arrived at Quebec in 1535 and discovered the village of Stadacona. After returning from Hochelaga (Montreal), Cartier anchored his ship, *La Petite Hermione,* in the St. Charles River—then called the Kabir Kouba, or "river of a thousand windings," by the Amerindians. The crew settled down for winter but were not prepared for the cold and hunger. They contracted scurvy, an illness that is caused by a vitamin C deficiency and results in the swelling of limbs and the rotting of flesh on the body.

Afraid of Donnacona, the chief of the "savages," Cartier pretended that nothing was wrong. He and a few healthy men made a show of working outside, while the dying men inside the ship knocked hammers and mallets against the hull. Their fear seems to have been unwarranted, for when some natives learned of the illness, they instructed Cartier how to make a cure from tree bark. However, the cure came too late for most of the crew.

With the arrival of spring, Cartier prepared to return to France. In an act of treachery, he kidnapped some children to take as presents for Francis I. Donnacona was at first angered by Cartier's actions, but was later convinced to see the marvels of Europe himself. Donnacona, "The King of Canada," was presented to the King of France, but soon died of a European disease against which he had no immunity. Six years later, Cartier returned to Quebec and told the Amerindians about the death of their chief; but because they were used to the hardships of life, they thought little of it.

205

The Stadaconans must have been rather more startled at Cartier's excitement when he thought that he had discovered gold and diamonds (thus giving Cap Diamant its name) and hurriedly returned to France. The gold turned out to be iron pyrites and the diamonds to be quartz crystals. Cartier's naïveté was laughed at in France; the court turned its back on the St. Lawrence River, and the expression "as fake as a Canadian diamond" has survived to this day.

Although fishermen, especially the Basques and Portuguese, made yearly visits to the Grand Banks of Newfoundland, it was more than sixty years before Quebec and Montreal were again visited by Europeans. By the 1590s, the process of felting fur had been invented and a great demand for beaver pelts developed. Hatmakers were especially keen for a trading post to be established in America. After a couple of failed attempts, including one in 1603 that retraced Cartier's route and during which Samuel de Champlain, a veteran soldier and geographer, noted that the towns of Stadacona and Hochelaga had disappeared, it was decided to build a colony on the Bay of Fundy. This too failed. It was not until 1608 that Canada—or any land north of Mexico—was permanently settled by Europeans. Champlain, with a charter from Henri IV and believing that he would find a route to China, chose to settle at Quebec. Its harbor, control of the river and surrounding arable land made it a natural choice. He built his *habitation* in what is now Place Royale in the Lower Town. Things did not go easily for him. In his first year, one of his men, Jean Duval, who wished to hand the trading post over to the Basques, led a mutiny. Champlain had him hanged and "his head was put on a pike to be planted in the most conspicuous spot of the fort." Of the twenty-eight men Champlain brought, twenty died of scurvy during the first winter and no Amerindian cure was found.

For twenty-seven years, until his death in 1635, Champlain planned for the future of New France. He sailed the Atlantic twenty-four times to lobby the court, convince the king that he could find a route to China and get financing for his dream of a French empire. On one of his trips, in 1610, when he was aged forty, he signed a marriage contract with Hélène Boulle, aged twelve, and invested the dowry in the colony. The fur trade grew as Champlain explored the Great Lakes and strengthened his alliances with the Algonquin and Huron tribes. As a result, however, the Iroquois were turned into dangerous enemies who would, in time, become allied with the Dutch and then the English on the Hudson River. In 1617 Champlain convinced a Parisian apothecary, Louis Hébert, and his family to become the colony's first agrarian settlers. They built a rude house on land close to what is now Montmorency Park. The little settlement now had two buildings.

Progress was difficult and the route to China ever more elusive, but there was money in the fur trade. In 1620, Champlain brought out his new bride, Hélène, and built a small fort, Château St-Louis, to defend the colony below Cap Diamant. In 1623 the Basques attacked but were defeated. Hélène de Champlain had tolerated three winters and went home (eventually to enter a nunnery), leaving her husband with his dogs.

Cardinal Richelieu, in France, organized and subsidized a ship filled with colonists, set to arrive in 1629. But England and France were at war. Two of the Kirke brothers, Huguenots or French Protestants, who were fighting for the English, captured the ship, and a third brother lay siege to Quebec. Champlain was forced to surrender and was escorted back to Europe. Under the peace settlement, Quebec was returned to France, but it was not until 1632, after Charles I had received his wife's dowry from the king of France, his brother-in-law, that Champlain was able to return to his small colony.

When he did return, he found a colony of 150 souls. The widow and family of Louis Hébert were still farming, but his trading post was in ruins. It was not much to show for twenty-four years of work. He began to build a large manor house but did not see it completed. In the fort on Cap Diamant, on Christmas Day 1635, while having feverish, religious hallucinations, he died.

Even if his colony was small when he died, it can be said that Samuel de Champlain was the founder of the greater part of modern North America. The direct and indirect results of his tenacity and drive eventually spread from Cape Breton to the Rockies and from the Gulf of Mexico to Hudson's Bay.

THE BATTLE FOR QUEBEC

The growth of Quebec, like that of Montreal, was slow during the French regime. Fifty years after its founding the population was only six hundred people. The town developed with a commercial section in the Lower Town and the religious, administrative and military headquarters in the Upper Town, but by 1690, when the English attack under Admiral Phips was resisted by Frontenac, there were still only 1,500 residents. In 1711, when the Royal Navy again attempted to take the town, there were still less than two thousand residents. The reasons for this slow population growth have been briefly mentioned in chapter 2.

In 1758, Louis-Antoine, Comte de Bougainville, who had come to Quebec as an aide to General Montcalm, wrote: "Woe to this land! It will perish the victim of its prejudices, of its blind confidence, of the stupidity or crookedness of its chiefs." Bougainville was right. The following year New France was conquered.

In early June 1759, the British fleet of forty ships (James Cook, who went on to claim Australia for England, was one of the pilots) was sailing up the St. Lawrence River and destroying every town within firing range of the ships. On June 17, nine thousand British soldiers with two thousand cannons arrived off Quebec. They set up camp on île d'Orléans, placed their cannons on the heights across the river and began bombarding the city. A devastating three-month-long siege ensued, but the French held their ground.

On September 12, with winter threatening, General Wolfe launched a bold and desperate last attempt. He had decided to use half of his army to make a mock attack at Beauport to the east of the city, and then, under cover of night, to have the other half climb, pulling their guns behind them, up some ravines to the Plains of Abraham to the west.

Montcalm, who had fallen for the ruse, rushed across the St. Charles River to defend Beauport. When he discovered his mistake he rushed his men back to the city to do battle. He did not await reinforcements and charged on to the Plains of Abraham, where he was met by a two-deep "thin red line" of soldiers that alternately loaded and fired. It was the first time in history that this military formation was used, and in less than an hour, Montcalm, mortally wounded, retreated behind the city's walls.

General Wolfe had been killed, but with the death of Montcalm the French army withdrew from the city to reorganize. On September 18, Ramezay, commandant of Quebec, on the advice of the citizens who had stolidly borne the months of bombardment and feared starvation during the winter months, surrendered the city. However, the war was not over—the French still controlled Montreal and had more than seven thousand soldiers there and at Trois-Rivières.

With the arrival of winter, military activities ceased and both sides awaited reinforcements from Europe. Quebec was in ruins. Even Brigadier James Murray, Wolfe's successor, called the destruction "shocking to Humanity." The conscience of the invaders was pricked. "The merchants and officers have made a collection of five hundred pounds Halifax currency and the Soldiers insist on giving one day's provisions in a month for the support of the indigent. General Townshend's troops go without pay to care for the French sick. And in return, the Ursuline nuns knit long woollen stockings for the kilted Highlanders."

With the arrival of spring, both the French and British prepared for a renewal of the war. In April, the French, under General Lévis, gathered an army of over six thousand men, moved up from Montreal and began to organize an attack on Quebec. The British got wind of his plans when a half-frozen French soldier, who had been accidentally carried downstream on a floating block of ice, arrived on the shores of île d'Orleans. Murray sallied out of the city with less than four thousand men. He tried to engage Lévis close to where Montcalm had been wounded in the previous battle, but the French fell back. The English charged. A spread-out battle, involving bayonet charges and hand-to-hand combat, lasted most of a day. Finally, Lévis's men circled around and forced Murray to fall back into the city. Lévis laid siege, hoping that the French navy would arrive to make the British position untenable, but British ships arrived first. The Battle of Ste-Foy, often called the Forgotten Battle, was the last French military victory in America. That summer, British general Amherst took Montreal. New France surrendered on September 8, 1760.

Some historians have said that the British never really conquered Quebec. They say that Quebec was abandoned by a corrupt France that had bled the colony dry and left 41 million livres of almost worthless paper money. Voltaire, who had previously called Canada "a few acres of snow," celebrated Wolfe's victory as the triumph of liberty over despotism, heralding the liberation of all America. He might have been right. If the Thirteen Colonies had continued to be threatened by New France, there might not have been an American Revolution. Whatever the speculation, it is certainly true that American colonists from New England participated in the conquest—one of General Wolfe's regiments was named the Third Royal American.

THE BRITISH AND CANADIAN PERIODS

On January 10, 1763, New France formally became a British colony with its capital at Quebec. It was a garrison town that protected the interior of a continent. The first governors, Murray and Carleton, were at ease with the French. The mostly illiterate colonists were led by priests and feudal landlords who were grateful for being allowed to keep their language, religion and land system. With no tradition of democracy, the replacement of one autocratic government by another made little difference to the poor *habitants* living on either side of the St. Lawrence River. They responded by having one of the highest birthrates ever recorded in human history.

Furs were the only export of any importance and the British and American merchants who came to take over the trade tended to settle in Montreal. In Quebec, many of the Scottish soldiers married Canadian women and became part of the French majority. Montreal was mostly ambivalent when the Americans invaded in 1775, but Quebec City supported the British. After the Treaty of Paris in 1783, when the United States formally gained independence, and during the War of 1812, Quebec remained loyal to the British crown. The linguistic tensions that were beginning to develop between merchants and Canadians in Montreal did not develop in the capital.

During the Napoleonic Wars, Quebec City began to develop as a port where vast amounts of lumber, which had come downriver in huge rafts, were loaded onto sailing ships. The economic benefits from this trade and from the British garrison contributed to the prosperity of a city that was considered to be one of the best postings that a soldier could have in the expanding British Empire.

Irish immigrants began to arrive in the 1820s, but since they were Catholics, they tended to have better relations with the French than did the Protestant Scots, English and Americans that settled in Montreal. The Rebellions of 1837 did not receive wide support in and around Quebec City.

For the first half of the nineteenth century, Quebec City grew steadily, but its position as Canada's most important center was beginning to be eroded by Montreal. In 1851, Quebec had a population of 52,000 residents while Montreal had 57,000. During the next fifty years, however, because of the advent of steamships and railroads, the decreasing threat of American invasion and the western expansion of Canada, the growth of the younger city completely outstripped that of Quebec. By 1901, Quebec had 68,000 residents while Montreal had 267,000.

Although Quebec remained a capital city after the Confederation of Canada in 1867, it was not until the growth of the civil service from the 1940s to the 1980s that the city began its economic revival. During this period, prosperity has been fueled by tourism. Today there are about forty thousand civil servants in a city that has more than a million visitors every year.

—— ❖ 10 ❖ ——

Four Short Walking Tours in Old Quebec

QUEBEC CITY AT A GLANCE

Churches: Basilique de Notre-Dame-de-Québec (6). **Chalmers-Wesley United Church** (21). **Chapelle des Jesuites** (23). **Chapelle des Ursulines** (10). **Chapelle des Soeurs du Bon-Pasteur** (37). **Holy Trinity Cathedral** (9). **Notre-Dame-des-Victoires. St. Andrew's Prebyterian Church** (8).

Harbor Cruises and Sailing: **The Old Port** (15)

Museums: **Amyot House**—contemporary art (12). **Artillery Park**—historical (25). **The Citadel**—military (43). **Le Grand Séminaire**—old masters, scientific instruments (5). **Interpretation Center of the Old Port**—maritime (15). **Maison Chevalier**—furniture (12). **Musée de la Civilisation**—cultural (14). **Musée du Quebec**—art (34). **Musée des Augustines de l'Hôtel-Dieu**—old masters, medical instruments (27). **Musée des Ursulines**—religious, historical (10).

Interiors: **The Citadel** (43). **The Clarendon Hotel** (9). **The Château Frontenac** (18). **L'Assemblée Nationale** (40).

Panoramas: **The Citadel** (43). **Dufferin Terrace** (1). **The Old Port** (15).

Shopping: **Quartier Petit-Champlain** (12). **Rue St-Paul** (16).

WALKING TOUR ONE: THE ST. LAWRENCE RIVER, CHURCHES AND MONASTERIES

The Champlain monument on **Dufferin Terrace** (1) is the place to begin a visit to Quebec City. The Château Frontenac, a grand hotel and Canada's most famous building, rises with its grandiose towers and peaked copper roof to Champlain's left. Behind him is the imperial sweep of the St. Lawrence River, which he knew was a gateway to a continent and hoped would become a route to China. Beneath the terrace are the foundations of his old fort. Rebuilt and enlarged several times, they helped support Château St-Louis, the governors' mansion, throughout the French Regime and until 1782, when Château Haldimand was built on the site of today's Château Frontenac. Château St-Louis was destroyed by fire in 1834. In 1838, Lord Durham inaugurated the first public belvedere, or lookout.

Directly below is the Lower Town, where Champlain's first *habitation* was built and where most of the commerce of the colony was transacted until well into the nineteenth century. The old port has recently been renovated for recreational purposes, but it was once the center of the fur, lumber and shipbuilding industries. Just upriver is the recycled old port and the entrance to the St. Charles River, where Jacques Cartier first wintered. The silver-roofed building to the left is the Grand Seminary, which was founded in 1663. In the distance, you can see Montmorency Falls, the suspension bridge to île d'Orleans, and on a clear day, the towers of the Basilica and Shrine of Ste-Anne-de-Beaupré. Mont-Ste-Anne is the largest of the rolling mountains beyond. As your eye returns, soothing itself on île d'Orléans, which Cartier called île Bacchus because of the abundance of wild grapevines there, it crosses the river to the modern shipbuilding yards at Lauzon. It was from directly across the river at Lévis that the British bombarded the city, destroying most of the Lower Town, in 1759.

Completing the panorama, your eye is drawn over the cliffs opposite and then back, across the river upstream, to the boardwalk and stairs that lead up to the Citadel and the Plains of Abraham.

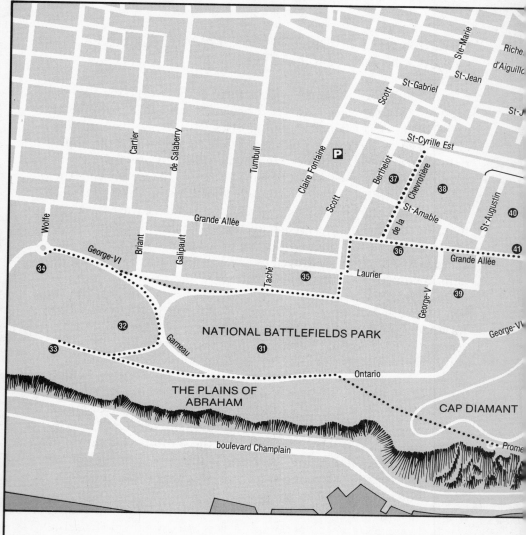

Old Quebec

---------- Walking Tour One
·········· Walking Tour Two
■■■■■■■■■ Walking Tour Three
•••••••• Walking Tour Four

1. Dufferin Terrace
2. The Laval monument
3. Montmorency Park
4. The Ramparts
5. Le Grand Séminaire
6. Basilique de Notre-Dame-de-Québec
7. Hôtel-de-Ville
8. St. Andrew's Presbyterian Church
9. Holy Trinity Cathedral
10. The Ursuline convent and museum
11. Break-Neck Stairs
12. Quartier Petit-Champlain

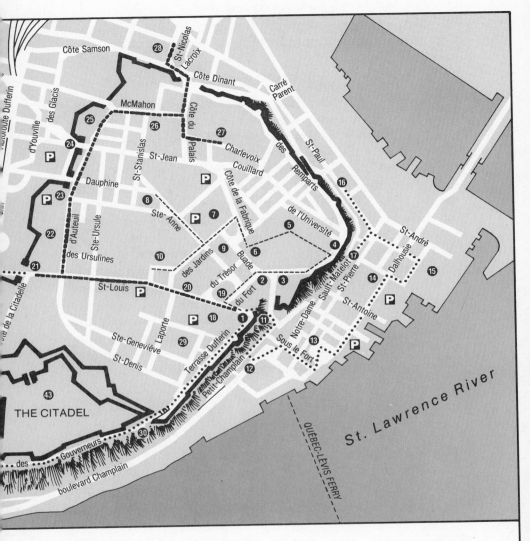

ACROSS THE RIVER

Until 1924, when icebreakers were introduced, a natural ice bridge would form almost every winter, making it possible to walk across the river. In summer, herds of cattle, bound for Quebec's abattoirs, were forced to swim the river. Today, this is where the famous iceboat races are held during Quebec's yearly Winter Carnival.

It is said that if you see a dismembered head in the ice, you are looking at the face of Pierre Soulard, an arrogant ferryman who was unrepentant after the drowning of his passengers and was, in retribution, crushed by the ice. It is said that if you see his head you will die before winter is over. It is also said that across these waters, many years ago, could be heard the wail of a siren. Not a mythical beast like the Lorelei of the Rhine, Lauzon's siren was named La Corriveau and was the soul of a woman who had been convicted of killing her husband, and who was hanged and left to rot in a body-shaped cage that was hung over the crossroads. It is said that she lured many a man to his death. In 1850, the cage disappeared, but suddenly reappeared in the United States as an attraction of Barnum's Circus.

The Champlain monument is the creation of two French artists, Paul Chèvre and Paul le Cardonel. It was erected in 1898. Because there exists no portrait of Champlain (he drew only one picture of himself—at a distance, shooting Iroquois), the face on the bronze statue is of Paritcelli d'Emery, a supposedly unscrupulous auditor. At least one historian has called this likeness "an insult to the energetic and vigorous soldier and sailor." In any case, today there is almost always a sea gull sitting on the statue's head. On the plinth there are full-breasted angels and cherubin.

The Laval monument (2) is outside the entrance to the domed Post Office Building. To get there, walk around the north side of the building and along rue du Fort, which quickly leads you to a bronze statue of Monsignor Montmorency de Laval, the first bishop of Quebec, who looks over to the great seminary he founded.

The 1908 monument was executed by Louis-Phillipe Hébert, a

descendant of the first settler of the colony. The three panels around the base illustrate seventeenth-century life and incidents in the history of Quebec.

Above the monument, incorporated into the post office's wall, is an old stone bas-relief on which there is a sculpture of a dog eating a bone. The quatrain underneath, in gold letters, translates:

> *I am a dog who gnaws the bone.*
> *While gnawing it, I am at ease.*
> *A time will come which has not come*
> *When I'll bite the one who bit me.*

The poem was originally installed on a merchant's house that was built in 1735 and eventually replaced by the present building, and the precise meaning of the inscription is lost. Speculation continues, but the most popular explanation was proposed by William Kirby in his nineteenth-century novel, *The Golden Dog*, in which he says that the one to be bitten was François Bigot, the corrupt intendant of New France at the time of the British conquest.

BISHOP LAVAL

Monsignor François de Laval was born in 1623, ordained in 1647 and named vicar apostolic of New France in 1658. He arrived in Quebec in 1659 and immediately quarreled with Governor d'Argenson over the placing of pews in the church. Both sensitive over their relative ranks, they quarreled again over the local tradition of soldiers playing flute and drum as the host was being offered. It was not long before d'Argenson was recalled to France and Laval began to dominate the colony.

Not all Laval's quarrels with the royal administrators were petty—he unsuccessfully fought to have the brandy trade with the Amerindians banned. He failed only because the interests of local fur traders, French hat and brandy manufacturers and Caribbean sugar plantations were too powerful for him. Laval was a man of stern doctrines—he disapproved of cards, theater, dancing and even ribbons worn by women. In 1683, when a visiting nobleman was introduced to a local priest, the priest violently grabbed and tore up a novel that the baron had been carrying. For much of the time that Laval led the clergy, Governor Frontenac, a friend of Louis XIV, led the soldiers. The two men were the same age, but completely different in temperament. Frontenac was lavish, passionate, liberal, in debt and loved the adventure of the fur traders (*voyageurs*). Laval was escetic, calculating, strict, wealthy and nurtured the religion of the settlers (*habitants*). For ten years, the two men were thorns in each others' sides. Laval gained more clout in 1674 when the diocese of Quebec (which stretched from Louisiana to the Great Lakes) was created. In 1682, Frontenac was recalled, but it must have been galling for Laval to learn in 1689, one year after he had resigned his episcopal duties, that his rival had been reappointed. From a retreat at St-Joachim, a few kilometers from the capital, the old bishop witnessed many of his policies being reversed. Some say that he slept in a vermin-infested bed and ate rotting food in his zeal for self-mortification. He certainly rose before dawn and spent hours on his knees in prayer. At last, in 1708, in a fireless chapel, the feet of the old priest were badly frozen during his devotions and as a result of the shock, he sickened and died. He was beatified in 1980.

Montmorency Park (3) is the unassuming park across the street. It was once part of Canada's first farm. Champlain granted the land to Louis Hébert, a Parisian apothecary who arrived with his family in 1617. He, in turn, gave the land to his daughter, Guillemette, and her husband, Guillaume Couillard. Before she died, Guillemette sold the land to the Church and Canada's first episcopal palace was built on the site in 1692. In 1792, the building became Quebec's first legislative assembly. It was from here that Louis-Joseph Papineau challenged the autocratic rule of British governors. From 1841 to 1854, when fire destroyed it, the building shared the distinction (with one in Toronto) of being the legislature of the United Canadas. In 1859, in a newly constructed building, the framework of the British North America Act, which would make Canada a unified, internally self-governing confederation, was drafted.

The George-Etienne Cartier monument is the work of the sculptor G. H. Hill. It was erected in 1920. Cartier was one of the most important architects of the Canadian Confederation in 1867. See the section on Old Montreal for more about Cartier.

The Hébert monument was designed and executed in 1918 by Alfred Laliberté. Louis Hébert, holding his first sheath of grain, is flanked by his wife, Marie, who is reading a book to her children, and his son-in-law, Guillaume Couillard, who was the first to use a plow in Canada (1628).

BIRTHPLACE OF A NATION

Marie and Louis Hébert had ten children, adopted two Algonquins and employed, for a while, Canada's first African slave, Olivier Le Jeune, whom they had bought from the Kirke brothers, who captured Quebec in 1629. (It was returned to France in 1632.) When Guillemette Couillard, one of their daughters, died in 1684, she had 250 living descendants—a full 3 percent of the population of the whole of New France. Considering demographics and that Guillemette had brothers and sisters, I wonder if there is a French-Canadian who cannot trace his or her ancestry to this plot of land. Olivier Le Jeune, the African, went off to live with the Montagnis.

The Ramparts (4) bristle with old cannons that once were ready to defend the city. Quebec did not become a completely fortified town until the 1820s. After the second English attack failed in 1690, the French built walls, redoubts, powder magazines and batteries, but they were a rather ad hoc sort of defense. Further building was going on when Wolfe attacked in 1759, but the intendant, François Bigot, was buying shoddy materials and paying cheap contractors so that he could embezzle funds to sustain his high-flying life-style. It was not until Americans began to talk of their "manifest destiny" to possess all of North America that Governor Craig, using a huge model of the city, was able to convince the Duke of Wellington and the British government to build the Citadel and complete the wall. The construction expenses for the defense of Quebec were the highest that the British ever encountered in any of their colonies. Medieval in concept, the plans (and their costs) must have been severely criticized. As it happens, the defenses were never needed.

Le Grand Séminaire (5) was founded in 1663 by Monsignor Laval. In spite of many fires (1701, 1705, 1865, 1888), it is still a fine example of seventeenth-century architecture. Enter through the gates opposite the Hébert monument. An archway will lead you to the **Musée du Séminaire** at 9 rue de l'Université. The collection (only a part of which is on display at any given time) includes 500 European paintings, 250 works by Quebec artists, 25,000 engravings, 300 gold and silver religious objects and household articles, 1,000 old scientific instruments, 155 pieces of oriental art and thousands of coins and medals. Many of the Old Masters came to Quebec during and just after the French Revolution. I especially enjoy the religious paintings of martyrs and saints and a Dutch school series on the seven deadly sins. The scientific instruments, which were used in the nineteenth century when the teaching of natural science was based on direct experience with phenomena, are grouped according to seven areas of study: optics, astronomy, heat, mechanics, acoustics, electricity and magnetism. There is a particularly macabre Egyptian mummy on the ground floor. Open: June 24 to September 30: every day 10:30 A.M. to 5:30 P.M.; October 1 to June 23: 11 A.M. to 5 P.M. Closed Monday.

Remaining inside the complex of buildings, you will come to the courtyard of a boys' school. In times past, the boys grew hops so that they could make their own beer under the supervision of the fathers. In the interior courtyard, on the old wing (1678), the sundial dates from 1773 and must have been read by the several hundred American prisoners of war who were imprisoned there in 1775 and 1776. The large chapel (1888–90) and the **funeral chapel,** where Bishop Laval is buried, can be visited all year long. In summer, **guided tours** visit the oldest part of the seminary, including the 1678 vaults, the site of Laval's kitchen with its huge fireplace and refectory. Monsignor Briand's 1785 chapel is an architectural and sculptural gem by Pierre Emond. Open: Monday to Saturday 9:30 A.M. to 5:30 P.M.; Saturday 12 noon to 5:30 P.M.

Basilique de Notre-Dame-de-Québec (6) faces City Hall and a small square. The first cathedral was built in 1650, enlarged several times, restored in 1748, and destroyed during the British bombardment of 1759. It was entirely rebuilt from 1768 to 1771. After a fire in

1922 (supposedly set by an American who wanted to rob the church) it was again rebuilt using the plans of 1766.

The interior is pure Baroque. It was designed between 1787 and 1827 by three generations of the Baillairgé family: Jean, François and Thomas. Within the cathedral are collections of old paintings, both original and copies, and silver from the French Regime. The canopy, Episcopal throne dias, stained-glass windows and chalice lamp, a gift from Louis XIV, are worthy of note. Governors Frontenac, de Call-ières and de la Jonquière, all the bishops of Quebec, and more than 850 other people are buried here.

THE SPURNED HEART

Louis Buade, Count Frontenac, was born in 1620. Louis XIII was his godfather. By the age of twenty-eight he was a brigadier general and a popular hero. He fell in love with Anne de la Grange-Trianon, whose parents forbade a marriage. The couple eloped and lived unhappily ever after. At court, their disastrous marriage was well known. Eventually Louis XIV sent Frontenac to Quebec and the couple found that distance made their hearts grow a little fonder. She supported him at court but they were never reconciled. Before Frontenac died, he charged his friends with removing his heart and enclosing it in a little silver casket that was to be taken to his wife—a last little humble tribute. She declared that she would have nothing to do with a dead heart that had not belonged to her while it had lived. She sent it back to be buried with the rest of his body, which was interred in the Recollet Church. When this church burned down, his body and heart were moved to the Basilique.

Hôtel-de-Ville (7) is across from the cathedral. In the Château style that was popular at the turn of the century, City Hall was built in 1895 on the site of the Jesuit college that the British had turned into barracks 136 years before. In the side entrance on côte de la

Fabrique is a small interpretation center in which the city mounts temporary exhibitions on Quebec's development.

The **Taschereau Monument,** by A. Vermare, is in the center of place de l'Hôtel-de-Ville. Monsignor E.-A. Taschereau was born in 1820. He was minister to the Irish typhoid victims during their 1847 quarantine on Grosse-Île (Canada's Ellis Island), was one of the founders of Laval University and became Canada's first cardinal in 1886. Some historians claim that his elevation was a direct result of London's pressure on the Vatican after the rebellion of Louis Riel in Manitoba had catalyzed French-Canadian nationalism after a fifty-year period of relative dormancy.

On rue Ste-Anne is a 1929 Art Deco skyscraper, the **Price Building.** Next door is the **Clarendon Hotel,** which has a wonderful Art Deco lobby and a perfectly preserved late-Victorian dining room. If your wallet is fat enough and you feel dignified enough, go in for lunch.

St. Andrew's Presbyterian Church (8), Quebec's kirk, is down and around the elbow of rue Ste-Anne (turning behind and away from City Hall). After the British conquest, many Scottish soldiers (and, later, businessmen) settled in Quebec. In fact, after the arrival of the Irish immigrants, by 1850 more than 40 percent of the population of Quebec was English-speaking. The Scots built their church, St. Andrew's, in 1809. Governor Dalhousie worshiped there. The building on the corner of St-Stanislas was Quebec's jail from 1810 to 1860, when the Presbyterians bought it to turn it into a college. Open: July and August, Monday through Friday 10 A.M. to 4:30 P.M.

Holy Trinity Cathedral (9) is on rue des Jardins, back up rue Ste-Anne. For thirty-seven years after the conquest, the Recollets shared their church on this site with the Anglicans. At ten-thirty the English drums would roll out a warning to prepare for service as soon as the Recollets were through with their mass. When Quebec was given an Anglican see and Bishop Mountain was appointed, they still had no church of their own; and when, in 1796, the Recollets' church burned to the ground, they were forced to use the old Jesuit chapel in what was then the military barracks.

The cathedral was completed in 1804. The Paladian style resembles that of London's St-Martin-in-the-Fields because George III, who paid for most of its construction, decided that it should be a copy of his favorite church. His request was not entirely fulfilled because the heavy snows of Quebec required that the pitch of the roof be steeper than that of the original.

The **interior** also owes much to George III. From the royal forest at Windsor, he sent the oak to make the pews. He also sent an altar facing that had been used at his coronation at Westminster, and ten pieces of valuable silver, all of which are still in the possession of the church. As a result of his patronage, on the balcony to the left there is a royal pew. Although William IV, Edward VII, George V and Edward VIII all visited Quebec as princes, the pew has never been used by a reigning monarch. George VI, who worshiped there in 1939, refused the honor by saying that he had come to pray, not to be stared at. Elizabeth II was saved the embarrassment; when the bishop invited Prince Philip to address the congregation it was deemed too awkward for him to have to descend from and return to the royal pew.

The bishop's throne (to the right of the chancel) is built out of an old elm tree that grew in the northeast corner of the close. Tradition has it that Champlain used to sit under this tree and smoke a pipe with his Montagnis and Huron allies. It was felled by a storm in 1846.

Three people are buried in the church: Jacob Mountain, first Anglican bishop of Quebec, who died in 1825; an anonymous child, whose body is thought to have been smuggled in by a workman when preparations were being made to bury the bishop; and the Duke of Richmond, who died in 1819 after having been bitten by a rabid pet fox.

A FAMILY MAN

The Duke of Richmond, a friend and fellow officer of the Duke of Wellington, was one of the most popular and genial fellows of his day. In Brussels, it was his duchess who gave the great ball on the eve of Waterloo, when, according to Byron, "bright eyes looked love to eyes that spake again," and "all went merry as a wedding bell" until the boom of distant guns called away the English officers to "the dance of death."

A family man, the duke brought six of his fourteen children to Quebec and arranged that his son-in-law, Sir Peregrine Maitland, be appointed lieutenant-governor of Upper Canada. His daughter Sarah had forced her parents to accept her marriage to Maitland by spending the night in his rooms and purposefully being discovered there in the morning. Three Ontario counties are named after her lap dogs.

The building at the corner of **rue des Jardins** and **rue Donnacona** is thought to be the narrowest in North America.

The Ursuline convent and museum (10) are on rue Donnacona, which is named after the Amerindian chief who died in France after Jacques Cartier had introduced him to the court of Francis I as the king of Canada. The Ursulines are a teaching order. Today their school in Quebec, with a student body of close to eight hundred, is one of the most famous in North America.

The **museum** is housed in an 1836 house that was built with the wood and stone of a building that had been first erected in 1644. The museum exhibits a collection of furniture, domestic tools, teaching aids, musical instruments, embroideries and religious objects that the nuns have preserved from the French Regime. The silk embroideries for which the Ursulines are justly famous are magnificent. Among the curiosities on display are one of the wooden boxes the nuns used to sleep in and General Montcalm's skull. In its own large carved reliquary is a sliver of wood that was once believed to have come from the true cross—it was authenticated in 1678 as coming from the Royal Treasury of England. Open: January 3 to November 24: Tuesday through Saturday 9:30 A.M. to 12 noon and 1:30 to 4:45 P.M.; Sunday 12:30 to 5:15 P.M. Guided tours on request.

The **Ursuline Chapel**'s building dates back only to 1902, but its interior is the work of sculptor Pierre-Noel Levasseur, and was created between 1726 and 1736. The gilding, wealth of ornament and hand-carved wooden statues are typical of the best of seventeenth- and eighteenth-century church decorations. Also note the altar screen, the pulpit with its trumpet-bearing angel and the tomb of Marie de l'Incarnation. Open: May through October: Tuesday through Saturday 9:30 A.M. to 12 noon and 1:30 to 4:45 P.M.; Sunday 12:30 to 5:15 P.M.

TWO DEAD GENERALS

After the Battle of the Plains of Abraham in 1759, the body of the Marquis de Montcalm was brought to the Ursuline chapel for burial. Debris covered the floor and shell holes gaped in the roof. Into the north wall, where a cannon ball had embedded itself, they thrust the dead commander and filled in the hole. A few days later, the British took over the city and Murray became governor. Across the river, the body of General Wolfe, who had been killed at almost the same moment Montcalm had been wounded, was waiting for the ship that was to carry him back to an English grave. In a strange twist of fate, his memorial service was held here, where Montcalm was buried.

At 10 rue Donnacona, behind a door on which is simply written "Bienvenue," is the Centre Marie-de-l'Incarnation, where a nun will personally welcome you to examine objects belonging to the reverend mother and tell you the story of the Ursulines. The love they have for their founder shines brightly! Open: Tuesday through Saturday 10 to 11:30 A.M. and 2 to 4:30 P.M.; Sunday 2 to 4:30 P.M.

TWO GREAT FRIENDS

Marie de l'Incarnation was born in Tours in 1599. In a dream at age seven, she gave herself to Christ, but to satisfy her father she got married. The marriage was brief and unhappy. She gave birth to a son and was widowed at age twenty. Soon after, she collapsed in the street and had a vision of being immersed in the blood that Christ was shedding for her sins. Again to satisfy her family, she pretended to marry another man; when her father died she revealed the deception. A talented businesswoman who managed the extensive affairs of her brother-in-law, she never gave up her desire to become a nun. In 1625 she had a five-hour-long vision during which she witnessed the workings of the Blessed Trinity in the nine Choirs of Angels and understood how the human soul is created to the image of God. She entered the Ursuline convent in Tours in 1631 and despite the passionate pleadings of her young son, who screamed "Give me back my mother!" outside the doors, she became a nun in 1633.

Two years later, she had a vision of meeting a young woman whom she took by the hand and with whom she traveled over land and then sea. They arrived in a vast, mountainous and mist-filled land, where they found a little church on which there was a marble statue of the Virgin Mary. The statue came to life, Marie de l'Incarnation stretched out her arms and the Mother of God kissed and caressed her three times. When she told her confessor about the dream, he told her that she would go to Canada. Two years later, a young, rich, childless widow, whom Marie recognized as the woman in the dream, arrived at the convent.

That rich widow, Madame de la Peltrie, had decided to use her fortune to educate the Amerindians. On August 1, 1639, she, Marie de l'Incarnation and five Ursuline nuns kissed the soil of Quebec. By coincidence, they arrived at the same time as three Augustinian nuns whom the Duchess of Aiguillon, niece of Cardinal Richelieu, had sent to found a hospital. That night, to celebrate the news that an heir to the throne had been born, the colonists, who numbered about two hundred, put on a fireworks display that totally astounded the natives.

The Ursulines built a two-room cloistered convent by the river. Madame de la Peltrie, who loved the "candor and simplicity" of the Amerindians, and her lady-in-waiting lived in an adjacent cabin to which their manservant's quarters were added. The winter was harsh; the lumber from France had not been seasoned, and gaps appeared in the walls and roof. To add to the hardship, the expedition had brought with it smallpox, which quickly became an epidemic among the Algonquins. The dedicated nuns ministered to the sick, but they could not save them all. Madame de la Peltrie adopted the orphans and gave them to the charge of the Ursulines. The school had been founded.

Because of Iroquois attacks it was decided to move the convent up to its present site. Plans were under way when Jeanne Mance arrived in 1651 with a mandate to build a hospital in a new colony, Ville-Marie (now Montreal), deep in Iroquois-controlled territory. Madame de la Peltrie took a great liking to Jeanne Mance and decided to take her household and all her furniture upriver. The Ursulines felt abandoned, and the convent and school were saved only by an unexpected donation from Queen Anne. After eighteen months, however, Madame de la Peltrie returned and built a house beside the convent. As the colony grew, so did the convent. Even the fire of 1650, which destroyed the first building, did not stop its growth. The nuns crowded into Madame de la Peltrie's house, and two years later a new building, which still stands, was completed.

For another twenty years Madame de la Peltrie and Marie de l'Incarnation worked together. In November 1671, the great benefactress fell ill and died; by May the next year, the mystic nun and teacher had followed her to the grave. They had been together for thirty-two years. Marie de l'Incarnation was beatified in 1980—and as one charming nun, her hands clasped together, told me: "We are lacking only one miracle for her to become a saint. We pray!"

WALKING TOUR TWO: THE LOWER TOWN

Introduction

Since Champlain first built his fort in 1620, Quebec has been divided into an Upper Town and Lower Town, with the governmental and ecclesiastical residences and offices above the commercial center below. In the seventeenth and eighteenth centuries, the fur trade and the port, where goods were unloaded to be carried upriver in smaller boats, dominated, and the merchants built themselves "lovely three-storey houses, in stone as hard as marble." Many of these buildings were destroyed by the British bombardment in 1759 but were soon rebuilt.

In the mid-nineteenth century, the merchants began to build houses in the Upper Town. Gradually the Lower Town deteriorated, and it was not until the tourist trade began in the 1950s and 1960s that this oldest part of the city began to prosper once again. In the 1970s, it was a lively convivial night spot, but today, because of restoration and renovation projects, parts of it, especially around Place Royale, have begun to resemble a beautiful and well-kept museum that preserves the old French patrimony.

* * *

As you descend the stairs that lead from **Dufferin Terrace** (1) (on the near side of the old domed post office), you come to a fair-sized shop that sells original Eskimo and Amerindian art. Porte Prescott was rebuilt in 1983 to replace the gate that was demolished in 1871. Continuing down the steps, you come to côte de la Montagne, which was once just the pathway that led from Champlain's *habitation*, past Louis Hébert's farm, to the fort. The large wooden cross on the other side of the street marks the site of Quebec's first cemetery, where Champlain's companions were buried during that terrible first winter of 1608–1609. Champlain is thought to have been buried in a chapel nearby.

Break-Neck Stairs (Escalier Casse-cou) (11) can be treacherous when covered with ice. Horses, cattle and sheep have been prohibited from climbing the stairs since February 22, 1698. They lead down past several levels of restaurants with patios. The first house at the bottom of the stairs was built in 1683 for Louis Jolliet, the discoverer of the Mississippi River. Renovated in 1977, it is now the entrance to the funicular that carries you up the cliff to Dufferin Terrace. First powered by steam, the funicular has been in operation, although twice rebuilt, since 1879.

Petit-Champlain (12) is a lively pedestrian street that claims to be the oldest shopping area in North America. The ground floor of the renovated and restored three-story buildings of the neighborhood house restaurants and over forty boutiques of artisans who sell original clothes, jewelry, decorative art and gifts.

An association of residents and store owners is very conscious of keeping the street attractive and full of fun. Clowns, magicians and musicians often perform during the day. At the end of the short street, where Petit-Champlain runs into boulevard Champlain, you can rent a scooter or a bicycle. The lighthouse outside the Coast Guard's docks and building has recently been brought to Quebec to remind people of the city's maritime heritage.

Boulevard Champlain runs beside the port. Amyot House, at number 24, houses a small but interesting museum of contemporary art. Open: Thursday and Friday 12 noon to 6 P.M.; Friday and Saturday 12 noon to 8:30 P.M.

The least expensive way to see Quebec from the river is to take the fifteen-minute ride on the car ferry to Lévis. Inaugurated in 1881, this crossing was once powered by two or three horses at work around a capstan that turned paddle wheels.

The *Louis Jolliet* leaves from a dock a little farther along. The largest excursion boat in Canada, it offers one-hour cruises to Lauzon at 10 A.M., a one-and-a-half-hour cruise to Montmorency Falls and île d'Orleans at 2 P.M. In the evening, musical cruises leave at 10 P.M. Sunday through Thursday and 10:30 P.M. Friday and Saturday. Reservations are not necessary.

Maison Chevalier, 50 boulevard Champlain, was built in 1752. The U-shaped building was converted into an inn, the London Coffee House, after the British conquest. Bought in 1966 by the Quebec government, it now houses a museum of domestic life, which traces not only the development of Quebec's unique, rustic-style furniture from Louis XIV and Georgian progenitors, but also the development of chests, armoires, commodes and glass-fronted furniture. It is well worth a visit. Open: every day 10 A.M. to 5 P.M.

When you turn into rue Notre-Dame and quickly right onto Sous le Fort ("Under the Fort"), you will come to Batterie Royale, which was built on the waterfront by Frontenac immediately following Sir William Phips's attack of 1690. Compare this primitive defense to the Citadel, which was built 130 years later up on Cap Diamant. Repeated landfill projects have moved the river away from the battery of cannons.

Quartier Place-Royale (13) has been lovingly restored. The cobblestone streets have been rebuilt, as have the mansard-roofed buildings. At 25 rue St-Pierre, the interpretation center, "Place Royale, 400 Years of History" is divided into six sections: "The Amerindians, the Founding of Quebec, Quebec City—a Strategic Site, Quebec Architecture, Wars in Quebec, and Population and Growth." The vaulted cellars date from 1735. Be sure that you pick up an English translation of the exhibits at the door, or ask to be given a guided tour. Open: mid-May to mid-September: every day 10 A.M. to 6 P.M.

FROM CONVICTS TO TOURISTS

By 1660, Champlain's *habitation* had been demolished (the outline of the foundations is marked) and Place-Royale had become Quebec's first market and public execution square. Quebec's first public executioner was a town crier of Montreal who, in 1648, had been convicted of engaging in "unnatural acts." During the strict reign of Bishop Laval, when the priests controlled the citizens and excommunication was frequently threatened, there seems to have been little need for other forms of punishment, for in 1680, when a man named Rathier was condemned to death for the murder of a young girl, his sentence was commuted on the condition that he become the officer for public discipline. Some years later, his wife and daughter were convicted of theft and he was forced to flog them in Place-Royale.

When the original, old, single-floored buildings were destroyed by a fire in 1682 and replaced by bigger stone ones, the square took on the aspect that it still maintains today. The roofs and interiors of the buildings were totally destroyed during Wolfe's siege, but many of the old walls still stood, ready for rebuilding. It was probably partially a result of the cholera epidemic of 1832, when Place-Royale was the scene of dead corpses and dying victims, that the last of the rich merchants moved to the Upper Town. It then became a center for prostitutes who worked the British soldiers and sailors.

The square economically stagnated for more than a hundred years, and it was not until the tourists began to arrive in the 1950s and 1960s that interest was rekindled. In the last twenty years, almost all the buildings have been renovated and restored. It is partially because this square escaped late-nineteenth- and early-twentieth-century development that the city of Quebec has been classified a World Heritage Site by the United Nations.

A bust of Louis XIV is in the center of Place-Royale. The first bust of the Sun King, who put New France under his direct supervision and paid for thousands of upright young women to emigrate to the mostly male-populated colony, was erected here in 1686. However, it was removed three years later because it interfered with traffic! The original bust was lost, but in 1928 France gave Quebec this second one (a duplicate of a work by Bervini). It was erected in 1931, but because of the protests of taxi drivers, it too was removed. It was not until 1948 (252 years after the original was installed) that the Sun King was permanently returned to his place of honor.

Notre-Dame-des-Victoires (Our Lady of the Victories) was built in 1688. The land for this church was granted by Louis XIV after Bishop Laval had written to explain that the harsh winter climate "made it difficult to bring the Sacred Host to the sick in the Lower Town," and that old people, children and the crippled "could not proceed to the Upper Town to attend Mass." It was first dedicated to the Infant Jesus, but two years later, while Phips was maintaining his five-day siege with firepower from thirty-four vessels, the Upper Town ladies, including Ursuline nuns, prayed to the Blessed Virgin and vowed to make a pilgrimage to the Lower Town church "to obtain their liberation." When Phips abandoned his attempt and prisoners of war (including Louis Jolliet, his wife and mother-in-law, whose small boat had been captured) were traded, it was considered a miracle, the pilgrimage was made and the church's name was changed to Notre-Dame-de-la-Victoire. When, in 1711, a second English fleet (this time with ninety-eight ships and twelve thousand men, who were to join two thousand more who had come up the Hudson River) floundered in storms, it was also considered a miracle, because Jeanne Le Ber, the hermit embroiderer of Montreal, had broken her silence and written a prayer to the Virgin. The name of the church was changed yet again—this time to Notre-Dame-des-Victoires.

Above the high altar, two frescoes, depicting the two victories, are on either side of Our Lady, who stands on the "impregnable Tower of David." The small chapel to the left is dedicated to Ste-Geneviève, patron saint of Paris. The large Old Masters hanging on the walls are old copies of paintings by Van Loo, Rubens, Boyermans and Wolfe. The model sailing ship that hangs from the ceiling is a miniature of *Breze*, which brought Quebec's first royal regiment to fight the Iroquois in 1664.

Place de Paris is down the short flight of stairs from rue St-Pierre. The open area received its name when Jean-Pierre Renaud's very intellectual, twenty-foot-tall, enamel-white, cubed *Dialogue with History* was erected on a design in the pavement. The sculpture was given to Quebec by the city of Paris in 1987. I heard one tourist guide say to some Americans, "The French gave you the Statue of Liberty; they gave us that!" In the summer, this square is also a performance center for a variety of small acts that can range anywhere from a troop of twelve miniature dogs to a one-man puppeteer whose stage and box are mounted on a moving tricycle. The information center provides guides to the area, will tell you the schedule of performances, has a model of Champlain's second *habitation* (the one that he did not see completed) and mounts a small exhibition outlining French-Canadian influences in California, Florida, New England and Manitoba. Open: mid-May to mid-September: every day 10 A.M. to 6 P.M.

Returning to rue St-Pierre, there is, to the right, a park for children that is designed to encourage historical and maritime fantasy play.

Le Musée de la civilisation (14) is a cultural museum that was designed in 1984 by the Montreal architect Moshe Safdie. This architecturally brilliant building settles into the neighborhood and brings, with its simple tower and copper roofs, a unity with the Upper Town. It also incorporates, without destroying them, two 1752 buildings on rue St-Pierre. On display inside are the old stone quays that were built before the landfill operations moved the river to where it now flows. In a pool with cascades in front of the quays is Astri Reusch's mammoth and powerful 1983 sculpture *La Débâcle*, which represents the movement of breaking ice on the river in spring.

The permanent multimedia exhibition, *Memoires*, which declares that "a nation without a memory is a nation without a future," draws on imagination, myth and history to stimulate the national consciousness of the Québecois. It is an extremely good exhibit, but can make the province's English-speaking minority groups feel marginalized. Visitors who do not speak French should ask for the translated "narrative" and examine it before entering—the interior lighting is not good for reading. The other galleries are dedicated to temporary exhibitions. There is a cafeteria in the basement. Open: June 24 through September 7: every day 10 A.M. to 7 P.M.; September 7 through June 24: Tuesday to Sunday 10 A.M. to 5 P.M. Free admission on all Tuesdays.

The Old Port (15) was completely redesigned as a park and marina to celebrate the 450th anniversary of Jacques Cartier's arrival in Quebec. Three old buildings, including the 1856 Customs House, have been preserved, but the new structures, which were to have housed boutiques and restaurants, have not been successful. Only the 6,000-seat amphitheater, l'Agora, which brings a wide range of entertainers to perform under the stars, lives up to its promise. Nonetheless, it's a pleasant walk along the river, and there is a splendid, multilevel wading pool and cascade for young children.

Croisière le Coudrière offers sightseeing cruises on the river at

10 A.M. and 1, 3, 4:30, 6, 7:30 and 9 P.M. **Croisière sur le St-André** (reservations: 659-4804) offers a one-hour cruise at 10 A.M., a one-and-a-half-hour cruise and a two-and-a-half-hour cruise at 10 P.M. **Les Croisières d'Anty** (reservations: 659-5489) offers six-hour cruises with buffet in a forty-nine-passenger powerboat.

The Louise Basin is a marina where **Vieux Port Yachting** offers three-hour cruises (departure: 1 P.M.) and sailing instructions in its yachts. It also rents boats for days, weekends and weeks, and offers guided two-day, five-day, one-week and two-week cruises down the St. Lawrence River and up the Saguenay River. Reservations: 692-0017; fax: 692-3728.

The Interpretation Center of the Old Port is a modern museum that exhibits artifacts and explains the industries, such as shipping, logging and shipbuilding, that have been the historical pulse of the port. Open: May 9 to June 23: Tuesday to Friday 9 A.M. to noon and 1 to 4 P.M., Saturday and Sunday 11 A.M. to 6 P.M.; June 24 to August 28: Monday 1 to 6 P.M., Tuesday to Sunday 11 A.M. to 6 P.M.

Rue St-Paul (16) is across the parking lot in front of the Interpretation Center. Walk back the way you have come, past the antiques shops and galleries. This area became a center of shoe manufacturing after the port went into decline, and Montreal benefited from the arrival of steamships and the dredged St. Lawrence River. In 1878, 1.3 million pairs of shoes were produced, but by the 1920s this industry was in decline and many residents sank into poverty, their children begging on the streets.

Rue Sault-au-Matelot (17) is a narrow old street. There are three stories as to why it is named Sailor's Leap. One says that Champlain's dog, Matelot, leaped off the cliff above; a second says that a drunken sailor crashed to his death here; and a third says that, before the landfill, sailors would leap from their ships to the docks to tie the hawsers. Whether or not dogs or sailors ever leapt or came flying down, it is certainly true that snow avalanches would fall into the street. In 1837, a biscuit salesman was killed after the noon salute of the guns in the Citadel set off such a slide.

At the corner of rue St-Jacques, Benedict Arnold was wounded when American invaders attempted to take Quebec in 1775. They threatened the city all winter, but the citizens built a wooden horse on the cliffs above and swore that they would only surrender when it began eating hay. When spring came, bringing with it British ships, the Americans retreated.

Sault-au-Matelot leads to Notre-Dame and Place-Royale, and finally to the funicular, which will take you back to Dufferin Terrace.

WALKING TOUR THREE: THE UPPER TOWN— MOSTLY SOLDIERS

The Château Frontenac (18) is probably Canada's most famous building. It was designed by the American architect Bruce Price in 1892 and was enlarged in 1924, when the central tower was added. In August 1943, and again in September 1944, FDR and Winston Churchill, both of whom were housed in the Citadel, came here to discuss war against Germany and Japan. The lobby of the old hotel is worth a visit, and there is no better place to have a drink than in the first-floor bar, which offers a splendid view of the river.

The Château Frontenac is built on the site of Château Haldimand, which was the residence of the British governor from 1784 to 1860. Frederick Haldimand, a native of Switzerland who spoke French better than English, marched with General Amherst against Montreal in 1760 and negotiated with the French for that city's terms of surrender. He was the British governor of Quebec from 1778 to 1786.

Place d'Armes (19) is the square across from the hotel. For 160 years it was Quebec's military parade ground. In 1665, the Marquis de Tracy, surrounded by royal guards, arrived with the famous Carignan regiment, numerous valets and pages, and an unprecedented twelve horses. He had been sent by Louis XIV to finally destroy the Iroquois menace for good.

With the construction of the Citadel in the 1820s, the army moved its displays of discipline and firepower to Parc de l'Esplanade, and Place d'Armes became the promenade for the wealthy, powerful and beautiful. In the 1880s, a column with a statue of a child, who held a fish that spouted water, was built in a basin surrounded by a chain fence. On Sunday, after the masses and services in the two cathedrals and the Scottish church, it was a matter of pride to be seen in your best clothes making *Le Rond des Chaînes.*

The present monument, Gaston Vennat's *Monument de la Foi* ("Monument to Faith"), was erected in 1915 in memory of the Recollets, who established Quebec's first religious community three hundred years before.

Rue St-Louis (20) was named after Louis XIV. It, and its extension outside the gates—Grande Allée—have always had the most prestigious addresses in the city. It was along this street that Governor Montmagny paraded the first horse to arrive in the colony. Horatio Nelson walked the street often in 1782—the future hero of the Battle of Trafalgar came to Quebec on a tour of duty and fell in love with a Miss Simpson, whose parents lived on Grande Allée. If it had not been for a friend named Davidson, he would have jumped ship for her. He vowed to return, but never did—he met Lady Hamilton in Naples and cuckolded her husband, who was more interested in Roman antiquities than his wife. Curiously, years later, two of his distant relations, Wilfred and Robert Nelson, became leaders in the Lower Canada Rebellions of 1837 and 1838. Robert went on to find and lose a fortune in gold in California, and Wilfred became a mayor of Montreal.

Maison Maillou, at 17 rue St-Louis, was built in 1736. The metal shutters hark back to a time when the night air was considered to spread disease. In the 1830s, the house was used as a treasury that could hold 100,000 pounds sterling—enough to pay the entire civil service for about five years!

The Duke of Kent's House, at 25 rue St-Louis, is one of the oldest in Quebec. Built in 1650, it was here that Ramezay signed the 1759 capitulation of the city to General Murray, General Wolfe's successor. It has gone through several transformations but attained its present size by 1791, when Prince Edward, Duke of Kent, the father of Queen Victoria, occupied it.

Jacob Mountain, the first Anglican bishop of Quebec, was another resident of Kent House. He hoped to assimilate the French when he offered free English-language schools to every parish in the colony. It is probable that he had learned of the effectiveness of education as a tool of assimilation from the establishment of English schools in Gaelic Scotland. The French priests of Quebec, because of a fear of Protestantism, refused his offer.

ROYAL RESIDENTS OF QUEBEC CITY

The Duke of Kent's three-year residence in Quebec is thought to have been the happiest period of his life. The year before he arrived, he had met the Baronne de St-Laurent, a refugee from the French Revolution and a descendant of the ancient Dukes of Normandy. They lived together for twenty-eight years until, in 1818, it seemed clear that the duke's two older brothers, George IV and Prince William Henry, later William IV, would die without legitimate issue (William had ten illegitimate children by an actress, Mrs. Jordan). As a result, Edward married a Protestant German princess, Victoria's mother, and Madame de St-Laurent retired to a convent in Smyrne.

During his stay in Quebec, the Duke of Kent befriended Charles Michel de Salaberry, who traveled the world as he rose through the ranks of the British army. He is most famous for defeating the Americans at Chateauguay, south of Montreal, during the War of 1812.

The Duke of Kent's brother William Henry also visited Quebec. When he arrived in 1787, he was honored with a ball at Château Haldimand. The guests, out of respect for his royal blood, were afraid to sit down—they stood for seven hours.

The *habitants* of Quebec were not as fearful. There is a story that says that once, when William Henry was on an exploratory mission on the heights of Lévis, across the river, he knocked on the door of a small cottage and asked for food. "I hope you're not like the other British soldiers, who left without paying," said the woman. "Have no fear," said the prince, and after eating, he handed her a gold coin. "So you're just like the others. You don't expect me to have change for that?" "Madame, you're talking to the prince," said one of the soldiers. "Even if you are the prince, I have to tell you what I think," she said. William Henry let her keep the gold.

Maison Jacquet, at the corner of St-Louis and des Jardins, is made up of two buildings. The one on the corner dates from 1677 and for many years was thought to be where General Montcalm died after being wounded in the Battle of the Plains of Abraham in 1759.

Joseph Bouchette lived at 44 rue St-Louis. He was surveyor-general and a colonel in the Canadian militia in the 1840s. It was his father who led the expedition that rescued Governor Carleton (later Lord Dorchester) from the American troops in Montreal in 1775.

A historic cannonball from 1759 is trapped in the roots of a tree between numbers 59 and 55 rue St-Louis. **Maison Pean,** at number 59, takes its name from a friend of the corrupt intendant, François Bigot. Pean and his wife (Quebec's most infamous "scarlet woman," who was reputed to have had many lovers, including Bigot) amassed a fortune and retired to France after the British conquest. Bigot also returned to France, but he was tried for misuse of funds, lost all his possessions and was banished from France for life.

The General's House, at 72 rue St-Louis, is named after Richard Montgomery, the American general whose body was brought to the building on this site after his death in 1775. He was buried near the St-Louis Gate, but his body was returned to the United States in 1818.

Up rue Ste-Ursule are two Neo-Gothic churches. The **Chalmers-Wesley United Church** was built in 1852 and, because of its stained-glass windows, woodwork and century-old organ, is considered one of the most beautiful in the city. Open: June 25 to August 18: Tuesday through Saturday 9:30 A.M. to 5:30 P.M. Opposite is the **Sanctuare Notre-Dame-du-Sacre-Coeur,** which was built in 1910 under the direction of François-Xavier Berlinguet. This sanctuary is also noted for its stained-glass windows. Open: daily 7 A.M. to 8 P.M.

Maison Cureux, at 86 rue St-Louis, dates from 1729. The old sloping roof with its dormer windows was replaced by the present mansard roof in 1890.

Maison Sewell, at 87 rue St-Louis, was built for Massachusetts-born Chief Justice Jonathan Sewell. The building, with its pediments, large windows and monumental sobriety, is a good example of English Palladian architecture. It was later used as a cavalry school, a council chamber for the government and a residence for army officers. The Garrison Club next door was founded in 1819 and is the oldest military club in Canada.

CHIEF JUSTICE SEWELL

Jonathan Sewell was a friend of Bishop Mountain and a powerful member of the Château Clique, a tight-knit group of business and Anglican church leaders that controlled Quebec in the early 1800s. He raised twenty-two children and rejoiced in an annual stipend of $12,688, when the colony's total budget for education was only five times greater. One of the most hated men to have ever lived in Quebec, he actively worked for the assimilation of the French and believed that Catholicism "debased the human mind." He was the bane of the liberal-minded governors Kempt and Aylmer, who were appointed by London to conciliate the interracial tensions. When the colony erupted in revolt in 1837, it was, in large part, because of Sewell's stranglehold on the government.

Monument aux Braves de la Guerre des Boers was erected in 1905. The Boer War was to galvanize French-Canadian political thought against the African imperialism of Europeans and focus Quebec's nationalism. Some people identified with the Boers (a colonizing people who were conquered by the British), but more important, their protest against involvement in "foreign" wars has led to Canada's role as a peacekeeping force for the United Nations.

Porte St-Louis (21) dates from 1878. It was designed by W. H. Lynn according to the plans of Charles Baillargé and replaced the 1693 gate through which General Montcalm rode, bleeding from his wounds and still striving to speak comfort to the frightened citizens who were preparing to accept the conquering British soldiers into the city. The old gate was demolished and reconstructed several times before the present structure was built.

The grounds between the walls and rue d'Auteuil were first a pasture and then, after the building of the Citadel, a military exercise ground. **The powderhouse** (at 1810) houses an interpretation center where the history of the building of the fortifications is recalled. Guided tours of the fortifications are offered. Open: May

14 to September 30: Monday 1 to 5 P.M., Tuesday through Sunday 10 A.M. to 5 P.M.

THE WALLS OF QUEBEC CITY

The building of the walls that surround Old Quebec began in 1690, but they were not very strong or secure until the 1820s, when Sir James Craig convinced the British to spend $37 million to fortify the city against possible American attack. When the British withdrew their garrison in 1870, the fortifications were handed over to Canada and the citizens of Quebec began using stone from the walls to build their own houses. The governor-general, Lord Dufferin, was dismayed and launched a series of projects to save and beautify the city. He not only rescued the walls and had two gates rebuilt, he was responsible for the construction of the boardwalk in front of the Château Frontenac.

Behind the powderhouse is an elbow-shaped postern, or small gate, that allowed defenders to gain entrance to the city without being open to enemy fire. Opposite it (at the corner of rue d'Auteuil and rue des Ursulines) is the old home of Quebec's Anglican bishops. Considered to be one of the most beautiful buildings in the city, this 1872 house has nineteen rooms, including a ballroom, and fifteen fireplaces, each made out of a different kind of marble. The staircase and mahogany and oak paneling are magnificent.

The Tourist Information Centre (22) is at 60 rue d'Auteuil. The small totem pole is by the British Columbian sculptor Mungo Martin. The statue is of Bonhomme Carnaval, the talking snowman of Quebec's Winter Carnival. A parking area for *calèche* drivers is adjacent for those who want a pampered tour of the city.

Porte Kent (23) was built in 1880. When Lord Dufferin was searching for money to restore the city's gates, Queen Victoria, in large part, paid for its construction. It is named in honor of her father, the Duke of Kent.

Chapelle des Jesuites has its entrance at 14 rue Dauphine. Originally built in 1818 for a lay order of men that had a special devotion to the Virgin, it was taken over by the Jesuits after their return to Quebec in 1850. Since 1925 the chapel has housed the devotional sanctuary of the Saints Martyrs Canadiens, which honors Fathers Brébeuf and Lallement, two Jesuits who were tortured and killed by the Iroquois. Beside the chapel of Brébeuf is a silver bust of the missionary and, beneath it, one half of his skull.

Next door is **Maison Loyola,** which was built in 1822 and became the Jesuits' chapel in 1904. It now houses a nightclub that presents a variety of rhythm and blues, rock and folk acts that star local, national and international talent.

THE JESUITS IN QUEBEC

The Society of Jesus (the Jesuits) was founded in 1534 by Ignatius Loyola and quickly grew in power as it led the Counterreformation in Europe. By 1610, there were twelve thousand members, organized into provinces that stretched as far from Europe as Brazil and India. Under Cardinal Bellarmine, they schemed, operated spy networks, and were accused of assassinations. Through their writings and fervent desire to "save the savages," they inspired much of the earliest colonization of Canada. Madame de la Peltrie, Marie de l'Incarnation, Jeanne Mance and Marguerite Bourgeoys were all deeply influenced by their Spartan heroism. Abraham Martin, after whom the Plains of Abraham are named, is thought to have been one of their secret agents. He is said to have operated under the code name The Scot and to have fled Europe because of his subversive activities in France, England and Scotland.

At the time of the British conquest of Quebec, the Jesuits owned one eighth of all the property in New France. Even in Europe they were considered to be too powerful—in 1773 the order was disbanded by the Pope. The revenue from the Jesuit estates in Quebec was used by the British to support local education. The order's religious relics were distributed. The skull and original silver bust of Father Brébeuf went to the nuns of the Hôtel-Dieu hospital.

The Jesuits were allowed to reorganize in 1814. They returned to

Quebec in 1850, but were not given back their estates. When they asked the Hôtel-Dieu for the relics, the nuns were reluctant to part with them. As a compromise, a duplicate bust was made and Brébeuf's skull was divided in two. The Jesuits did not receive any compensation for their land until 1889.

Porte St-Jean (24) was built in 1939 to replace one that had been torn down in 1898 to let in tramcars. It, in turn, had been built in 1867 to replace the original of 1720.

Artillery Park (25) overlooks the plateau to the west of the city. In the 1970s, the federal government began a program of restoration and has created an important park that describes both military and manufacturing activities of the area. Between the buildings are grassy areas, where a puppet theater and numerous other activities are staged. Open: May 9 to October 31: Monday 1 to 5 P.M., Tuesday through Sunday 10 A.M. to 5 P.M.

The Interpretation Centre is housed in a converted foundry and workshops that were built over a military parade ground between 1903 and 1908. Of special interest in the foundry is a huge scale model of Quebec City in 1808. It was built by two men, By and Duberger, and was sent to England by Governor Craig to convince the Duke of Wellington, and others, of the need for stronger fortifications.

The rest of the park is across rue McMahon. **The Dauphine Redoubt** houses a "labyrinth," which depicts everyday life in the early eighteenth century. In the officers' quarters, children (and adults) can dress up in seventeenth-century uniforms to be guided back to the past through games and disguise.

THE HISTORY OF ARTILLERY PARK

When Admiral Phips attacked Quebec in 1690, the area was defended only by the Bourreau Redoubt, a masonry structure that was integrated into the earthen walls of 1693 and 1697. Plans to build five towers were drawn up, but problems in construction slowed progress. By 1712 only the Dauphine Redoubt was in place, and it was not completed until 1745, when it became the barracks for the Troupes Franches de la Marine and a detachment of Swiss mercenaries. Behind it, Les Nouvelles Casernes ("The New Barracks") were built against the fortifications between 1749 and 1754 by Chaussegros de Léry. The 525-foot-long building contained armories, stockrooms, a guardroom and six prison cells.

The British maintained the military purpose of the area and added a powder magazine, a shed for gun carriages, storehouses, stables, workshops, latrines and a pumping station. In 1879, however, the Canadian government turned the barracks into a cartridge factory, the Dauphine Redoubt serving as the director's residence. During both world wars, thousands of women manufactured ammunition there for the Allied armies.

When the factories closed in 1964, the federal government sold the barracks to the Hôtel-Dieu Hospital for $1. They are used as a staff parking garage. Since the area has been turned into a park and all the other buildings have been restored, the government regrets the sale, but the hospital will not give the building back.

The Irish Quarter (26) used to lie on the other side of rue McMahon from the park. From 1830 to 1870, the Irish were fully 20 percent of the population of the city. Le Quartier Petit-Champlain and Cap-Blanc were Irish bastions when their union controlled the stevedores of the port. In the 1850s, they began to move into this area, and, in 1866, they built St. Patrick's Church, which was closed in 1959, when most of the community had moved beyond the city walls. It burned down soon afterward, but its stone walls still stand.

The Musée des Augustines de l'Hôtel-Dieu de Québec (27) is at 32 rue Charlevoix, just up the côte du Palais from rue McMahon. The Hôtel-Dieu is the oldest hospital in North America. Still located on its 1644 site, the present buildings reflect little of the original one. The hospital was founded by Augustinian nuns, who were sponsored by the Duchess of Aiguillon, Cardinal Richelieu's niece. The first buildings burned to the ground in 1755. Two disgruntled sailors were blamed for setting the fire. In 1759, British troops occupied the new building, returning it to the nuns only in 1784. The building was much altered in 1816, 1892, 1925, 1930 and by the fifteen-floor addition of 1954.

Robert Giffard, son-in-law of Louis Hébert, was the first Quebec doctor. The first surgery was performed in 1700, when a Montreal nun, Sister Marie Barbier, had a cancerous breast removed by Dr. Michel Sarrazin. To perform the successful operation, she was put to sleep with Gallice wine. She lived another nineteen years. The museum presents a collection of antique furniture, including an old chest that belonged to the founders (1639), as well as seventeenth-century ornaments, a collection of antique medical instruments, copperware and many paintings. The convent's library contains 3,500 books from the seventeenth century. On request, people can visit the arched cellars (1695) and the church (1800). Catherine de St-Augustin is buried at the center named after her. Paintings and religious works of art recall moments in her life. Open: Tuesday through Saturday 9:30 to 11:30 A.M. and 1:30 to 5 P.M., Sunday 1:30 to 5 P.M.

Côte-du-Palais once led to the Intendants' Palace at the bottom of the hill. It was here, under the nose of the nuns of the Hôtel-Dieu Hospital, that Bigot threw his lavish balls and decadent parties. Only the **palace vaults** remain. The **archaeological digs** (28) on the site of the palace reveal the foundations of Quebec's first brewery. Open: Tuesday through Saturday 12:30 to 5 P.M.

WALKING TOUR FOUR: THE PLAINS OF ABRAHAM AND THE CITADEL

This walking tour is mostly through parkland. I suggest that you start it with a visit to the **Musée du Fort** at 10 rue Ste-Anne (just off Dufferin Terrace), where they use a large model of the city as it was in 1750 to describe the six sieges of Quebec, including the Battle of the Plains of Abraham. Open: every day 10 A.M. to 6 P.M. Half-hour shows alternate in English and French.

Le Jardin des Gouverneurs (29) has a monument that honors Wolfe and Montcalm, the opposing generals who died fighting for Quebec in 1759. The monument was the brainchild of Governor Dalhousie, who was looking for ways to bring French and English together. It was erected in 1827.

La Promenade des Gouverneurs (30) was opened, in 1960, by John Diefenbaker, prime minister of Canada. The first public lookout over the St. Lawrence was built, under the direction of the governor of Lower Canada, Lord Durham, in 1838. Forty years later, the city created the toboggan run and the boardwalk that was named after the governor-general of Canada, Lord Dufferin. The newest extension runs under the walls of the Citadel to National Battlefields Park, which includes the Plains of Abraham.

The land for the park was assembled through several purchases made from 1908 to 1954. Overlooking the St. Lawrence, the initial park was designed by Frederick G. Todd, who was also responsible for the park on île Ste-Hélène in Montreal. It offers wooded areas, trails, roads, lawns, gardens, lookouts and sports fields.

Martello Tower (31) is about a five-minute walk from the Citadel. After you pass the top of a long staircase that cuts down through woods and down the cliff to Cap Blanc, cut across the lawns and keep to the height of land until you see the round tower.

In 1805, Governor Craig, without gaining London's approval, began the construction of four defensive towers to the west of the walls of the city. The word "Martello" is an English corruption of Mortella, a point in Corsica where such a tower had so impressed the English forces, when they attacked it in 1794, that they used the design to build two hundred of them throughout the world. To protect them from mortar bomb attacks, the roofs were five- to six-feet thick, but the cleverness of their design rests in the fact that if they were to be taken by the enemy, they could easily be destroyed by cannon fire from the rear. A free exhibition in Martello Tower 1 gives a good impression of what it must have been like for the up to twenty soldiers to live in these defensive facilities. Open: June through early September: Tuesday through Sunday 10 A.M. to 5 P.M., Monday 12:30 to 5 P.M.

The Centennial Fountain (32) was built to celebrate the hundredth anniversary of the confederation of Canada. The eastern-standard-time sundial was installed in 1987.

Earl Grey Terrace (33) is named after Canada's governor-general (1904–11) who gave the cup that is annually awarded to the country's best professional football team. His father gave his name to a Mandarin tea that he imported to London.

Forming a large semicircle behind the terrace are the Price guns, which were bequeathed to the park by William Price in 1913. The guns date from 1711 to 1890. The cannons, with their narrow muzzles, were designed to shoot iron balls over long distances. The heavier carronades were mounted on British ships and were designed to shoot shot, rubble and balls; the short, squat mortars were used to lob bombs, fireballs and flares over the top of fortifications. The guns to the east of the terrace were captured from the Germans during World War I.

Behind the guns is a jogging track and playing field where an old horse-racing track used to be.

Musée du Québec (34) was designed by Wilfred Lacroix in 1927. The spacious stairwells, galleries and atriums reflect a mixture of Classical and Art Deco styles. Emile Brunet designed the great bronze doors and the fourteen aluminum bas-reliefs on the exterior. This building has recently been connected to the old provincial jail, which was designed by Charles Baillargé in 1867 and now, retaining much of the old interior architecture, is an annex to the museum. These two completely different buildings are joined by a half-submerged, Postmodern structure. The three buildings together reflect 120 years of very different architectural styles, yet they manage to complement one another.

The Wolfe monument, outside the new entrance to the museum, stands on the spot where General Wolfe is thought to have died. In the 1790s, a meridian marker was placed there. It was replaced, in 1832, by a simple column, which was replaced, in 1849, by a monument similar to the present one. It, in turn, was replaced in 1913, but was dynamited in 1963 by the Front de Liberation du Québec. The present monument dates from 1965.

The collections of the museum are made up of traditional, classical, modern and contemporary Quebec art dating as far back as the seventeenth century. Its paintings, sculptures, gold and silver objects, drawings and engravings make it one of the most important museums in the country and give it an international reputation. Open: September 15 to June 14: Tuesday through Sunday 10 A.M. to 5:45 P.M. (Wednesday closing is 9:45 P.M.); June 15 to September 14: every day 10 A.M. to 8:45 P.M.

Le Jardin Jeanne d'Arc (35) is a beautiful formal garden. The equestrian statue of the warrior-saint was donated, in the 1930s, by an anonymous New York couple who had fallen in love with Quebec. It is a copy of one in Jeanne d'Arc's birthplace and identical to another in San Francisco.

───────────────■───────────────

JOAN OF ARC

It could not be more fitting that a monument to Joan of Arc should be on the Plains of Abraham. The French-English animosity can be traced to 1066, when William of Normandy conquered England and his French-speaking ancestors went on to control (especially after Eleanor of Aquitaine married Henry II in 1152) the greater part of present-day France. By 1420, the king of England had occupied Paris and virtually controlled France. But nine years later Jeanne d'Arc went into battle at Orléans and began the process of unifying the country under the Bourbon kings. Nonetheless, Calais still owed allegiance to London when Jacques Cartier discovered Quebec.

───────────────■───────────────

Martello Tower 2 is at rue Taché and avenue Laurier, at the northwest corner of the flower garden. To the northeast is Place Montcalm, where, in the shadow of the Loews-Concorde Hotel with its revolving restaurant on top, stands a monument to the defender of Quebec. The statue, which faces Grande Allée, is a copy of one in Candiac, France, Montcalm's birthplace, and was given to Quebec in 1911.

Grande Allée (36) was once so exclusive a residential street that people were expected, no matter how much money they had, to ask permission to live on it. Today, the large old houses between Place Montcalm and the parliament buildings have been converted into restaurants, bars and discotheques, most of which, in summer, spill out onto the patios facing the street.

The Chapelle des Soeurs du Bon-Pasteur (37) is at 1080 rue de la Chevrotière. The exterior facade, with its turrets and belfries, was designed by François-Xavier Berlinguet in 1909. The actual building is by Charles Baillargé and dates from 1868. The chapel's interior is a mix of Romanesque and Baroque styles. The carved wood and gold-leaf-finished main altar is by Lavasseur (1730) and the side altars were crafted by Florent Baillargé in 1800. The large painting of the Assumption is by Antoine Plamondon, and the thirty-eight smaller works are by the Bon-Pasteur Sisters, who were famous for their canvases at the turn of the century. The chapel offers several series of concerts, as well as an artists' mass at 11 A.M. on Sunday. Information: 641-1069. Open: May through September: Tuesday through Sunday 12 noon to 5 P.M.

Anima G (38) is a modern office tower with a free observation deck on the thirty-first floor.

The Drill Hall (39), on avenue Laurier, is in the Château style that is a hallmark of Quebec's late-Victorian architecture. It was designed in 1885 by E. E. Taché, who also designed the National Assembly opposite. In the park in front is a monument to two soldiers, Short and Wallick, who were killed in 1889 while attempting to blow up a building and stop the spread of a fire that had already destroyed four hundred houses.

The modern structure on the square is nicknamed the Bunker because it was there that Quebec premier Robert Bourassa "hid" from the media when he was, in 1976, deeply unpopular with both English and French constituents.

The larger-than-life statue across the street is of Maurice Duplessis, premier of Quebec from 1936 to 1939 and 1944 to 1959. Duplessis was not universally loved even in Quebec. Born in Trois-Rivières, he was, above all, a canny politician. He founded his own political party and courted the business and religious communities by being violently anti-Communist. He caught the emotions of the ordinary people by being a nationalist. His opponents accused him of having Fascist tendencies when he used the Padlock Laws against the Jehovah's Witnesses. During a strike in the asbestos mines, even the bishop of Montreal opposed him. The statue was commissioned soon after he died in office in 1959, but mysteriously "disappeared" when the Liberal party came to power. It was "found" twelve years later when the Parti Québecois was elected. The quotation on the statue reads: "We do not wish the legislature of Quebec to be in the tow of Ottawa. It must be led by the citizens of Quebec."

L'Assemblée Nationale (40) was designed in 1884. Its French Renaissance style is by Eugene-Etienne Taché, a former prime minister of Canada. The inscription over the entrance is the province's motto, "Je me souviens" (I remember), and the statues on the facade are a lesson in Quebec history. Wolfe and Montcalm occupy niches directly above the main entrance. Above them are Champlain and de Maisonneuve, the founders of Quebec and Montreal. Above them are the teachers, Marguerite Bourgeoys and Marie de l'Incarnation. To the left, running along the building at the ground-floor level, are Lord Elgin, the governor-general who refused to overturn the constitution; Louis Buade, Count Frontenac, who fought with Laval and refused to surrender Quebec to Phips; Intendant Talon, who built the first brewery, shipped timber to France and worked the iron forges in Trois-Rivières; Lafontaine, the prime minister who played a major part in the implementation of responsible government in 1848; La Vérendrye, the first white man to cross the prairies; and Iberville, who was born in Montreal, fought naval battles in Hudson's Bay, founded New Orleans and died in Havana. On the right of the entrance are Lévis, who won the Battle of Ste-Foy; de Salaberry, who defeated the Americans in the Battle of Chateauguay; and Lord Dorchester, who guaranteed the rights to use the French language and worship in Catholic churches.

The central bronze statues in front of the building are dedicated, in the words of Taché, to the "proud aboriginal tribes of Canada." Above, a family is tensely engaged as one of them shoots an arrow at some forest prey; below is a fisherman with a spear poised above a wriggling fish. They are the work of Louis-Phillipe Hébert.

The visitors' entrance to the National Assembly Building is on the left. Because, in the 1980s, a Canadian soldier, a French-speaking native of Quebec, went on a rampage with a semiautomatic gun in the assembly (it was not in session at the time), you have to pass through a metal detector before joining a guided tour.

You'll find history as present inside the building as it is outside. In the lobby, the fleur-de-lis of France, the rose of England, the shamrock of Ireland and the thistle of Scotland are carved into the mahogany wainscoting. The two main chambers, save for the color of the walls and furnishings, are identical in their French Renaissance design. Both have second-floor galleries for the general public.

The fresco on the ceiling of the Salon Bleu (Blue Chamber), where elected members debate and vote, is titled *Je me Souviens* and illustrates the march of Quebec's history from Jacques Cartier until the first decades of the twentieth century. It took Charles Huot, who was in his seventies, four years to complete, working on his back for three hours a day. He then went on to paint the canvas that covers the far wall and that illustrates the debate of 1793 that reaffirmed the legality of the French language. When parliament is in session, the premier and his government sit to the right of the ornate and crowned dais of the president's (speaker's) throne; the leader of the opposition and his party sit opposite, and on the table between them lies a silver-headed mace of authority.

The Salon Rouge (Red Chamber) was the home of Quebec's legislative council, an unelected senate that was abolished in 1968. Charles Huot died in 1930 before he completed the painting *The Sovereign Council of New France*, which hangs over the speaker's chair. The room now serves eight standing committees: Institutions; Budget and Administration; Social Affairs; Labor and Economy; Agriculture, Fisheries and Food; Planning and Infrastructures; Education; and Culture.

The restaurant of the National Assembly is open to the public. The decor is better than the food, but prices are cheap. Eating there was described to me as "spaghetti with the premier!"

When in session, the National Assembly sits on Tuesday and Thursday, 2 to 6 P.M. and 8 to 10 P.M., Wednesday 10 A.M. to 1 P.M. and 3 to 6 P.M. Visitors are welcome to watch debates. For information, telephone 643-7239. Guided tours: September 4 to June 23: Monday through Friday 9 A.M. to 4:30 P.M., June 24 to September 3: every day 10 A.M. to 5:30 P.M.

The Mercier monument (41) is by the French sculptor Paul Chèvre. It honors Quebec's first nationalist premier, Honoré Mercier, who swept to power in 1887 on the wave of French-Canadian indignation that followed the hanging of Louis Riel, a French-Métis leader in Manitoba. During his mandate (1887–92), he organized Canada's first Provincial Premiers' Conference, founded libraries and night schools, gave free land to men with more than twelve children and opened the Laurentians to greater settlement. His friendship with the Jesuits and his pro-France and pro-papal stands gained him the hatred of the Orangemen of Ontario. Accused of graft and corruption, he was swept out of office as quickly as he had come into it. The monument shows him holding out his hand; cynics say that he honors tip-searching *calèche* drivers that wait for their customers in front of him.

The François-Xavier Garneau monument (42), just outside Porte St-Louis, is also by Paul Chèvre. It honors Quebec's first great historian. In 1828, while Garneau was working as a clerk in a law office, one of his English colleagues said, spouting a common sentiment of the time, that Quebec had no history. Garneau supposedly replied: "I shall write the history which you do not even know exists. You will see that our ancestors yielded only when outnumbered. . . .

There are defeats which are as glorious as victories." His three-volume masterpiece, *Histoire du Canada,* was published in 1845, 1846 and 1848, giving rise to accusations that he was anticlerical and freethinking. His history of Quebec to 1789 asserts that the essential relationship between "our language, our laws, and our customs," and between faith and nationality, are necessary parts of ethnic and cultural survival.

The Citadel (43) has its entrance at the end of côte de la Citadelle, just inside Porte St-Louis. The continued presence of the Royal 22nd Regiment (the "Vandoos"—a corruption of *vingt-deux,* or "twenty-two") makes it the largest group of fortified buildings still occupied by troops in North America.

Samuel de Champlain first proposed building a citadel in 1634, but it was not until 1693, when a small redoubt was constructed, that any attempt was made. Chaussegros de Léry, New France's most important engineer, drew up plans for more permanent fortifications in 1720 but by the 1750s only a powder magazine had been added. The British began some work in the 1790s, but it was not until the 1820s that the present star-shaped Vauban-style structure was built according to the plans of Colonel Durnford.

The military museum, the Quebec residence of Canada's governor-general, the historic guns, the prison cells, the subterranean firing range and the view from 402 feet above the river are all worth seeing. The daily Changing of the Guard at 10:00 A.M. reflects the British heritage of the Canadian army, and the Beating of Retreat, at 7:00 P.M. on Tuesday, Thursday, Saturday and Sunday in July and August, is great theater. A cannon is fired daily at noon and 9:30 P.M. from the Prince of Wales bastion. Guided Tours: March, April and October: weekdays 9 A.M. to 4 P.M.; May through mid-June and September: daily 9 A.M. to 5 P.M.; mid-June to Labor Day: daily 9 A.M. to 7 P.M.; November: Monday through Friday 9 A.M. to noon; December, January and February: daily 10 A.M. to 2 P.M. Reservations: 648-3563.

ESCAPE FROM THE CITADEL

The most interesting story I have found about the Citadel involves a group of Americans who were held prisoner there. The Hunter

Lodges were loosely connected organizations of freedom-fighters that sprang up from Vermont to Michigan after the Rebellions of 1837. Dedicated to liberating Canada, they gave themselves military ranks, stole arms from at least one American arsenal, and in the spring of 1838 undertook a series of raids across the border. Their most spectacular success was setting fire to an empty ferry boat and sending it, in flames at night, crashing over Niagara Falls. Poorly organized, the ragtag "armies" were soon dispersed, and a number of their "officers," including General Sutherland, General Theller and Colonel Dodge, were captured, brought to Quebec and imprisoned in the Citadel.

At the time, it was unclear whether or not individuals could be tried for acts of war. President Van Buren wanted as little to do as possible with the case and agreed that the precedent-setting trial would be held in London. As the prisoners waited for their ship, they were kept in one spacious room. Because they were "gentlemen," they were allowed to employ a washerwoman; have newspapers, books and liquor sent to them from town; and see visitors. Using these contacts, Theller and Dodge made plans to escape, but Sutherland, who claimed to be the friend of U.S. vice-president Johnson, was against the idea. Afraid that Sutherland would tell the British of their plans, Theller, who was a doctor by profession, used an array of psychological techniques to gradually drive Sutherland insane. Sutherland finally attacked a guard and was removed to solitary confinement.

Theller and Dodge swung into action. On a dark and stormy night, they hypnotized and then drugged their guard with opium, managed to cross the moat and scale the walls and made their way down into the Lower Town. In one hilarious episode, as recounted by Theller, they were hidden under the floor of a stable housing a horse that had been given a diuretic. With excrement dripping down on top of them, they escaped detection. Finally, with the help of Charles Drolet, the elected representative for Saguenay, they reached the American border.

Life in Quebec City

ACCOMMODATIONS

There is no better way to visit Quebec than to stay in one of the numerous small hotels inside, or just outside, the walls of the Old City. Most of them will give you a sense of history, warmth and charm. If they don't have their own lots, all of them will give you a discount for twenty-four-hour parking in the nearby municipal garages. I find Tourisme Québec's ratings do not take into account such intangibles as charm, and I am of the opinion that a two-star hotel in Quebec would get three stars in Montreal, though I do use the standard rating system. There are no networks of bed-and-breakfasts in Quebec City.

Abbreviations

PB = private bathroom
AC = air-conditioning
K = kitchenette
W = whirlpool bath
F = fireplace
Tel = telephone
TV = television
P = parking
P$ = parking fee
AmEx = American Express
DC = Diners Club
MC = MasterCard

The numbers in parentheses do not refer to exact positions, but only to those *closest* on the map of Old Quebec (see page 214–15).

The Very Expensive

Château Frontenac (18): *1 rue des Carrières. Tel.: 692-3861, 1-800-268-9420.* 524 rooms with PB, AC, Tel and TV. P$. If you have the money or a liberal expense account, there can be no better place to stay in Quebec City than at the Château Frontenac. This famous copper-roofed and towered hotel has dominated the skyline since it was built. Its public rooms are worth visiting in their own right and its bar, because of its magnificent view of the St. Lawrence River, has no equal. It is a grand hotel that is owned and managed by Canadian Pacific. AmEx, MC, Visa. ★ ★ ★ ★ ★

Manoir Victoria (27): *44 côte du Palais. Tel.: 692-1030, 1-800-463-6283.* 142 rooms with PB, AC, Tel and TV. Indoor swimming. Fitness center. Sauna. P$. Recently renovated, this hotel provides luxury accommodations. AmEx, MC, Visa. ★ ★ ★ ★

Expensive

Hôtel Clarendon (7): *57 rue Ste-Anne. Tel.: 692-2480, 1-800-361-6162.* 89 rooms with PB, Tel and TV. P$. The centrally located Clarendon has been in business since 1870. Its spacious, elegant dining room, Le Charles Baillargé, is the oldest continually operated restaurant in Canada, and the beautiful, beamed, Art Deco lobby dates from 1925. To be renovated, restored and refurnished by 1991, the rooms will reflect the hotel's heritage. I'm sure that its rating will rise. AmEx, MC, Visa. ★ ★ ★

Hilton International Québec (40): *3 place Québec. Tel.: 647-2411, 1-800-268-9275.* 563 rooms with PB, AC, Tel and TV. Indoor swimming. Sauna. Fitness center. P$. Just outside the city walls, this first-class hotel is integrated into the convention center, and is as you would expect a modern Hilton to be. AmEx, MC, Visa. ★ ★ ★ ★ ★

Loews le Concorde (36): *1225 place Montcalm. Tel.: 647-2222, 1-800-463-5256.* 409 rooms with PB, AC, Tel and TV. Outdoor pool. Fitness center. Sauna. P$. Quebec's newest, big, top-of-the-market hotel, with its revolving restaurant on top, is extremely popular for graduation balls and similar celebrations. Close to the Plains of Abraham, it offers quality accommodations and panoramic views. AmEx, MC, Visa. ★ ★ ★ ★ ★ ★

The Medium Priced

Au Manoir Ste-Geneviève (29): *13 rue Ste-Geneviève. Tel.: 694-1666.* 9 rooms with PB, AC and TV; 2 with K. P$. Across Governor's Park from the Château Frontenac, this hotel's fine rooms are furnished with antiques. CAA and AAA approved.   ★ ★ ★

Cap Diamant (29): *39 avenue Ste-Geneviève. Tel.: 694-0313.* 9 rooms with PB, AC and TV. P$. Florence Guillot has furnished this beautifully restored 1826 house with a splendid selection of antiques. The rooms have been individually and tastefully decorated. Some have marble fireplaces and some have small refrigerators. There is a small shaded courtyard in the back. Completely charming.   ★ ★

Château Bellevue (29): *16 rue Laporte. Tel.: 692-2573, 1-800-463-2617.* 57 rooms with PB, AC, Tel and TV; 5 with K. P. This modern hotel occupies a newly converted row of houses close to the Château Frontenac. Some of the front rooms have good views. AmEx, MC, Visa.   ★ ★ ★

Château de la Terrace (29): *6 place Terrasse Dufferin. Tel.: 694-9472.* 18 rooms with PB, Tel and TV; 4 with K. P$. This hotel offers its guests a terrace and splendid views of the St. Lawrence River. The front rooms share the view and some have private balconies. One wonderfully large room, suitable for a family, has both balcony and kitchenette. AmEx, MC, Visa.   ★ ★ ★

Hôtel au Jardin du Gouverneur (29): *16 rue Mont-Carmel. Tel.: 692-1704.* 17 rooms with PB, AC and TV. P$. Once the home of Sir Lormer Gouin, one of Quebec's former prime ministers, this well-located hotel has lovely big rooms. One on the top floor, with its garret windows, is especially pleasant. CAA and AAA approved. AmEx, MC, Visa.   ★ ★

Hôtel du Vieux Québec (27): *8 rue Collins. Tel.: 692-1850.* 27 rooms with PB, K, AC, Tel and TV. P$. Just off busy rue St-Jean, this three-year-old hotel, with its efficiency units, is one of the best for young families. AmEx, MC, Visa.   ★ ★ ★

Hôtel le Manoir d'Auteuil (22): *49 rue d'Auteuil. Tel.: 694-1173.* 16 rooms with PB, Tel and TV. AC in most. P$. This is a wonderful Art Deco building with Art Deco furnishings and a comfortable, wainscoted public lounge. Edith Piaf stayed twice in a splendid room that has one of the most magnificent bathrooms I have ever seen. Maximum occupancy per room is two, and no children under twelve are allowed. Some rooms are reserved for nonsmokers. In winter, a large breakfast is served.   AmEx, MC, Visa.   ★ ★ ★

Maison du Fort (29): *21 avenue Ste-Geneviève. Tel.: 692-4375.* 10 rooms with PB, AC and TV. P$. This Georgian-style house was built in 1810 by Thomas Baillargé, who was the architect of Quebec's basilica. His particular style was personalized by a rose, which you can still see on the door frames of this hotel. The rooms are comfortable and large, and some have stone walls. There is a suite that can accommodate six. Trouble-free pets are accepted.   ★ ★

Maison Marie-Rollet (8): *81 rue Ste-Anne. Tel.: 694-9721.* 10 rooms with PB, 6 with AC. TV. P$. Host Fernand Blouin is an educated man who likes peace and quiet. He accepts neither groups nor students. His hotel is part of a row of houses built in 1875 by J. F. Peachy. This magnificent Second Empire house has maintained its original charm, and several of the rooms are furnished with antiques. One beautiful wainscoted room on the ground floor and a pair of rooms in the basement are rented at bargain prices; others seem overpriced. The European-style tariffs mean that two do not stay as cheaply as one. There is a laundry.   Visa.   ★ ★

The Inexpensive

Auberge de la Chouette (22): *71 rue d'Auteuil. Tel.: 694-0232.* 10 rooms with PB, AC, Tel and TV. P$. Just inside the city wall, this 1845 converted house maintains its original charm. Above the quiet Apsara Restaurant, one of the best in the city, and up a beautiful, curving staircase, the well-appointed rooms are furnished with antiques. One has a fireplace.   AmEx, MC, Visa.   ★ ★

Au Petit Hôtel (20): *3 ruelle des Ursulines (just off rue Ste-Ursule. Tel.: 692-2487.* 15 rooms with PB, AC, Tel and TV. P$. Your host, Sottho, runs a quiet, welcoming hotel inside the city walls and close to the St. Louis Gate. He occasionally accepts well-behaved pets. Good value.   AmEx, MC, Visa.   ★ ★

Hôtel Château de Léry (29): *8 rue Laporte. Tel.: 692-2692.* 19 rooms, 17 with PB, 2 with K. AC and TV. P$. Facing Governor's Park, the front rooms offer a good view. One large room sleeps 6.   AmEx, MC, Visa.   ★ ★

Hôtel le Clos St-Louis (20): *71 rue St-Louis. Tel.: 694-9491, fax 694-1311.* 29 rooms, 12 with PB, 1 with AC, 15 with TV. P$. Built in

1854 for a Mr. Boswell, a local brewer, the building, with a beautiful wooden staircase, maintains a romantic atmosphere. Good value.   AmEx, MC, Visa.   ★ ★

Hôtel Maison Doyon (8): *109 rue Ste-Anne. Tel.: 694-1720.* 19 rooms, 11 with PB, 12 with TV, 4 with refrigerators. P$. Robert Turcotte and his staff run this hotel with affection. The large terrace, in the back, overlooks the garden and small orchard of the Ursuline nuns; the front lounge has a beautiful view to the northeast. The hotel seems to attract a young clientele. One two-room suite, with a bathroom separating the rooms, is perfect for two couples or a family. Well-behaved pets are accepted. MC, Visa.   ★

Maison Acadienne (20): *43 rue Ste-Ursule. Tel.: 694-0280.* 28 rooms, 21 with PB. Tel and TV. P$. Built in 1822 as three houses, this well-located hotel maintains a sense of the past without sacrificing modern conveniences. The rooms are attractive and there is a patio. Good value.   AmEx, MC, Visa.   ★

La Maison Demers (20): *68 rue Ste-Ursule. Tel.: 692-2487.* 7 rooms, 4 with PB, 3 with TV, refrigerators, hot plates. P$. Jeanine and Jean-Luc Demers opened their home to tourists twenty-eight years ago. They clearly love being hosts, for there are wonderful, welcoming touches, like a silk rose on every door and a bowl of candies in every room. You really feel at home—as if you're visiting a friend. There are balconies both back and front, and a continental breakfast is included in the price. One of my favorites.   MC, Visa.   ★

La Maison Ste-Ursule (20): *40 rue Ste-Ursule. Tel.: 694-9794.* 15 rooms, 12 with PB, 7 with K. TV and refrigerators. P$. The main house, with five rooms for rent, was built in 1756. The much newer, two-level motel units in the back have been built, with balconies and patios, around a tree-shaded yard. Very pleasant.   AmEx, MC, Visa.   ★

Manoir des Ramparts (4): *3½ rue des Ramparts. Tel.: 692-2056.* 35 rooms, 22 with PB, Tel and TV; 2 with K. P$. This newer building offers an excellent view of the harbor. There is a good suite with a terrace overlooking the harbor for a very modest price. Public rooms with TV. If the corridors are a little rundown, the prices more than make up for them.   AmEx, MC, Visa.   ★ ★

The Least Expensive

Hôtel la Maison General (20): *72 rue St-Louis. Tel.: 694-1905.* 12 rooms with TV and refrigerator. P$. This friendly hotel is a little run-down, but it's the least expensive in the city.

Manoir de la Terrace and Hotel Beau Site (29): *4 and 6 rue Laporte. Tel.: 694-1592.* 15 rooms, 9 with PB. P$. Half the clientele of these adjacent hotels (which are managed by the same man) is gay.   MC, Visa.

Manoir Lasalle (20): *18 Ste-Ursule. Tel.: 647-9361.* 9 rooms, 2 with PB. P$. The owner, Therese Lachance, is quite a character. She claims that she keeps the rates down because the building is paid for and she doesn't need to pay any more income tax. She has cats and will accept pets.   ★

Rooms and Flats

Appartements Riendeau (36): *1216 place Montcalm. Tel.: 529-2484.* 11 apartments and rooms. Kitchen facilities. TV in some rooms. P. Bruno Riendeau manages five well-maintained, comfort-able, old, neighboring houses just outside the St. Louis Gate and close to the Plains of Abraham. Because the houses have not been con-verted, individual rooms share the bathrooms and well-equipped kitchens. One 7-room apartment can sleep 16. Long-term rates can be arranged.

Youth Hostels

Centre International de Séjour (20): *19 rue Ste-Ursule. Tel.: 694-0755.* 270 beds.

Auberge de la Paix (27): *31 rue Couillard. Tel.: 694-0735.* Smaller than the above, but the same low prices.

RESTAURANTS

Unlike Montreal, Quebec City does not have publications that rate restaurants. In my research, I asked over one hundred Quebec resi-dents which were their favorite restaurants and where they would dine in order to celebrate a special occasion. I then went and visited all the recommended places. These restaurants were the winners of the survey. The number after each name refers to the closest number on the map.

Inexpensive

Chez Temporel (7): *25 Couillard.* Tucked away behind rue de la Fabrique, this unassuming restaurant is famous for its croissants and soup. Perhaps the best restaurant for lunch or a light supper, it's a favorite with students. Downstairs is a small room where people can comfortably dine alone. Upstairs is a larger room for couples and parties. Open until 2:30 A.M.

Le Casse Crêpe (8): *1136 St-Jean. Tel.: 692-0434.* This is easily the most recommended crêperie in Quebec. Here you can watch the superthin pancakes being made and stuffed with meat and fruit fillings. Open until 3 A.M. on the weekends.

Le Cochon Dingue (12): *46 Petit Champlain. Tel.: 692-2013.* The steaks, quiches, salads, pâtés and sandwiches are recommended for their good value and atmosphere. A children's menu is offered.

Le Mille Feuille (20): *1996 St-Louis. Tel.: 681-4520.* This recommended vegetarian restaurant is housed on two floors of a 200-year-old building. Downstairs is reserved for nonsmokers.

Moderately Priced

L'Apsara (22): *71 rue d'Auteuil. Tel.: 694-0232.* The Cambodian, Vietnamese and Thai cuisine makes this the most highly recommended oriental restaurant in the city. The front room of this nineteenth-century house is subdued and formal. The larger room in the back is decorated with large color slides of Angor Wat.

Chez Pepé le Fouineur (36): *585 Grande Allée. Tel.: 524-7612.* This French-Italian restaurant is noted for its mussels.

L'Elysée Mandarin (22): *65 rue d'Auteuil. Tel.: 692-0909.* This restaurant serves Hunan, Szechuan and Pekinese cuisine. The furniture and decor make you think you're in China. Simon Cho, who is from Hong Kong, is the chef. Prices are surprisingly low.

Pub d'Orsay (7): *65 rue Buade. Tel.: 694-1582.* This pub-restaurant claims to be the "only real English pub" in Quebec. With its mahogany wainscoting and granite-surfaced bar, it is certainly very pleasant, but I was reminded more of Paris than London. It's very popular and has a good wine list.

Moderate-Expensive

À la Bastille—Chez Bahauaud (29): *47 Ste-Geneviève. Tel.: 692-2544.* Saus-Vide cuisine was created by the French chef Paul Bocuse, who invented a new way of transporting produce in vacuum packs. This restaurant was founded in 1982 by Bernard Bahauaud, who is originally from Breton. He is especially proud of his seafood dishes. In a converted house, the large Edwardian room still feels like a home. Original paintings by Luc Archambault hang on the wall. There is an excellent wine list. Outside there is a terrace and bar.

L'Astral (36): *1225 Place Montcalm. Tel.: 647-2222.* This revolving restaurant on the top of the Loews-Concorde Hotel gives splendid panoramas of the city. The buffet food is thought to be good value, but à la carte is not considered exceptional for a first-class hotel.

Aux Ancienne Canadien (20): *34 rue St-Louis. Tel.: 692-1627.* Quebec dishes are served by costumed waiters in one of the oldest buildings (1675) in the city. Traditional woodcuts and old wooden tools decorate the walls. The restaurant has been owned and managed by the same family for twenty-five years. It offers good, honest value. The chef is Raymond Bilodeau.

Le Café de la Paix (7): *44 Des Jardins. Tel.: 692-1430.* After forty years, this restaurant is still so popular that it is necessary to reserve a table. Game and salmon dishes are the specialties of the chef, Clermont Berzeron. Service is excellent.

Le Paris Brest (36): *590 Grande Allée. Tel.: 529-2243.* French, with an emphasis on nouvelle cuisine. Phillipe Bourdet opened this restaurant in 1982. It has an excellent French wine list, and professional reviewers have given it an excellent reputation.

Sault au Matelot (17): *17 Sault au Matelot. Tel.: 692-0526.* This small French restaurant makes a speciality of young turkey and evolutive cuisine.

Expensive

La Cremaillèrie (8): *21 rue St-Stanislas (off St-Jean). Tel.: 692-2216.* Continental cuisine is offered in this restaurant that has an old charm and excellent service. It is noted for its frogs' legs.

La Marie Clarisse (12): *312 rue Petit Champlain. Tel.: 692-0857.*
This French restaurant, noted for its seafood, is located near the
bottom of the Break-Neck Stairs, and the old stone arches and
beamed ceiling give it a good atmosphere.

La Ripaille (6): *9 rue Buade. Tel.: 692-2450.* The French and
Italian cuisine is excellent. Don't be fooled by the unimaginative
decor and background music. The chef, Serge Dusseault, cooks for a
loyal and demanding clientele.

Le Biarritz (8): *136 rue Ste-Anne. Tel.: 692-2433.* The Basque and
Landaise cuisine is created by R. L. Lacoste, who sits down and eats in
his own restaurant. The decor is unpretentious—the food is the
thing.

Le Charles Baillargé (7): *Clarendon Hotel, 57 Ste-Anne. Tel.:
692-2480.* Dating from 1890, this very elegant and formal French
restaurant is the oldest to be continually operated in Canada. It is
noted for its refined table and its costumed operetta singers.

Le Continental (20): *26 rue St-Louis. Tel.: 694-9995.* Louis Sjobba
is the chef of this family restaurant that has been in business for
thirty-four years. Its Italian and continental cuisine is highly recommended by professional reviewers. It has a good wine list and a
pleasant window that looks down the street.

L'Échaude (17): *73 Sault-au-Matelot. Tel.: 692-1299.* The French
nouvelle cuisine is highly recommended. The Art Deco decoration of
this restaurant in the Lower Town is very attractive. Seafood, especially eel, is considered exceptional.

Le Saint Amour (20): *48 St-Ursule. Tel.: 694-0667.* French
nouvelle cuisine is offered. Owner-chef Jean-Luc Boule's restaurant
proved to be the most popular in my survey. The wine list takes your
breath away. In winter, a *menu de dégustation* is highly recommended.
In summer, ask for the chef's recommendation. The decor is light,
airy and very attractive; a retractable roof covers a garden in the
back.

Very Expensive

À la Table de Serge Bruyère (7): *1200 rue St-Jean. Tel.:
694-0618.* Reservations are required a week in advance to eat in this
internationally recognized French nouvelle cuisine restaurant.
Bruyère is a very adventuresome chef of the highest order. There is
one lunch and one dinner service.

Le Champlain (18): *Château Frontenac, 1 rue des Carrières. Tel.: 693-3861.* Continental cuisine is served by waiters dressed in seventeenth-century costume while a classical harpist plays. The antique wood paneling is beautiful. When recommended by Quebec citizens, they had a tendency to giggle—perhaps because of the prices and the fact that the Château Frontenac is one of the grandest hotel institutions of the city. The restaurant is noted for its adventuresome table d'hôte and Sunday brunch. It also offers a low-calorie menu. The wine list is disappointing.

La Closerie: *1648 chemin St-Louis, Sillery. Tel.: 687-9975.* This French restaurant is not within walking distance of Old Quebec, but is one of the best in the metropolitan area. Take Grande Allée, which becomes chemin St-Louis. After St-Sacrement (3 kilometers from Porte St-Louis), chemin St-Louis is no longer the main road but winds south.

Le Croquembroche (23): *Hilton International, 3 Place Quebec. Tel.: 647-2411.* The French cuisine is considered, by some, to be the best offered in a hotel. The restaurant has a noted chef, an excellent wine list and a formal decor. Reservations are suggested—especially for Sunday brunch.

Le Tanière: *2215 rang St-Ange, Ste-Foy. Tel.: 872-4386.* This restaurant serves venison and game food adapted to nouvelle cuisine. Not within walking distance from the Old City. Reservations only.

SHOPPING

Although Quebec has a number of good antiques shops on rue St-Paul (16), it has to be said that Quebec City, unlike Montreal, is not a great place to shop. The best area is in Le Quartier Petit-Champlain (12), where many local artisans have shops where they sell original jewelry, clothes and gifts. L'Iroquois has a fine collection of Inuit (Eskimo) and Amerindian art. For less specialized shopping walk along rue St-Jean (24) and côte de la Fabrique (6).

QUEBEC AT NIGHT

Theaters and Shows

Le Soleil newspaper prints a calendar of what is going on in Quebec City. The symphony orchestra plays the **Grand Théâtre de Québec,**

269 boulevard St-Cyrille, Tel.: 643-8131. The **Palais Montcalm,** *995 place d'Youville, Tel.: 670-9011,* presents popular entertainment, as does **Agora du Vieux Port,** an open-air theater in the Old Port. **Théâtre de la Bordée,** *1091½ rue St-Jean, Tel.: 694-9631* and **Théâtre du Grand Dérangement,** *30 rue Stanislas, Tel.: 692-3000,* are the city's theaters.

Clubs and Dance Bars

If you walk from côte de la Fabrique and along rue St-Jean, which continues outside the city to just beyond rue Ste-Geneviève, you will pass most of Quebec's clubs; some are within the walls, but most lie outside. I have arranged them geographically because the majority provide live music at least on the weekends. The greatest concentration of dance bars is just behind the National Assembly on Grande Allée. Unless noted otherwise, there is no cover charge.

Le Petit Paris (7): *48 côte de la Fabrique. Tel.: 694-0383.* Not as small as the name might imply, this club is owned and managed by a Spaniard. It presents Quebec singers to a lively crowd that varies in age from twenty to fifty. Every night there are two singers or groups who entertain almost continuously from 9 P.M. until 1:30 A.M. From a balcony on the second floor you can watch the acts below. On the third floor is a separate, quieter bar that is usually open only on weekends.

The Clarendon (7): *57 rue Ste-Anne. Tel.: 692-2480.* There is a dignified, but pleasant, jazz bar on the ground floor of the Clarendon Hotel.

Casablanca (7): *1169 rue St-Jean. Tel.: 692-4301.* Tucked away behind the street, this bar, with its small dance floor, plays reggae and African music.

Les Yeux Bleus (8): *1117 rue St-Jean. Tel.: 694-9118.* Presenting Quebec's blues singers every night from 10 P.M. to 2:30 A.M., this bar seems to be partially built into a cave. It is small, lively and fun.

Bar Entre Mise (8): *30 rue St-Stanislas (just off St-Jean). Tel.: 692-0708.* Small rock and rhythm-and-blues bands play here Thursday through Saturday. Attracting a student crowd, this club has a small dance floor, pool table and dart board.

Bar Chez Son Père (8): *24 rue St-Stanislas. Tel.: 692-5308.* Overlooking St-Jean, this *boît aux chansons* presents local musicians. The audience will often sing along. It's lively and enthusiastic.

Obsession (24): *1018 rue St-Jean. Tel.: 692-1313.* It's young. It's funky. It's poorly appointed and it's fun—even if the clientele has notably less money than that of the more fashionable discos on Grande Allée.

Alexandre Pub (24): *1017 rue St-Jean. Tel.: 694-0015.* Beautifully reconditioned, the building was designed by Boluguet. The bar offers nineteen different draft beers from seven countries and has over forty bottled beers from seventeen countries. During the theater and jazz festivals, shows are presented here.

Le d'Auteuil (23): *35 rue d'Auteuil. Tel.: 692-2263.* Quebec City's most important nightclub for live musicians occupies an old chapel. Le d'Auteuil presents a wide variety of international, national and local acts. The price of entrance varies from $1 to $20, depending on the fees that the artists charge.

Faxx: *873 rue St-Jean. Tel.: 648-1653.* Outside Porte St-Jean, this large, popular, multilevel discotheque has a large dance floor, a balcony from which you can watch the crowd and a third-floor bar where one can talk, play pool and watch rock videos. It has the reputation of being "mixte," with gay and straight clientele.

Le Ballon Rouge: *811 rue St-Jean. Tel.: 647-9227.* Almost exclusively gay, this discotheque has a balcony over the dance floor and an upstairs bar that leads out onto a large patio.

Drag Taverne and Drag Bar: *Corner of rue St-Augustin and rue St-Joachim. Tel.: 647-7413.* Around the corner and behind Le Ballon Rouge is a second gay bar. During the day, half of the space is a tavern, which closes at midnight. The bar half, which closes at 3 A.M., is on two levels—the lower level has tavern tables and chairs and the upper is dominated by a huge screen on which rock videos play.

Cent Limites (36): *670 Grande Allée. Tel.: 529-3565.* This is a small complex that includes an intimate American-type bar, a restaurant and a relaxed, spacious bar that has a small dance floor and ample place for talking.

Dagobert (36): *590 Grande Allée. Tel.: 522-0393.* This discotheque, which calls itself *un disco monstre,* is indeed huge. It occupies a large Victorian mansion, the inside of which has been totally torn out. On the ground floor there is a nightclub of the type you might find in gangster films of the 1940s. Live music plays every night. Upstairs is a huge discotheque with plenty of space for cruising, and on the third floor the bar looks down on the dancers. It accommodates nine hundred people, but there can be long lines outside on a Friday or Saturday night. It must be seen to be believed!

Brandy (39): *690 Grande Allée. Tel.: 648-8739.* With two large dance floors, and a bar connecting them, Brandy attracts a well-heeled young crowd. Behind the central bar is a bank of video screens that show the activity on the dance floors. One of the more interesting things about the screens is that when the infrared and blue lights replace regular lighting, the dancers take on eerie, even ghostly, qualities. The music is loud and conversation is pretty much limited to outside on the patio. As one of the customers told me, "C'est flyé" (which means "crazy fun").

Vogue (39): *1170 rue d'Artigny. Tel.: 529-9973.* Three buildings down from Brandy, Vogue has a large bar on the ground floor where there is a pool table—and plenty of space, with nooks, for talking. Upstairs is a small but good and lively dance bar. There is a terrace in the back, and a balcony from which you can watch the revelers on the street in front.

✤ 12 ✤

Vacation Areas
Outside Quebec City

ÎLE D'ORLÉANS

How to Get There

Autoroute Dufferin-Montmorency (Highway 440) starts just outside the walls of Old Quebec and quickly leads to the bridge, built in
1935, to île d'Orléans, which is thirty-four kilometers long and eight
kilometers wide. It is a perfect place for easy bicycling.

History

The Algonquin Indians called this bucolic island Minigo, or "en-
chanted place." In 1535, Jacques Cartier called it île Bacchus because
of the numerous grapevines that he found. The following year he
renamed it île d'Orléans, in honor of the birth of the Duke of Orléans,
the third son of Francis I. The agricultural potential of the island was
quickly recognized, and when de Maisonneuve and Jeanne Mance
arrived, in 1641, Governor Montmagny suggested that they found
their colony here rather than at Montreal. They refused, but ten years
later settlers began to be granted fiefs and subfiefs by the seigneur
and, in 1661, the parish of Ste-Famille opened its registers. The
population grew quickly; in 1679 St-Pierre, St-Paul (now St-Laurent)
and St-François became villages. By 1685 the census reported 1,205
inhabitants, making it the most extensively cultivated area in New
France.

265

St-Pierre

This town has grown considerably since the opening of the bridge. It was the home of Felix Leclerc, one of Quebec's most beloved singers and songwriters, who died in 1988. The church, the oldest in Quebec, was built in 1717. It was declared to be a national monument in 1954. The altar and sculptures in the sanctuary were created between 1732 and 1740 by Charles Vezina. Behind the building is an arts and crafts shop.

PRIESTS' WAY

In 1703 the villagers of St-Pierre accused the villagers of St-Laurent, across the island, of stealing a religious relic—a bone from the arm of St. Clement that would heal injuries when placed on a wound by a priest. The people of St-Laurent said that they were only taking back what was rightfully theirs. For thirty years the two villages quarreled. Finally, the bishop of Quebec decided in favor of St-Pierre and instructed the priests of the two villages to take their flocks to the border of the two parishes and witness the return of the relic. A large white cross was erected and blessed by the bishop. Since that time, the road between the two parishes has been known as *Route des Prêtres* ("Priests' Way").

Ste-Famille

The oldest parish on the island has the greatest concentration of architecture from the French regime and reflects three centuries of rural architecture. The convent that was founded in 1685 is close to the church (1743), which, with its three bell towers, is considered to be one of the most beautiful examples of Quebec's religious architecture. Maison Eudor-Morency, 4403 chemin Royal, was built in 1680 and now houses **l'auberge l'Atre** (Tel.: 829-2474), an inn that is a loving re-creation of an early farmhouse—it has no electricity. Maison Canac-Marquis (at number 4466), with its dormer windows, shows how seventeenth-century French architecture adapted to Quebec's climate. Maison Premont, at number 3584, is a Victorian home. Its neighbor, with the mansard roof, shows American influence.

St-François

Unfortunately, the 1734 Norman-style church of this most easterly parish burned in 1988. The village is best known for the thousands of migrating ducks and geese that arrive in April and October. The observation tower gives a splendid view of the river. The eight-room **Auberge Chaumonot** (425 chemin Royal, Tel.: 829-2735) is beautifully quiet and one of the highest-rated small inns in the province. The island's best site for camping, Camp Orléans, is on the southern shore.

St-Jean

The church was built in 1732 overlooking the river. Its walled cemetery is the final resting place of many sailors and river pilots. The French-style **Mauvide-Genest Manor** (1451 chemin Royal, Tel.: 829-2915) was built in 1734, withstood direct cannon fire from the British in 1759 and now houses an interesting museum of period furniture and everyday objects. The restaurant specializes in smoked sturgeon, and ham with maple syrup. The yellow bricks that were used to build some of the other houses were imported, as ballast in the timber ships, from Scotland.

St-Laurent

The most maritime of the island's six towns was, in the last century, a great shipbuilding center, where up to four hundred *chaloupes* (long rowing boats) were built every year. The **Moulin de St-Laurent** (754 chemin Royal, Tel.: 839-3888) is an excellent gourmet restaurant in a converted, seventeenth-century water mill, Moulin Gosselin. Guy Bel makes and sells beautiful statues, weather vanes and jewelry at the forge de Pique-Assaut, at 2200 chemin Royal. The island's only golf course is at 758 avenue Royale (Tel.: 829-3896).

Ste-Petronille

In 1759, the British army occupied the *bout de l'île* ("end of the island") to launch its siege of Quebec. The grove of red oaks is the most northerly in North America, and the strawberries grown in the parish are said to be the sweetest in the world. The village, which was part of St-Pierre until 1870, owes much of its development to the building of the quay, in 1855, which enabled produce to be easily transported to Quebec and wealthy merchants from the city to build fine summer houses in the Regency style (called Anglo-Norman in Quebec). **L'auberge La Goéliche** (Tel.: 822-2248) is a twenty-four-room hotel that was built in the last century.

THE DEVIL AT THE DANCE

Île d'Orléans is famous for its legends and stories. This is one of the best loved.

The family of François C. had decided that on the eve after the Twelfth Day of Christmas they would throw a party to welcome home their son, who had been traveling for several years. Word had spread, and after supper a large party of young people arrived. They were led by Dede. All the new guests were in high spirits, and Madame C. was slightly disturbed by the amount of brandy that they had brought. However, since they were all her son's childhood friends, she welcomed them and even allowed the furniture to be put to the side of the room so that the dancing could begin.

Now Dede, although a young man, was already considered to be the greatest fiddle player on the island. They said that after he had had a little shot, he played like one possessed—he tapped his heel to rhythms and counterrhythms that only the most skillful dancers could follow. The evening went like wildfire.

It was just about eleven o'clock when there was a short lull, and Madame C. was hoping, just a little, that the guests would leave. But instead, there was a sound of sleigh bells outside and then there was a knock on the door. "Come in!" said Pierre, in whose honor the party was being thrown. A tall handsome man, dressed in a beaver cloak with a sealskin cape, entered. His black eyes sparkled and his curly hair shone. He looked like a real gentleman.

"I heard the sound of the fiddle," he said, and pointed his foot to show that he was wearing caribou moccasins decorated with beads and dyed porcupine quills. His eyes seemed to throw sparks. The young women were watching, wondering, wanting to know if they would have the honor of dancing with him. The young men were jealous. Dede knew instinctively that he would have to play his fiddle as never before.

The stranger approached Blanche, the oldest daughter of the house. She trembled and acted shyly, but she was a very good dancer. No matter how quickly Dede played his intricate rhythms, the couple seemed infallible.

Blanche began to tire, and the stranger took all the best dancers in turn. All the girls danced better than they had ever done before. The young men were becoming annoyed. Several tried to replace the stranger, but they lost their steps and he waved them aside. The game became solely one between the fiddler and the stranger.

Dede was sweating heavily. He was much too proud to slow up. Then suddenly—*twang*—a broken string! Dede had done it on purpose. Baby François, just three years old, could be heard crying from the bedroom. Grandmother Catherine went to comfort him. Dede replenished himself with a good shot of brandy, and as he began again, he seemed as fresh as at the beginning of the party. Reel followed reel.

Eventually, Grandmother Catherine, unable to get the child to sleep, sat at the door to the bedroom with him on her knee. But each time the stranger passed before her, the young François gripped her around the neck. "Bur-burning!" he cried. Grandmother Catherine at first thought the child's utterances were just silly, but then she noticed that the stranger would stare with hatred as he passed.

Twang! Another string had broken. Dede, now sure that he was losing the contest, took another long shot of brandy for one last fly on the fiddle. But as he restrung his instrument, Grandmother Catherine overheard the stranger offer to trade a jewel-encrusted locket with his portrait inside for a gold cross that one of the girls was wearing. When the music began again, still carrying the child, she walked into the bedroom, where a small jug of holy water stood at the end of the bed. She dipped her trembling hand into the jug and returned. She waited for the stranger to come swirling by and then, making the sign of the cross, spattered the water over him.

The result was frightening. The Devil—for that is who it was—leaped to the ceiling and screamed a cry from Hell. Steam came out of his ears and eyes. He wanted to spring through the door, but saw, above it, a temperance cross mounted on a holy bough. Mad with rage, he threw himself through the stone wall, and thunder crashed as he staggered into his silver sleigh. The Devil and his horse disappeared in a trail of flames that flashed into the night sky.

Of course, the party broke up; and even Dede was sober as he returned home. The next day, a mason came to fill in the hole in the wall, but each stone, as if possessed, immediately fell out. The house still stands. Today, the hole is still there. Inside the room, there is always a chest of drawers mounted by holy candles; outside there is always a pile of wood. And there has never ever been dancing again in the old house of François C.

AN AFTERNOON'S DRIVE TO STE-ANNE-DE-BEAUPRÉ

The most attractive way to get to Ste-Anne-de-Beaupré is to take Highway 440 out of the city, turn off at the **d'Estimauville exit** (exit 24) and then turn left onto chemin Royal (it later changes its name to avenue Royale), Route 360, just after you pass the huge old mental asylum. This road wanders along the heights, which give splendid views over the river, and through the attractive towns of Beauport, Ange Guardien and Château Richer.

Beauport

Maison Bellanger-Girardin, 600 avenue Royale, is a Norman-style farmhouse built in 1722. Restored in 1983, it now houses exhibitions of the work of local artists. Opposite are a number of fine Victorian residences, and a little way east is the Greco-Roman Notre-Dame-de-la-Nativité parish church, which was built in 1916 using the remains of the walls of its predecessor, which had been destroyed by fire. The presbytery was built in 1903 in the French-provincial style, and the nearby convent, with its corniced roofs and turreted facades, was built in 1886.

Montmorency Falls

The Manoir Montmorency, overlooking the eastern side of the eighty-five-meter-high waterfalls (thirty meters taller than Niagara), was first built in 1780 as a summer house by Governor Haldimand. For many years it was known as Kent House because the Duke of Kent, Queen Victoria's father, lived here with his mistress, Madame de St-Laurent. It is now a sixty-four-room inn (Tel.: 663-2877, 1-800-463-5573) set in its own spacious grounds and with a restaurant named **La Femme Blanche.**

THE LEGEND OF MONTMORENCY

In 1758, Louis Gauthier became engaged to Rose, a girl from Beauport just upriver from the falls. That autumn, to earn some money before the marriage, he guided the canoe of a fur trader with plans to return in the spring. Rose, meanwhile, collected her trousseau of linen for their new home. Not long after the curé had published their marriage bans, news came that the English, under General Wolfe, were approaching by river. When Louis did not arrive home, Rose knew that he had joined the army.

General Wolfe landed at Montmorency and took the heights above the falls; the French retreated. After the battle, Rose became worried because she still had had no news of Louis. She vowed that if the Virgin Mary protected him, she would always dress her firstborn girl in white. The next day, the count of the dead and wounded soldiers was made, but there was no trace of Louis. Rose became very morose and spent her days walking on the shore, searching for the body of her lover. When she finally found him on the banks of the Montmorency River, he was dead. His companions told her that he had dragged himself there to drink and then died calling out her name. Filled with despair, Rose could not keep from returning to the falls of

Montmorency. Then, at the end of autumn, after Quebec had surrendered, she disappeared.

Several years later, people who would go at night to cut the reeds or hunt the birds at the base of the falls said that they had occasionally seen a white shadow walking and crying "Louis, where are you?" The ghost of Rose still walks in the spray of Montmorency.

Route 360 continues over a bridge at the top of the falls and leads to **Parc Montmorency,** where there are lawns, picnic tables, the foundation of a redoubt built by General Wolfe, a handicraft center and a trail that leads down to the smaller park at the bottom of the falls, where you can walk deep into the spray. In winter, the continual spray forms a mountain of ice over the river. In the last century it was considered an act of daring to climb this "sugar loaf" and slide down. There is at least one account of a tourist having done this during spring thaw—moments before the whole "loaf" collapsed into the river.

Château-Richer

Continuing east through L'Ange Gardien (Guardian Angel), you pass old farmhouses and the continued mix of Quebec's residential architecture that overlooks the river and île d'Orléans. At 7007 avenue Royale, in an old mill that was built in 1695, is an audiovisual presentation of the history and cultural development of Côte-de-Beaupré.

Ste-Anne-de-Beaupré

The basilica at Ste-Anne-de-Beaupré is the most important shrine in Quebec. Miraculous cures have been attributed to this religious site for more than three hundred years. The cornerstone of the present Neo-Romanesque church was blessed in 1923 and the building was officially opened on July 26, 1934. The stained-glass windows were installed from 1949 to 1963, the spires and main altar in 1962, and the floor paving in 1968. The basilica was consecrated in 1976.

THE SHRINE OF ST. ANNE

In 1659, Etienne Lessard offered a plot of land for the construction of a church or chapel, and that same year it was built and dedicated to St. Anne, the mother of the Virgin Mary. Three years later, because of flooding, Bishop Laval had the chapel relocated and rebuilt of wood with stone siding. In 1662, he presented the church with a statue of St. Anne, and according to Marie de l'Incarnation, "from that moment, God began to perform miraculous cures in this place." That same year, shipwrecked sailors were saved after making a vow to St. Anne, and by 1667 accounts of these and other miracles were well known in France.

In 1676, a new stone church was built. It was restored and enlarged in 1694. In 1759, when the British destroyed the town, it was regarded as a miracle that the church was left unscathed. Miraculous cures continued, and by 1778, one hundred pilgrims were arriving every month. With the advent of steamship and rail transportation, the number of pilgrims grew. In 1872, it was decided to build a much larger church, which was opened four years later. On March 29, 1922, it burned to the ground. Construction of the present church began the following year.

OUTDOOR ACTIVITIES ON MONT STE-ANNE

Taking Route 360 past Ste-Anne-de-Beaupré, you come to Mont Ste-Anne, Quebec's greatest skiing and mountain bike center. A little farther on, at St-Féréol-les-Neiges, there is excellent camping.

Close to the mountain park, both the 252-room **Château Mont-Ste-Anne** (Tel.: 827-5211, 1-800-463-4467) and the 110-room **Hôtel Val des Neiges** (Tel.: 827-5711, 1-800-463-5250) are highly rated.

The surrounding region also offers various other attractions. **The**

Grand Canyon is a picturesque gorge with waterfalls, trails and pedestrian bridges. **Les Septs Chutes** is a retired, but preserved, company town and hydroelectric facility that harnessed the St. Anne River as it fell over seven waterfalls. The national wildlife reserve of **Cap Tourmente** is where thousands of snow geese gather during their migrations in the spring and fall.

Camping

Located eight kilometers east of the alpine ski center are 166 sites for either trailers, trailer-tents or tents. *Outdoor activities:* swimming, fishing, hiking, swings, game areas. *Indoor activities:* billiard and Ping-Pong table, projection room, video games.

Golf

Le Beaupré: Tel.: 827-3778. Has 18 holes. Par 72. Length: 6,713 yards. All facilities.

Le St-Féréol: Tel.: 827-3778. Has 18 holes. Par 72. Length: 6,135 yards. All facilities.

Mountain Biking

From the ski center, there are 250 kilometers of trails, ranging from easy to very difficult. Bikes can be rented by the hour or day. Lessons. Tel.: 827-4561.

Skiing

Downhill: Tel.: 825-4561. 50 slopes, 12 open at night—easy to very difficult. Vertical drop: 625 meters. Longest slope: 4,831 meters. 6 chair lifts, 5 T-bars, 1 gondola. Equipment rental, dining, nursery, ski boutique and school.

Cross-country: Tel.: 827-5727. 22 trails—easy to very difficult. 208 kilometers of trails. Heated relay stations. Equipment rental, dining, nursery.

PICTURESQUE CHARLEVOIX

Introduction

Highway 138 climbs, winds, dips, dives and then plunges into Charlevoix, which, because it encompasses four ecosystems (boreal forest, tundra, peat bog and taiga), is the first inhabited area in the world to be named a "world reserve of the biosphere" by the United Nations.

The area was first populated in the seventeenth century, when *seigneurs* were granted the land and divided it into thin bands (*rangs*) so that each farm had easy access to the river. Later, as the population grew, second *rangs* were cultivated behind the first, then third and so on. In 1855, the seigniorial system was abolished, and the county of Charlevoix, named after the Jesuit father and historian François-Xavier de Charlevoix, was created.

The country, sprinkled with small villages with colored roofs and silver-spired churches, is, in turn, austere and soft. Long isolated, the area is renowned for traditional friendliness, refined cuisine and landscapes that have inspired generations of artists.

Baie-St-Paul

At the point where the Gulf of St. Lawrence becomes the river is the picturesque village of Baie-St-Paul, which was once part of a *seigneury* belonging to the Seminary of Quebec. In the twentieth century, the town is most famed for the artists who have adopted it. There are about a dozen art galleries, and the **Centre d'art de Baie-St-Paul,** *4 rue Fafard,* has an important permanent collection. Joseph Tremblay, 18 rue de la Lumière, makes superb model boats and ships—especially coastal schooners—costing from $30 to $2,500. In August, a yearly symposium of young Canadian artists is held. The Centre Histoire Naturelle, 152 rue St-Jean Baptiste, is open from June to the end of October and gives a geological history of the area. **Maison Otis,** *23 rue St-Jean-Baptiste* (Tel.: 435-2255), is a beautiful Quebec inn that has one of the province's most famous restaurants (reserve in advance).

Parc des Grands-Jardins (north on Highway 381) is home to a herd of caribou. A trail to the summit of Mont du Lac des Cynges (Swan

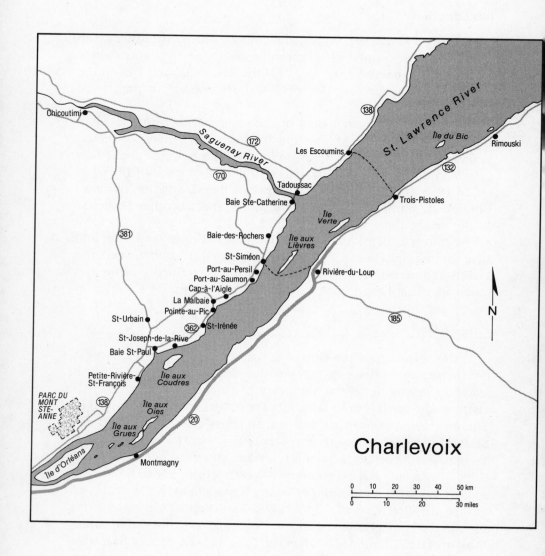

Charlevoix

Lake Mountain) gives a clear picture of taiga and northern vegetation.

SAVED BY GEESE

In 1759, the invading British army and navy were burning all the villages along the shores of the river as they headed up to conquer Quebec. The villagers of Baie-St-Paul hastily dug a trench, from which they planned to mount a defense. They sent the women, children and livestock into the forest and waited. The soldiers landed. The villagers shot, but it was clear that the British would soon take the town and burn it to the ground. Suddenly, there was a clamor of noise from the forest. It sounded remarkably like the war cries of a great army of Montagnis Indians. The British hastily retreated, leaving the village still standing. They were unaware that the frightening war cries were nothing more than the honking of geese that the women and children had purposefully excited.

St-Joseph-de-la-Rive

A spectacular descent sweeps down into this village that lies between the mountains and the sea. Two small inns, **Maison sous les pins,** *352 rue Principale* (Tel.: 635-2583), and **Auberge L'Ete,** *chemin du Quai* (Tel.: 635-2873), are both recommended. At the papeterie St-Gilles, they make paper using seventeenth-century techniques and have a small museum dedicated to the use of paper throughout the ages. At the Ancien Chantier Naval, the history of boats on the St. Lawrence is traced.

Île aux Coudres, a small (twenty-six kilometers in circumference) friendly island is a free, fifteen-minute ferry ride away. Families of St. Lawrence River pilots make up one-third of the population of the three parishes—St-Louis, St-Bernard and La

Baleineand—and are called *les Marsouines* ("the Porpoises") by mainlanders.

In St-Louis, visitors are invited to see the adjacent water and wind mills, which were built in 1826 and 1836, and a small maritime museum. La Baleine has an extensive artisans' center and a good inn, **La Roche Pleureuse** (The Crying Rock), which is named for a girl who waited so long for her fiancé, a sailor, to return from sea that she turned into a rock with a spring at its feet. At St-Bernard, where you can rent bicycles to tour the island, is **La Maison Croche** (Tel.: 438-2733), an eccentric inn that is filled with amusing old objects and where the dining room is papered with old newspaper articles. The favorite pastime of the island is traditional Quebec dancing— visitors are more than welcome to join in.

Les Eboulements

Back on the mainland, the next village, Les Eboulements (the Landslides), has a spectacular view of the St. Lawrence and rustic old houses, some of which can be rented. (Tel.: Lyne Tremblay: 678-2353.

The villages of Charlevoix East, because they, soon after the conquest, became the property of two Scots, Malcolm Fraser and John Nairn, have an entirely different character than those such as Baie-St-Paul. By the 1900s they had become a favorite resort area where large summer homes were built for both Montrealers and Americans.

Ste-Irénée

This town hosts an annual dance, jazz and classical music festival (Tel.: 452-8111), which runs from the end of June to the end of August. **L'Auberge des Sablons** (Tel.: 452-3594), a restaurant on the shore of the river, is noted for its beautiful setting and excellent Quebec cuisine.

Pointe-au-Pic

The luxurious, 334-room **Manoir Richelieu** (Tel.: 1-800-463-4495) was built to cater to wealthy visitors, who would often arrive by boat or steamship at the beginning of this century.

High above the river, it has maintained its magnificent public rooms and offers golf, tennis, swimming, horseback riding and a summer theater. Surrounded by trees, the neighboring **Auberge des Falaises** (Tel.: 665-3731) offers more intimate accommodations, a splendid view of the bay, a refined and British decor, and a restaurant that specializes in fish and home-smoked meats.

Parc régional des Hautes-Gorges de la Rivière Malbaie is on Route 138. Just outside the park, you can take a riverboat or stroll along trails to discover the gorges of the Malbaie River Valley.

Cap-à-l'Aigle

This town is noted for its inns. **Auberge la Pinsonnière** (Tel.: 665-4431) has a gourmet restaurant. **Auberge des Peupliers** (Tel.: 665-4423) is renowned for its warm and friendly atmosphere. The Port-au-Saumon Ecological Centre in Ste-Fidèle and the Palisades Forest Study Centre provide activities revolving around the preservation of local fauna and flora.

Port-au-Persil and St-Siméon

The first of these two villages is considered to be the prettiest on the coast. Just outside St-Siméon is Baie-des-Rochers, a beautiful cove with a tiny uninhabited island in the center.

Baie-Ste-Catherine and Tadoussac

Perched atop cliffs on either side of the mouth of the magnificent Saguenay River, these two towns are Quebec's whale-watching capitals. A three-hour cruise will take you to see the white belugas and a six-hour cruise will show you the huge blue whales. Six-and-a-half-hour cruises (they depart at 9:30 A.M.) will take you one hundred kilometers up the magnificent fjord of the Saguenay. Don't forget to take a sweater or windbreaker.

A NOTE ABOUT TOURING THE GASPÉ

Tourisme Québec's free guide of the Gaspé is perfectly adequate for any visitor who wishes to see the natural beauty of the peninsula.

However, it is best to drive on the side of the road closest to the coast. This means traveling along the north shore of the St. Lawrence River from Quebec City to St Siméon, taking the ferry to Rivière-du-Loup and then cutting across the peninsula to Restigouche and La Baie des Chaleurs. Many visitors make the error of driving in the other direction. One further hint: If you plan to stay a night in Percé, where the motels and hotels give a splendid view of the cliffs and sea, telephone in advance of your arrival—accommodations can be impossible to find by late afternoon.

Appendix

READING A FRENCH MENU

Restaurants in Montreal and Quebec are required to post their menus outside, but if you don't speak French or have not studied European cuisine, you may be no further forward. Here is a little guide to dining in French.

First Perusal

à la carte: each dish is priced separately.

entrée: main course.

hors d'oeuvre: appetizer.

menu du dégustation: a taster's menu consisting of a series of gourmet dishes. This means that the chef is being creative, having fun and wishes to play with your palate. Serge Bruyère, in Quebec City, who is considered to be one of the great chefs of the world, is not above calling his creations "concoctions."

prix fixe: includes soup, main course, dessert and coffee at a fixed price.

table d'hôte or *menu du jour:* the daily menu. This can mean either that the chef has had a fancy to cook a special dish, often using the freshest seasonal ingredients, or that the manager has bought a large quantity of a certain food. The price relative to the *à la carte* menu will usually tip the diner off as to which it is, but remember that some of the better restaurants will change their entire menu every week.

Meats

agneau: lamb
boeuf: beef
porc: pork
veau: veal

Poultry

caille: quail
canard: duck
dinde: turkey
poulet: chicken

Seafood

calmar: squid
crevettes: shrimps
flétan: halibut
homard: lobster
huitres: oysters
morue: cod
moules: mussels
palourdes: clams
saumon: salmon
thon: tuna
truite: trout

Vegetables

asperge: asparagus
aubergines: eggplant
champignons: mushrooms
chou: cabbage
épinard: spinach
fèves: broad beans
haricots: string beans
laitue: lettuce
oignons: onions
petits pois: peas
poireaux: leeks
poivrons: peppers

Seasonings

ail: garlic
estragon: tarragon
laurier: bay leaves
moutarde: mustard
persil: parsley
poivre: pepper
romarin: rosemary
sel: salt

Preparations

à la meunière: floured, then gently fried with lemon and parsley
au four: baked
au gratin: covered with bread crumbs and browned
boeuf à la mode: braised beef
en croûte: wrapped in pastry to seal in the juices
florentine: contains spinach
frit(e): fried
fumé: smoked
grillé: grilled
mariné: marinated
poché: poached
provençal: contains tomatoes and garlic, perhaps mushrooms, green onions, bay leaf and thyme
ragoût: stew
vapeur: steam
véronique: includes seedless grapes

Steaks

bleu: very rare
saignant: rare
à point: medium
bien-cuit: well-done

Soups

à l'oignon: onion soup with
cheese-encrusted bread on
top
aux pois: French-Canadian
pea soup
bisque: chowder
bouillon: clear soup
Condé: mashed red beans
Crecy: pureed carrot soup
crème de: cream of . . .
Dubarry: puree of
cauliflower
julienne: shredded vegetables
paramentier: pureed potato
potage: soup

Saint Germain: fresh green
peas, often with ham
veloute: thick soup
Vichyssoise: cold leek and
potato cream soup

Desserts

crème caramel: baked custard
crème glacé: ice cream
crêpe Suzette: thin pancake
flavored with orange juice
or liqueur and then
flambéed at the table
fromage: cheese (usually
served before a sweet
dessert)
gâteau: cake
Paris-Brest: pastry ring baked
and filled with praline
and whipped cream
patisserie: pastry
tarte au sucre: sugar pie
tarte Tatin: upside-down
apple pie

Index